Arise Ye Mighty People!

Gender, Class and Race in Popular Struggles

Arise Ye Mighty People!

Gender, Class and Race
in Popular Struggles

Edited by Terisa E. Turner
with Bryan J. Ferguson

Africa World Press, Inc.

P.O. Box 1892
Trenton, New Jersey 08607

Africa World Press Inc.

P.O. Box 1892
Trenton NJ 08607

Copyright © Terisa E. Turner, 1994
First Printing, 1994

Cover Design by Carles J. Juzang

Library of Congress Cataloging - in - Publication Data

Arise Ye mighty people! : gender, class, and race in popular struggles
/ edited by Terisa E. Turner with Bryan J. Ferguson.
    p. cm
Includes bibliographical references and index.
  ISBN 0-86543-300-3 (hardback). -- ISBN 0-86543-301-1 (pbk.)
  1. Social movements 2. Feminism. 3. Nationalism. 4. Ras Tafari
movement. I. Turner, Terisa E. II. Ferguson, Bryan J.
HN18.A75 1993
303.48'4--dc20   93-36486
                                                  CIP

Permission to reprint the following materials is gratefully acknowledged:

Turner, Terisa E., "Women, Rastafari and the New Society: Caribbean and East African roots
of a popular movement against structural adjustment." *Labour, Capital and Society* 24:1 (April
1991): 66-89. Chapter Two is a longer version of this article.

Peters, Hollis (Brother Book). "Message to intellectuals from the grassroots." *The Optician.* San
Fernando, Trinidad: Vangaurd Publishing, 1977.

Tobocman, Seth. "The history of America and Tompkins Square Park." *World War 3 Illustrated*,
#11 (the Riot Issue), Fall 1988, New York.

Yawney, Carole D. "Moving with the dawtas of Rastafari: from myth to reality." *El Caribe y
America Latina*, Ulrich Fleischmann, and Ineke Phaf, editors, Verlag Klaus Dieter Vervuert,
Wielandstr. 40, D 6000 Frankfurt/M1, Germany, 1987: 193-199.

Yawney, Carole D. "Rasta mek a trod: symbolic ambiguity in a globalizng religion," in Thomas
Bremer and Ulrich Fleischmann, editors, *Alternative Cultures in the Caribbean*, Frankfurt:
Verlag Klaus Dieter Vervuert, 1991.

Grace Nichols, 'Taint,' a poem published in Grace Nichols' collection of poetry, *i is a long
memoried woman.* published in 1983 by Caribbean Cultural International, Karnak House, 300
Westbourne Park Road, London W11 1EH. This poem appears in Terisa E. Turner's Chapter
Two on Rastafari and the new society.

Tunde, Carmen, 'Dreadlocks Lesbian,' published in Shabnan Grewal, Jackie Kay, Lilaine
Landor, Gail Lewis and Pratibha Parmar, (eds.). *Charting the journey: writings by black and third
world women.* London: Sheba Feminist Publishers, 1987: 205-206. This poem appears in Terisa
E. Turner's Chapter Two on Rastifari and the new society.

For Laura Zimmerman Turner, F. T. Bear, Rusell Hewit Turner, and Arminta Turner.

Table of Contents

Chapter 1

The New Society

Terisa E. Turner

The central premise of this book is that ordinary people are struggling, now silently, now loudly, to give birth to a new society. Bob Marley, who did more than anyone to promote Rastafari globally, sang *"Arise ye mighty people! There is work to be done."* He got the words from the biblical psalms. The work is midwifery, maternity and paternity, the bringing forth of a new society out of the debris of the old. The making of this new society has deep historical roots, but its *global* making was accelerated 500 years ago when Columbus unified the world market, thereby establishing the trade framework which fostered and fuelled modern capitalism. How then are people arising and working to realize the new society? And by what theory do we grasp this process? And how do we appreciate its complexity of class, gender and race?

This book was conceived in Kenya where, in the late 1980s and early 1990s, I researched Mau Mau women and carried on discussions with politically engaged people, especially from the grassroots. It is shaped by the questions which arose in Kenyan 'reasonings,' or discussions. The chapters were assembled with students in mind, in particular those in Kenya and their counterparts in Trinidad, Jamaica, Nigeria, Canada and the USA. The collection was also influenced by the Trinidadian revolutionary intellectual, CLR James (1901-1989), who Edward Said has called "that great champion of liberation." The book attempts to apply James' specific version of marxism. In 1937 CLR James published the twentieth century classic of popular history, *Black Jacobins*, the story of the first successful slave revolution which established the second new world republic in San Domingo (Haiti) in 1791. For James, *Black Jacobins* was not only an intervention to internationalize the historiography of the French Revolution. It was most centrally, an intervention in the struggle of colonized peoples against twentieth century empire and occupation. *Black Jacobins* demonstrated what slaves had done. And this demonstration was an intervention into an intellectual wasteland of

1

nihilist existentialism which, in the 1930s, found the colonized 'unready for self-rule.' In the same way that *Black Jacobins* was written to fuel the anti-colonial independence struggle, *Arise Ye Mighty People!* is intended, however humbly, to strengthen the anti-imperial struggles against structural adjustment and capital's resurgent attack on women, all exploited peoples and the earthly commons.

A further goal of *Arise!* is the elaboration of a new kind of marxism which is here called Jamesian marxism. It is fundamentally global, recognizes the revolutionary capacity of a broad range of actors, eschews doctrinaire formulae for open-ended conceptions of *what* constitutes resistance and *who* are the agents of transformation. It centralizes Marx's insight that capitalism shapes its successor society on a global scale. It recognizes with Gramsci that the contention between new and old, between socialism and barbarism is the fundamental dynamic of the century. And it draws theory from the struggles of those who understand and respond to forces of class, gender and race relations of power.

Class is employed here to delineate the great division and dialectic between exploiters and exploited. All the world's people have, with the globalization of capitalism 500 years ago, been drawn into this bifurcation and this struggle. While the class of exploiters includes many factions and a small proportion of women and men of colour; this relatively small group of capitalists consists overwhelmingly of white men. The geographical polarization between the rich north and the poor south obscures the reality of the north in the south and the south in the north. In short, the international character of capital has created an international bourgeoisie of exploiters which is represented in every society. And it has created dispossession worldwide such that exploited peoples in the so-called south share with their northern sisters and brothers, a similar fundamental relationship with the profit takers.

Among the exploited are many differences including those between women and men, and between black and white. What I call a 'hierarchy of labour power' structures the dynamic relationship among the exploited. The most privileged of the exploited are white men, and beneath them are black (all non-white) men. The gender line divides men from women who are still further down in the hierarchy, supporting capital and exploited men with the unpaid work of the production of life. This, under capital is the unparalleled strategic work of producing labour power, the precondition for profits. White women have been structured into this hierarchy in a position above black women, who are institutionalized at the very bottom to underpin the world capitalist order. The global division of labour between northern white women and southern black women of the exploited class, has varied but involves for all, different degrees of dispossession and separation from the means of sustenance and production. In the contemporary period, exploitation has meant for white women, enforced specialization in consumption and reproduction; while for black women it has meant enforced specialization in the production of cheap wage goods, export crops and services. Thus we see that the imperial US state and its allies simultaneously pursue a pro-natalist, anti-abortion policy in the north and an anti-natalist policy in the south. Official culture propagates an ideology which reinforces and champions a particular myth of the traditional, patriarchal nuclear family. At the same time it promotes the Hardin falsehood that 'too many people cause underdevelopment,' and the genocidal demographic engineering which follows from this misconception.

Race became important with the slave trade, the 'curse of Columbus.' Racism was fostered to rationalize the brutal trade and then to justify European invasion of the African continent to establish direct overrule in the 19th century. Racism and sexism structure the hierarchy of labour power and are essential to capital's level of profits and to capital's security in power. Official culture maintains, reinforces and reproduces divisions among the exploited class in the hierarchy, along gender and race lines. In contrast popular culture, with which *Arise!* deals, is that expression of the exploited which unites people across ethnic and gender divisions, but on the basis of the expressed interests of those at the bottom of the hierarchy. It is increasingly recognized that women of colour, from the grassroots, are at the forefront of many popular struggles and new social movements. The interests of those at the bottom, of black women, are being articulated through a wide range of struggles and are finding expression through virtually all types of media.

Just as official culture perpetrated racism and elaborated a 'scientific' ideology of racial superiority and inferiority; popular culture as of the 19th century celebrated African race pride and gave rise to pan Africanism and the Marcus Garvey movement in the early years of the 20th century. This grassroots internationalism around the affirmation of African people grew directly out of the material organization of capitalism which structured black people into positions in which they were subjected to super exploitation, under the discipline of whites. It arose at the time, in 1917-1918 when peace movements and peace associations were formed throughout the world. The black internationalism of the Pan African Congresses and Garveyism could be understood as the first great internationalist movement in the capitalist epoch. It was much more grassroots and powerful than its predecessor, the First International (1864-1876), organized by Karl Marx, or the Second International (1889) which today persists in a loose network of social democrats. In the inter war years, the pan African internationalism of Garvey and his more class conscious challengers and successors gained strength. It fuelled the anti colonial upsurge despite the support which the Comintern or Third International, (1919-1943) extended to the colonial powers. Women of colour organized at the base of the pan African Garveyist international. However, they were constrained by Garvey's essentially pro-capitalist philosophy which sought a place for the black man alongside white capitalists and which maintained a bourgeois Victorian ideal of the black woman as housewife in the nuclear family. Despite this view from the top of the Garveyist international, women of African origin mobilized in their own and their community's interests; and thereby strengthened an organized affirmation of pan Africanism.

Fundamental to the Jamesian marxism which this book seeks to elaborate, is the premise that popular struggles are organized not by a vanguard party, but by capital itself. This is to reject both stalinism and anarchism. How has capital organized popular struggles? Resurgent popular movements, it is contended, are the outcomes of contemporary neo-liberal capitalist strategies of structural adjustment and free trade. As the oneness of the world market becomes more pronounced, the oneness of the exploited, unwaged and waged, becomes more tangible. As the state is weakened by structural adjustment, it becomes less of an obstacle to grassroots mobilization and international coordination amongst such mobilizations. Popular movements are expressions of class struggle. They are not to be confused with multiclass populism which is essentially reformist as is black nationalism. However, populist expressions may be present within and weaken popular movements.

4

The emphasis here on a simultaneous analysis of class, gender and race in popular struggles is also an attempt to show the inadequacies of 'analysis' which leaves out treatment of any of these crucial structural, relational divisions within the hierarchy of labour power on which profit accumulation depends. *Arise!* includes four chapters on Rastafari because it is one powerful contemporary expression of the earlier internationalist movement of the exploited that was pan Africanism. Further, Rastafari has, in its globalization, been taken up by some groups of indigenous people in their struggle to take back alienated land and to protect nature and natural resources. It is also one nexus through which some indigenous peoples link up with intellectuals who recognize that global survival has, as its prerequisite, the enforcement of an end to ecological destruction.

Rastafari is an important expression of the new society, and consequently historical, universalizing and contradictory trends within the social movement demand attention. In chapter two on the new Rastafari and its feminist historical roots, I address gender division and 'the male deal,' while highlighting some bases for gender unity. In chapter three, Bryan Ferguson presents a chronology which roots Rastafari in the construction of the capitalist system from 1492 to the present. In chapter four Carole Yawney documents the early gender discussions within Rastafari and among feminist theorists. In chapter five Carole Yawney accounts for Rasta's international expansion by reference to spiritual power and nihilism. Rastafari recalls the alienation of captivity and of the loss of a landbase in Africa. A similar sense of alienation experienced by most people is the basis for the global receptivity enjoyed by Rastafari. In chapter six, Seth Tobocman illustrates the 500 years of land grabs which have galvanized resistance in the new world. His prescient theme is rape and the fightback against new enclosures, especially in the inner cities of the imperial metropole. He treats the urban insurrections which since 1988 have rocked New York city's Lower East Side and which presaged the 1992 Los Angeles uprising. From New York to Nairobi, squatters have been struggling to hold onto the scraps of terrain from which they make their physical fight to survive. In chapter seven Trinidad's rapso poet, Hollis Peters (Brother Book) provides a message to the intellectuals from the grassroots. Brother Book elaborates a prominent Jamesian theme in calling for the unity of producers and revolutionary intellectuals to carve out 'a most beautiful history.' In chapter eight the political culture of Kenya is reviewed in a poem by Sophie Striker. The poem was written before the 1992 turmoil and provides a context within which to understand the forces which continue to be played out in the Kenyan struggles. Striker's focus on exploited grassroots women enabled her to virtually predict the 1992 popular uprising in Kenya associated with the pro-democracy movement and the women-led refusal to participate in export crop production under IMF discipline. Susan Ward's poem in chapter nine rejects post modernist indulgence in favor of *"feet drumming the land, hands drumming the earth, poets drumming the mind, swaying, moving, crashing down, burning up, those brothels of separate rooms."*

In chapter ten I develop the theme of confrontation between exploiters writ large in the form of multinational US petroleum corporations; and black women at the very bottom of the hierarchy of labour power. Nigerian peasant women won ecological gains from big oil, assisted by the solidarity of a faction of their menfolk. This presentation of the 1984 and 1986 women's uprisings against the Nigerian oil industry considers how class formation involves change in gender relations. It shows how capitalism is simultaneously destructive and constructive with respect to the organization of social power. The more successful social movements, it is suggested, are those characterized by gender relations in which women, acting in their own interests, are supported by some men who appreciate that both justice and their own self interest are embodied in grassroots women's initiatives. Hilary Rouse-Amadi's chapter eleven dramatizes the devastation which the Nigerian oil boom has visited on ordinary women of Eastern Nigeria in domestic labour in the urban centres. She documents the class relations through which bourgeois women exploit ordinary girls and women in the household. Hilary Rouse-Amadi's chapter twelve shows how, with the breakdown of Nigerian society under 'the corrosive acid' which is oil capitalism, young Nigerian women struggle to pursue those limited opportunities created by the capitalist market. Leigh Brownhill, in chapter thirteen, shows how some men join women to resist the sexist backlash that is domestic discipline imposed by violent men. Finally, in chapter fourteen I place the 1991 Gulf war in the trajectory of uprisings in the USA, the Mideast and globally in the late 1980s. Capital fought back with Desert Storm, but has not won, and was put on hold midway into another adventure of bombing Libya by the April-May 1992 Los Angeles uprising which spread to dozens of other cities in the US and internationally. The battle between the rulers' 'new world order' and the new society is on.

Arise ye mighty people! is about the battle through which the new world society is emerging from the disarray of the old. It is about Caribbean revolutionaries including Bob Marley and CLR James who invoked and documented uprisings of the people, and in so doing, strengthened the new cycle of working class struggles emerging in the late twentieth century. This collection documents expressions of the new society from Nigeria's oil belt, North America's urban insurgents, the Middle East's intifada, the Caribbean's free villagers, and Kenya's Mau Mau, ecology and democracy movements. Rastafari, one of many such movements, is presented in *Arise ye mighty people!* as an international force within which women are expressing their own interests. The chapters contrast the divisiveness of official culture with the unifying power of revolutionary popular culture. Through case studies of popular struggles, *Arise!* identifies a growing internationalism of grassroots people who are appropriating global media and markets to unite across gender, race, ethnic and national divides. One popular counterforce to global capital's drive for private profit and power is this emerging unity, forged by movements in which women are prominent.

7

Chapter 2

Rastafari and the new society: Caribbean and East African feminist roots of a popular movement to reclaim the earthly commons

Terisa E. Turner

Extending the view of CLR James that the Jamaican Rastafari movement is an expression of a new society emerging from the contradictions of post WWII capitalism, this chapter argues that a black feminist movement has grown up to shape a 'new Rastafari.' The origins of this development are traced to East Africa and the Caribbean during three crises of capitalism: the early 20th century, the period of the 1930s through to the nationalist struggles to the 1960s, and the current period of structural adjustment programs. Using the concept of the 'male deal' to examine dynamics during each crisis, the chapter concludes that the 'new Rastafari' is part of a broad egalitarian social movement of resistance to structural adjustment and affirmation of communal control over resources.

"Anyone who knows anything of history knows that great social changes are impossible without the feminine ferment." Karl Marx

"...the real fundamental human difference is not between White and Black, it is between man and woman." CLR James, reviewing Morrison's Sula, 1981.

"You who know what the past has been, you who work in the present tense, you who see through to the future, come mek wi work together. Come sit here with me, an mek wi drink tea, a mek wi talk, a mek we analyse. You who have been burned by vanguardism, come mek wi give you little nurturing. Come sit awhile, a mek wi drink tea, a mek wi talk, a mek wi strategise. You who believe in the future and in transforming your labour, Let the future be in good favour." Lillian Allen, Revolutionary Tea Party, 1985.

Terisa E. Turner

Introduction: Rastafari, old and new

"Having survived fifty years of social and religious in-
tolerance, discrimination and harassment, the Rastafari movement is poised between becoming a part of world history,
contributing to a universal culture, and being a passing
phenomenon of the 20th century" [Campbell 1987:234].

The perspective here is that the place of Rastafari in a universal
culture, a new society, depends not only on it becoming more informed by class analysis, as Campbell contends, but also on the
nurturing of the feminist ferment which here is called 'the new
Rastafari.' Original Rastafari is uncompromising in its commitment
to 'chant down Babylon,' the capitalist system. However, it is bound
by the 'capitalist male deal.' Sexism is the key defining feature
distinguishing the old Rasta from the new. And it is also a fetter
limiting the old Rasta to a black nationalist accommodation with
capitalism. In contrast, the defining feature of new Rastafari is the
affirmation that class consciousness cannot exist without gender
consciousness.

This study considers gender and class relations in Caribbean and
East African popular struggles during three crises of capitalism in
the 20th century. It argues that with the growing internationalization
of the world market, capital has sought to develop through establishing class alignments characterized by specific gender relations.
Using the concept of the 'male deal' to examine gender dynamics
during each crisis, the study concludes that the 'new Rastafari' is part
of an international social movement of resistance to structural adjustment and affirmation of a new society which transcends the
limitations of the male deal.

Rastafari, organically rooted in the overthrow of slavery, crystallized
as a Caribbean movement in 1930 when Haile Selassie was crowned
Emperor of Ethiopia. In 1964 CLR James wrote that Rastafari is "the
sect of Jamaican Negroes who reject the bastardised version of British
society which official and educated Jamaica seeks to foist upon them.
They have created for themselves a new world, in which the Emperor
of Ethiopia, Haile Selassie, is God on earth. His kingdom in Africa is
the promised Heaven to which all the Rastafari elect will go, not
when they die but when they can raise the money for the passage"
[James 1984:163].

10

James emphasized that the importance of Rastafari was not only their rejection of official society but their creation of a new one. This comes, he says, from their being West Indians, a "new people [who] came into existence only three hundred years ago...." Hence, "their world is just beginning. They do not suffer from any form of defeat. That is not in their history" [1984:163-164]. CLR James has underlined the special international force which Caribbean history has bestowed upon its accomplished sistren and brethren. He pointed out in 1975 that the "Africans transported to the West Indies had to develop or improvise a culture suitable to their new environment because the chief industry which necessitated their arrival in the Caribbean was systemised agriculture. ... The concentration of labourers on the plantation was combined with the ability to work in the factory process which transformed the cane into material which could ultimately be refined. ... The sugar industry in the Caribbean was one of the most developed industries of its time. The very food which the slaves ate was imported and, at that early date, it was impressed upon them that what they produced was sent abroad. Thus, as far back as the seventeenth century, they were at the centre of a great international industry. ... [And for the slaves so organized] The primary effort was a struggle for freedom" [James 1984:218-219].

The creativity of new world slave societies can be appreciated only after a rejection of that omnipresent theme in development theory, both Weberian and marxist, that everywhere tradition or precapitalist social relations exist and act as a fetter. In 1852 Marx introduced *The 18th Brumaire of Louis Bonaparte* with his now famous observation that people "make their own history, but they do not make it just as they please; they do not make it under circumstances chosen by themselves, but under circumstances directly encountered, given and transmitted from the past. The tradition of all the dead generations weighs like a nightmare on the brain of the living" [Marx 1963:15]. But this is not the case in the new world. Because the Caribbean peoples were ripped from their motherland, transported and assembled by merchants and planters for the sole purpose of sugar manufacture, they were relatively free of the fetters of tradition. At the same time those cultural retentions of use to enslaved Africans and sustainable under sugar factory production, were kept alive; usually in a syncretic blend with European forms.

11

The creative power of Rastafari, dub and political reggae music derives from the unique sociology of new world slave society. On the one hand is the ultra modernity of Caribbean peoples, unburdened by the dead weight of the past. On the other hand is the society's beginnings in slavery and hence its focus on the fight for freedom. Especially for African women, the focus included a fight for freedom from sexual enslavement [Beckles 1989, Bush 1990, Turner 1982]. The focus on the fight for freedom is lucidly presented in CLR James' 1960 independence lectures in Port of Spain, Trinidad [James 1960]. With a broad historical sweep, James tells a popular audience of the successive leaps forward in the social organization of the fight for freedom. One leap was taken by early Christianity. James treats St. John of Revelations, in the manner of Rastafari, as a great anti-imperialist predicting the battle of Armageddon when Babylon (Rome) would fall: St. John "had a sense of historical development. ...the fifth monarchy would be the Kingdom of God on earth. ...there would be a new world after the Romans had been defeated, and everybody would be happy. ...the lion and the lamb would lie down in peace. ...St. John was dominated by the vision of a peaceful and harmonious society" [James 1960:7-8]. More recently the Jamaican historian, Orlando Patterson has traced this history of freedom from the 5th century BC to the Middle Ages in an account which elaborates the work of James and is consistent with Rastafari historiography [Patterson 1991]. In the Caribbean the imperative of a highly modern people to fight for freedom by abolishing private property in people has generated astonishing creativity, not least in the sphere of gender relations.

The plantation organization of capitalist agriculture empowered new world slaves to spearhead the overthrow of slavery. CLR James centralized the orthodox marxist perspective that "the working class is united, it is disciplined and it is organized by the very mechanism of capitalist production itself; and the more progressive capitalist production is, the more it unites those who are destined to be its grave-diggers" [James (1960) 1973:53]. But the new system of wage slavery and the exploitation of vast multitudes of unwaged gave rise to a more international organization of capital and with it a more globalized drive to democracy. In 1985 James drew attention to the objective, physical capacity of capitalist technology to unite people: "The means of communication, means of information today are such that it is impossible to believe that as time goes on it does not mean greater and greater communication between people, which means, ultimately, a democratic system of some sort. ... I'm speaking in particular about the objective materials, physical means of living, means of communication, means of spreading information. That is going on every day. That's what I look at and say the tendency towards a democratic relation between people is bound to follow. I believe that's what Marx and Engels meant ... There is an absolutely remorseless movement towards democratic relations between people. That I learned early, and I've never seen anything to make me change it. Television, in my opinion, is one of the greatest strengths of democracy, because the people who are working for television think of the whole public; that is what they have to [do]" [James 1986:26,29]. The communications revolution is central to the emergence of the new society. Among the more dramatic examples of this is in the rapid spread of Rastafari. And reggae music was its harbinger, riding the wave of technological globalization.

A decade before Bob Marley made reggae a powerful weapon for revolution, James pointed to the future in the present. He saw that the rejection of capitalist mainstream relations by Black Muslims, Rastafari, Africa's Mau Mau and white proto hippies or beatniks constituted a global watershed from which would emerge a new global society. In the early 1990s with Spike Lee's release of the film *Malcolm X*, popular culture expressed a link between Malcolm X and Rastafari through music, colours, clothes and publications. This resurgence of revolutionary black counter culture from the 1960s among a new generation in the very different context of the 1990s was presaged by James. In the early 1960s while reviewing Patterson's *Children of Sisyphus*, he argued that Rastafari expressed "a universal feature of contemporary life. The Rastafari are one example of the contemporary rejection of the life to which we are all submitted. The Mau Mau of Kenya do the same. The Black Muslims of the United States are of the same brand. And for the time being we need go no further than the beatniks of the most advanced countries of Western civilisation. 'Anywhere, anywhere out of the world, the world that they know'" [1984:164]. James recognized that Rasta was part of the new world society emerging from the disarray of the old [James 1984:73-84]. And he linked Rastafari with other expressions of the universal new society: Mau Mau, black power and the revolt of white youth.

Twenty years later Honor Ford-Smith of *Sistren*, the Jamaican feminist theatre collective, pointed to the emergence of a secular, new

Rastafari. "The culture has influenced many who are not believers in Selassie to adopt elements of the way of life such as vegetarianism, locksed hair (as is worn by the Masai warriors of Kenya), and the use of words developed within the group e.g. 'irie' - all right" [Ford-Smith 1987:314].

The tremendous expansion of Rastafari as a secular movement in the 1970s was impelled by the teachings of CLR James [James 1984, Grimshaw 1992], Walter Rodney [1969, 1972] and especially by Bob Marley who "used his music as a vehicle of mobilisation" [Campbell 1987:143; Cooper 1987]. Campbell's unparalleled treatment, *Rasta and resistance: from Marcus Garvey to Walter Rodney*, retells the history of world revolution in the twentieth century from the perspective of black men. Campbell places Rastafari in the mainstream of this trajectory. While he is virtually silent on gender and the new Rastafari, the Jamaican historian does organize invaluable material on the old Rastafari, including a treatment of Bob Marley and reggae. Marley's 1979 album *Survival* "linked Rastafari to the advanced struggle for liberation at the frontline of racism and imperialism with its songs *Wake up and live, Africa unite, So much trouble, Babylon system*, and especially *Africans 'a liberate Zimbabwe*.... African guerillas who were in the bush fighting Ian Smith heard this reggae song and claimed it as their own. ... Countless reggae singers had linked the struggles of the African peoples to their own plight, but Marley's song actually intervened in an ongoing struggle against technological inhumanity, atomic misphilosophy, [insisting that] we are the survivors" [Campbell 1987:144].

Through their lyrics, Marley, the Wailers and the I-Threes dissected and analyzed the barbarity of late capitalism. They affirmed the vitality, health and power of a new society of fighting survivors. Marley "centralised the idea of armed struggle as his view of Rastafari." As for Nigeria's Fela Anikulapo-Kuti, for Marley, "the music is the weapon." In introducing Campbell's book, Kwayana states that "such is the power of art that Bob Marley's music has done more to popularise the real issues of the African liberation movement than several decades of backbreaking work of pan Africanists and international revolutionaries" [Kwayana 1982 in Campbell 1987:xii]. Reggae is a weapon of revolution because of the power of art but also because of the power of capitalist communication technology. Reggae cannot be banned, censored or repressed because audio cassettes and duplication are available to everyone. The severe repression by third world military cabals in the post independence period cannot silence the analysis and upliftment contained in dub and rapso poetry, political reggae and in 'world music' of the 1990s. The 1991 police beating of Rodney King in Los Angeles was videoed, aired by US television and employed by dread Sister Souljah as the music video accompanying her rap song which encouraged people to resist police brutality. This popular appropriation of capital's global communication technology was a vital input to the April-May 1992 Los Angeles riots and complementary upheavals in dozens of other cities. Marley sang freedom songs as did Paul Robeson in the 1940s, but to hundreds of millions of people, amplified by computer technology and the super villagization of the globe.

Rastafari is a political, cultural and social movement. It is not being treated here as a millenarian or religious phenomenon [Bakan 1990:16, Campbell 1987:3, Post 1978] but rather as way of life which emerged when peasants were faced with land seizures and forced into cities, especially in Jamaica in the period since 1930, but also in Africa since the turn of the century. Far from being a millenarian flash in the pan, Rasta has grown exponentially in the last half of the 20th century. George Lamming states that Rastafari has extended into "a dominant force which influences all levels of [Jamaican] national life" [1980 in Campbell 1987:1]. In Kwayana's view, "Rastafari culture is perhaps the most influential cultural movement in the Caribbean today.... " [1982 in Campbell 1987:xii]. And Campbell points to the "massive spread of the culture inside Jamaica, in the English-speaking Caribbean, and ultimately as the most dynamic force, among the children of black immigrants in the United Kingdom" [1987:4]. Today Rasta is one of many expressions of indigenous people fighting for their rights. It unites first nations peoples with those of the African diaspora, including exiles, migrants, refugees and their children. For instance some of the aboriginal peoples of New Zealand are identifying themselves as Rastafari and are pursuing land claims. New Rastafari is a global cultural practice, an expression in particular of black people and especially of black women, but one which is also inclusive of revolutionary white women and men.

New Rastafari came from the old male-identified Rastafari and its antecedents in the jubilee of emancipation from slavery. It came from radical religious movements in Jamaica in the 1800s, from Ethiopianism, Garveyism, pan Africanism, struggles of 'the sufferers,' and from nationalist insurgency in Africa and Caribbean. It has emerged from but also *against* these antecedents. The new Rastafari has come from a global fightback against IMF and World Bank

15

structural adjustment programs (SAP) especially by women because SAP hits women and children so hard [Antrobus 1989:26, 1991:3, Beneria and Feldman 1992, Elson 1992, Sparr 1993]. It has come from media globalism and the music so purveyed; and from international feminisms, including the excavation of the history of women's militancy and centrality to each phase of capitalist expansion and to the struggles characteristic of that phase [Silvera 1983, Mohanty et al 1991]. New Rasta has come from the recognition that central to the struggle for women's rights is the resistance of black women, north and south, against "the gendered, racial and racially-gendered hierarchies" of slavery, colonialism and today's super-exploitation [Brand 1987:29, Young and Dickerson 1993]. In sum, new forces have adapted and transformed Rastafari into a different and even more potent world social movement.

This chapter argues that a new society is emerging from the grassroots of international capitalism. At the forefront are black women and their allies who, by pursuing their social aspirations, embrace those of more powerful echelons of what is here called the 'hierarchy of labour power,' which includes white women, black men and white men from the exploited classes. By embracing the interests of all the exploited, black women's revolutionary practice articulates for the first time what Marx called 'the general class interest.' Such an articulation is the precondition for unity across race and gender lines, of the exploited class worldwide. It is a unity based on structural links between the strata of exploited with the interests and initiatives of black and third world women at the forefront. The argument then is that the new society of which the new Rasta is only one element, has the practical potential to supplant and transform the contemporary world order. Other elements of this new society include the many types of social movements focused for instance on such issues as indigenous land rights, ecology, peace and human rights [Eckstein 1989, Escobar and Alvarez 1992]. New Rasta's prominence derives in part from its capacity to express the individual's historical connection to other social forces (class, race, gender) locally and internationally. In this way, new Rasta is an influence for the transformation of elements of the existing global 'class in itself' into a 'class for itself.'

A methodology which is adequate to the task of tracing the emergence of the new society has to have an international scope. It has to embrace the links between the various actors while being sensitive to gender relations as they undergo change in the process of class formation. This analysis attempts to employ such a methodology in understanding the international emergence of a particular social movement, Rastafari. A small school of contemporary feminist (and I would say, Jamesian marxist) scholars including Mies and Reddock, have begun to recast in an internationalized and gendered mode, the historiography of the slave period, the triangular trade among Europe, Africa and the new world, the social transformations attendant upon the rise of capitalism in Europe and the process of colonization. The methodology employed here is patterned after that used by such scholars and it is applied to the twentieth century.

A full historical analysis of the rise of Rasta feminism would be global and would include pre-capitalist social relations in Africa and elsewhere. Such an historical methodology I call 'feminized marxism' or gendered political economy and define as the analysis of the formation and interaction of social classes historically and on a world scale [Turner 1976:64-70; 1980:202-208; 1989:61]. Class formation and struggle are fundamentally gendered and ethnicized. A pathbreaking global analysis of this type is Maria Mies' study, *Patriarchy and accumulation on a world scale: women in the international division of labour* [1986]. Another is Martha Mamozai's 1982 study of the impact of German colonialism on African women which includes the effect of this process on gender relations in Europe [Mamozai 1982]. A global analysis is essential in order to "perceive more fully the double-faced process of colonization and housewifization" [Mies 1986:97]. These links are traced in Reddock's study of gender under Caribbean slavery and into the 20th century [Reddock 1984]. A brief review of Reddock's analysis will both illustrate the methodology and provide an historical foundation for understanding the global emergence of Rastafari in the 20th century.

Reddock points out that by the 1700s, "Africa was incorporated in the capitalist world economy only as a producer of human labour" [Reddock 1984:18], and Caribbean slaves were actively discouraged from having children. Rather, planters worked them to death in an average of seven years and purchased new slaves from Africa. Mies points out that "These more than a hundred years that 'slave women in the Caribbean were neither wives nor mothers' were exactly the same period that women of the European bourgeoisie were domesticated and ideologically manipulated into wifehood and motherhood as their 'natural' vocation. While one set of women was treated

17

as pure labour force, a source of energy, the other set of women was treated as 'non-productive' breeders only" [Mies 1987:92 citing Reddock 1984:18 and Badinter 1980]. In West Africa a third set of women, those in the grip of 18th century African merchant princes, produced people for export as slaves to the new world, thereby relieving capital of the cost of producing labour power [Dike 1956:153-165; Rodney 1972].

However, in the late 1700s and into the mid 1800s, bonded labourers and slaves revolted in West Africa, while in the Caribbean enslaved African women refused the new demands of metropolitan governments and plantation owners that they reproduce the labour force on site [Reddock 1985:70-74]. There is evidence that during this period of rising global opposition to slavery, "women resisted having children and did not regard motherhood as an instinctive or automatically natural role" [Ellis 1985:28]. Despite inducements such as those legislated in 1798 in Tobago, that payment of $1.00 be made to a midwife for "every child which she delivers alive," and that "mothers of six or more children be granted a total exemption of all labour;" [Williams 1964:60-62 cited in Reddock 1985:71] slave women remained "hardened in their anti-breeding attitudes with the result that most of the schemes for increasing the population by greater reproduction failed" [Patterson 1967:112]. Patterson quotes Sabina Park, an enslaved woman in Jamaica who killed her three year old child, as defending herself in Slave Court, by asserting that "she had worked enough for bukra (master) already and that she would not be plagued to raise the child...to work for white people" [1967:106 cited in Reddock 1985:73].

This study of Rastafari employs a methodology in opposition to that method which divides up poles of exploitative relations to present them as separate entities without visible structural connections. It follows Mies who tries "to trace the 'underground connections' that link the processes by which nature was exploited and put under man's domination to the processes by which women in Europe were subordinated, and examine the processes by which these two were linked to the conquest and colonization of other lands and people" [Mies 1986:77]. This integrative methodology links the historical emergence of European science and technology, and its mastery over nature, to the European witch killings and the attendant deskilling and economic marginalization of women. And both the persecution of the witches and the rise of modern science are linked to European slave based triangular trade and the destruction of self sufficient, autonomous economies in Africa and the new world. As capitalism developed in the 20th century, and especially after WWII with the more pronounced unification of the world market, first world women were concentrated in the work of reproduction and consumption. At the same time, third world women were forced to produce cheap export and wage goods, according to specific demands of colonial and imperial capital.

Documentation of the emergence of the new Rastafari needs to be informed by a deep history of capital's differential shaping of genders in all the regions of the world simultaneously. However, the present treatment is limited to three periods: the early 20th century, the period of the 1930s through to the nationalist struggles to the 1960s, and finally the current period since 1980 of struggles around the implementation of structural adjustment programs. Because the crises of these three junctures were global, a more complete treatment would draw from all regions of the world. While the dynamics of global power establish the context for this discussion, the actual analysis concentrates on gender in class struggles in East Africa and the Caribbean. The discussion begins with the crisis of capitalism at the turn of the 20th century when East Africa's women centred Nyabingi movement rose against colonial occupation and local male collaboration. At the same time in Jamaica, ex-slaves who had formed a free peasantry developed further a pre-existing pan Africanism [Thomas 1988:72-81] and the Garvey back-to-Africa movement. These two regions were central to the rise of Rastafari. They also provide two distinct cases of the operation of the 'male deal.' East Africans were organized by pre-capitalist male deals to which reactionary male-led political movements hark back when challenging European male imposition [Presley 1992, White 1990, Murray 1974]. And the Caribbean, in the absence of an indigenous traditional culture, is without precapitalist male deals. Consequently the cases drawn from the Caribbean reveal struggles around the creation of a dynamic between men and women which is radically modern, global and new.

This chapter seeks to trace some of the ways in which capital, in the throes of three crises, organizes exploited peoples to resist. The emphasis then is on both the relations of exploitation and the relations of liberation. This follows CLR James' insistence on Marx's originality residing in his perception that capitalism organizes a

19

successor society. While Mies' 1986 study emphasized patriarchy as essential to exploitation, this study emphasizes feminisms' centrality to the transcendence of capitalism. Fundamental is the perspective that the working class is organized, disciplined and united by the process of production itself. However, the prevailing notion of *who* constitutes the working class and *what* is encompassed by the production process are much too narrow. It is necessary to act on CLR James' urging to "extend Marx" [James 1989] to embrace the fightback against intensified exploitation of 'nature' or the earthly commons and of women, north and south. I try to show that this fightback, while global, has for at least this century been spear-headed by third world women. And out of resistance and fightback is maturing a new society, the 'future in the present.' The unprece-dented globalism of transformational initiatives is strengthened by open economy free trade policies in structural adjustment programs, the 'new enclosures' by contemporary capital which threaten the last remaining scraps of terrain from which resistance may be mounted [Midnight Notes 1990, 1992, Sparr 1993].

Capital depends for the exploitation of women on the male deal. It is posited here that each arrangement among classes entails a par-ticular form of 'the male deal.' Dauda defines the male deal as an arrangement typical of pre-capitalist societies, or those with many pre-capitalist kinship remnants, in which men agree to a kind of joint solidarity around the exchange of women. The male deal ensures access for all men to fertile women [Rubin 1975, Dauda 1992:20]. Dauda's analysis may be extended to conceptualize a capitalist male deal. A product of rigorous socialization, the capitalist male deal is a tacit, assumed, 'natural' agreement that all men will have a specific type of power in relationship to women. In general this takes the form of patriarch in a nuclear family in which men are the heads of household.

The centrality of the male deal to profit making requires an apprecia-tion of the revolution in marxist theory achieved in the mid-1960s by Dalla Costa, James [1972] and Federici [1973]. They developed the insight that labour power is the strategically most crucial commodity under capitalism and that this is the special product of women. Organized under male discipline in the nuclear family, women are socialized and forced to produce and service, without pay, this precious commodity the character of which changes with capital's changing needs. Mies summarized Dalla Costa's analysis: "The housewife and her labour are, in other words, the basis of the process of capital accumulation. With the help of the state and its legal machinery women have been shut up in the isolated nuclear family, whereby their work there was made socially invisible, and was hence defined - by marxist and non-marxist theoreticians - as 'nonproductive'. It appeared under the form of love, care, emotionality, motherhood and wifehood. Dalla Costa challenged the orthodox left notion, first spelt out by Engels, but then dogmatized and codified by all communist parties, and still upheld today, that women had to leave the 'private' household and enter 'social production' as wageworkers along with the men if they wanted to create the preconditions for their emancipation. Contrary to this position, Dalla Costa identified the strategic link created by capital and state between the unpaid housework of women and the paid wage-work of men. Capital is able to hide behind the figure of the husband, called 'breadwinner', with whom the woman, called 'housewife', has to deal directly and for whom she is supposed to work out of 'love' not for a wage. 'The wage commands more work than what collective bargaining in the factories shows us. Women's work appears as personal service outside of capital'" [Mies, 1986:31-32 citing Dalla Costa 1972:34].

Women are exploited by capital in other ways, but in the production of people as labour power, they are irreplaceable. This strategic power gives women revolutionary capacities, but the full potential of these are blunted by the equation of 'manhood' under capitalism with control over women, with disciplining a wife. Profit making depends on the male deal in two essential ways. Solidarity among men through the male deal is vital to capital first, because "all modern means of production, all classes of societies depend, for the supply of labour power, on the domestic community ... and on its modern transformation, the family, which still maintains its reproductive function although deprived of its productive ones" [Meillassoux 1975:81]. Second, capital needs a male deal because it mediates class struggle by reassuring men that they have a stake in power relationships through their continued subordination of women [Dauda 1992:144].

A thorough political economy analysis would address at least the following questions with regard to the capitalist male deal: What is the content of the male deal? How does this content define menwomen relations in specific periods? How does this form of the male deal condition and promote capitalist strategies at the particular historical juncture globally? How do exploited men, by conforming to the male deal's terms, avoid confronting their real class enemies while venting their frustration downward against those weaker than themselves? How does the male deal not only foster capitalist exploitation, but protect capital from challenge? How does conscious adherence to the male deal compare with unconscious adherence? How do women resist the male deal or seek to position themselves to be a part of it, seeking 'protected woman' status? And finally, how do some men exempt themselves from and resist the deal usually as part of a struggle against capital? In the present treatment of the new Rastafari, only some of these questions are addressed. The capitalist male deal is useful in this analysis because it conceptualizes the class specific dynamics which capital sought to create among men, among women and between men and women at each historical juncture in the three periods under examination.

The early 20th century

East African Nyabingi

Europe and North America at the turn of the century were marked by competition among national capitals, expressed in part through the scramble for Africa and its formal parcelling out to European powers in 1885. This competition and globalization of industry spurred infrastructural investments in the third world, notably ports and railroads. The capitalist crisis of the late 19th century generated serious pressures from the European working class which could only be solved by massive emigration. In East Africa, the construction of a railroad, beginning in the 1890s from Mombasa on the Indian Ocean to Kampala inland on the shore of Lake Victoria was designed to hold the territories for British settlement. Africans responded to European contact and overrule by attacking British officials and their indigenous allies. Nyabingi was a women-centred popular movement in Uganda which led this resistance at the turn of the century [Hopkins 1970:258-336; Rutanga 1991].

The Nyabingi movement, influential in southwestern Uganda from 1850 to 1950, was centred around a woman healer, Muhumusa, who was possessed by the spirit of Nyabingi, a legendary 'Amazon Queen.' Muhumusa organized armed resistance against German colonialists and was subsequently detained by the British in Kampala, Uganda from 1913 to her death in 1945. The spirit of Nyabingi possessed mostly women, but also men, who led uprisings against the British in 1916, 1919 and 1928 among the Kiga in Kigezi, along Uganda's borders with Congo and Ruanda. British occupation involved imposing foreign African Ganda intermediaries on the egalitarian, patrilocal Kiga agriculturalists. The Ganda's exactions of land, labour, food and money for poll tax galvanized the Nyabingi movement to rebel both against European and Ganda men and win major concessions. Nyabingi was a woman-led movement against oppression of all the community but specifically of women who did the farming and food preparation and hence were directly affected by colonial demands.

British efforts to crush Nyabingi involved criminalizing it as witchcraft through the Witchcraft Ordinance of 1912, promoting Christianity and encouraging other indigenous anti-Nyabingi cults. In labelling Nyabingi 'witchcraft' the British were resuscitating the witch burnings of 1500-1650 that were central in the move from pre-capitalist to capitalist relations in Europe. In this move, the power of women, especially over reproductive sciences, had to be crushed [Federici 1988]. Christianity produced Kiga men who replaced Ganda Agents as British intermediaries by the 1930s and who enforced colonial exactions from Kiga women and men. A capitalist male deal was struck between Christianized Kiga men and British colonialists for their mutual aggrandizement. This rise of the male deal was effective in forcing the woman-centred Nyabingi movement underground and depriving Kiga and other African peoples of their autonomy and wealth. With the emergence of colonial class relations, women suffered disempowerment to a much greater degree than men. Land loss reduced women's food self-sufficiency and trading capacities while the anti witchcraft campaign delegitimized Nyabingi women's work as healers and seers. Ironically, out of the colonial schools and churches rose male African nationalists who through a campaign against racism, challenged not the system of capitalist exploitation but the European men's exclusive privileges within it. In the Kigezi area of Uganda, church schools produced the 'Twice Born,' who like Nyabingi were proscribed as seditious by the British and led two revolts in the 1940s. Ultimately the nationalist men formalized a class arrangement with the departing British which included a capitalist male deal giving land ownership to men, not women and which centralized political

23

power in the hands of men. Nyabingi remained powerful in Kigezi, Uganda throughout the 1930s, where resistance involved arson. In Jamaica in 1937 it was reported in a local newspaper that the Nyabingi spirit moved on to Ethiopia and possessed Haile Selassie who fought Mussolini's fascist invasion.

Jamaican roots of Rastafari

In tracing the roots of Rastafari, the resistance of captured slaves in Africa must be a starting point. The social relations from whence they came are the sources of the resistance's early tenacity. African class and gender relations were developed for some 350 years around the European slave trade [Dike 1956:1-46]. The treachery of what was one of the earliest male deals is remembered by Guyanese poet Grace Nichols [1983:19] in her poem *Taint*.

> But I was stolen by men
> the colour of my own skin
> borne away by men whose heels
> had become hoofs
> whose hands had turned talcons
> bearing me down
>   to the trail
> of darkness
>
> But I was traded by men
> the colour of my own skin
> traded like a fowl like a goat
> like a sack of kernels I was
> traded
>   for beads for pans
> for trinkets?
>
> No it isn't easy to forget
> what we refuse to remember
>
> Daily I rinse the taint
> of treachery from my mouth

Malcolm X recalls the toll of the middle passage. "I know you don't realize the enormity, the horrors, of the so-called *Christian* white man's crime...*One hundred million* of us black people! Your grandparents! Mine! *Murdered* by this white man. To get fifteen million of us here to make us his slaves, on the way he murdered one hundred million! I wish it was possible for me to show you the sea bottom in those days - the black bodies, the blood, the bones broken by boots and clubs! The pregnant black women who were thrown overboard if they got too sick! Thrown overboard to the sharks that had learned that following these slave ships was the way to grow fat! Why, the white man's raping of the black race's women began right on those slave ships!" [Malcolm X 1965:311 quoted in *Sparerib* May 1992:30]. And from the time the first African slave set foot on land in the new world, rebellion was on the agenda. In 1503, only eleven years after Columbus' voyage, a complaint was sent back to Spain by the governor of Hispaniola (Haiti and San Domingo), Ovando. Basil Davidson reports that Ovando "told the Crown that fugitive 'Negro' slaves were teaching disobedience to the 'Indians', and could not be recaptured. It would, therefore, be wise for the Crown to desist from sending African captives: they would only add to troubles already great enough. But the Crown, naturally, did no such thing. Even by now, there was too much money at stake" [Davidson 1992:18].

Women fought rape. Native American women, "part of the bounty due the conquering Europeans" [Sale 1990:141], like their African sisters, "were victims of sexual terrorism as part of the larger scenario of conquest and colonisation" [Ransby 1992:84]. A sailor in Columbus' crew, recorded his exploits on landing at Santa Cruz island: "I captured a very beautiful Carib woman whom the Lord Admiral [Columbus] gave me, and with whom, having taken her into my cabin, she being naked according to their custom, I conceived desire to take pleasure [rape her]. I wanted to put my desire into execution but she did not want it and treated me with her finger nails in such a manner that I wished I had never begun...I took a rope and thrashed her well, for which she raised such unheard of screams that you would not have believed your ears" [Sale 1990:140 cited in Ransby 1992:84]. European invaders projected their inhumanity onto indigenous peoples and enslaved Africans. It was the depiction of Africans as inhuman, as 'heathen' which rationalized for the Spanish, the vicious trade and genocide in the Americas. Just months before Columbus sailed, the Spanish expelled Islamic Africans and Jews from Spain and used their property to finance conquest. In 1550 the Dominican friar Bartolome de las Casas argued that before the arrival of the Christian Spanish, the new world people "were in-

25

volved in every kind of intemperance and wicked lust" [Berkhofer 1979:12 cited in Stevenson 1992:30]. Amerigo Vespucci averred that "The women...are very libidinous...When they have the opportunity of copulating with Christians, urged by excessive lust, they defiled and prostituted themselves" [Berkhofer 1979:9 in Stevenson 1992:31]. Indigenous and captive women, the victims of rape, the survivors of slave hunt and middle passage, were labelled licentious and therefore, in the European slaveowners' lexicon, legitimately enslaved.

Slavery existed before Columbus. But the mass commodification of people entailed in the Atlantic trade and plantation slavery constituted an escalation of the commerce in labour power that provoked horror and resistance in Europe. The pursuit of a global trade in African people required what Basil Davidson calls "an ideological transition." He reports that "the first auction of African captives imported into Portugal in the 1440s 'was interrupted by the common folk, who were enraged at seeing the separation of families of slaves'" [Davidson 1992:22 citing Saunders 1982:35]. The Catholic Spanish and Portuguese justified chattel enslavement as "the means of Salvation to pagans otherwise condemned, ineluctably, to the fires of Hell." But this was "meagre stuff at the best, and almost from the start it was seen that something more was needed if the slave trade were not to be threatened by abolition" [Davidson 1992:22-23]. The racism of superstition and deviance became transformed into the racism of hard cash. Captives "were fitted for enslavement because they lacked the capacities to know and use freedom: they belonged in truth to an inferior sort of humanity; in short, they were 'primitives' whom it was practically a mercy to baptise and enslave" [Davidson 1992:23]. The 'scientific' and religious rationalization for slavery expanded in the measure that the 'curse of Columbus' grew. The ideology of racism "was enlarged again when the overseas slave trade, in itself the product of a proto-colonial relationship between Europe and Africa, was transformed into the imperialism of the nineteenth century. Racism had been useful to the justification of mass enslavement. It was to be still more useful to the justification of invading and dispossessing Africans in their own lands, Africans at home, at a time when invading and dispossessing Europeans in their own lands, Europeans at home, was stridently deplored as an act of barbarism" [Davidson 1992:23].

Between 1700 and 1830 British merchants and planters made tremendous profits from industrialized sugar plantations in Jamaica.

African slaves provided the labour which financed British capital's leap from mercantile to industrial capitalism [Williams 1944]. While slaves such as the woman warrior Ni in Jamaica fought for territory under Maroon control, European rural populations fought land enclosures through the late 18th century. Slaves and the new European working class challenged capital through the French and Haitian revolutions at the end of the 1700s and brought forth the era of free trade and free wage labour. In this context of world ferment, Jamaican slaves negotiated more time and more land under their own control for provision grounds and 'higglering' or the marketing of their own production. In Jamaica, African women controlled much of free Maroon agriculture. Slave women were very much in charge of both independent agriculture and, possibly before but "definitely" after emancipation, in internal marketing or 'higglering' [Mintz 1974:216-217, cited in Reddock 1985:76]. With the Sam Sharpe slave uprising and the overthrow of slavery in the 1830s women and men established a revolutionary peasantry of "Free Villages." Labour short plantations went bankrupt and were absorbed by land invasions into the revolutionary peasantry.

Fierce defense of land and other resources so seized was articulated through a militant quasi-religious 'Ethiopianism' which included Baptist sects in which women were in the majority. In the 30 years after abolition remnants of the old planter slaveholder class were joined by local merchants, in recapitalizing plantation agriculture for export crops (bananas, pimentos or allspice, coffee). From the outset women, who constituted 70 per cent of the cane cutting gang in post-emancipation Jamaica, were paid one half as much as men for equivalent work [Craton 1978:287]. Some free peasants also produced cane, bananas and other export crops profitably. As a result, by the 1860s resurgent agro-industrial capitalists were joined by some richer peasants to confront the poorer independent peasantry and a large class of unemployed and landless people. This was also a gender division as men gained access to capital and market outlets for cash crops while women were pushed off the land and denied waged work (locally and abroad in Nicaragua, Cuba and Panama) in favour of men. New technology such as the plow also displaced women agricultural wage workers. The planters and colonial state viewed the African ex-slave woman, not as the producer of commodities for exchange on the world market, but as producer of the labour force, which formerly was the concern of the slave plantation owner [Reddock 1985:76; Augier et. al. 1961:188]. In

27

Turner

1865 Paul Bogle led the Morant Bay peasant uprising for land around the Africanist slogan "cleve to the black!" From its repression grew an even stronger Ethiopianism around Bedward (1859-1930) who in 1895 told the black poor that "Hell will be your portion if you do not rise up and crush the white men" [Napier 1957:14]. Beward's movement constituted the vital link between the Morant war and the powerful Back to Africa mobilization of Marcus Garvey during WWI. In 1902 the early black feminist, Mrs. James McKenzie, served as secretary of the Kingston Branch of the Pan African Association. Through these movements 'the sufferers' and rural women in particular, elaborated the culture of the Free Villages.

The struggle for land and economic independence was fuelled by the rise of Garveyism coinciding with the relative power of the Jamaican poor during the commodity boom of WWI. Marcus Garvey (1887-1940) a printer and journalist, promoted race pride, African unity and political independence through armed struggle. Pledging "One God, One Aim, One Destiny!" and "Africa for the Africans," hundreds of thousands joined the Universal Negro Improvement Association (UNIA) which became the 'largest mass movement among black people this century, with 996 branches in 43 countries and over five million members" [Campbell 1987:54]. This massive moblization took place in the context of the formation of an international anti-war movement in 1917-1918. Amy Ashwood-Garvey, an early black feminist, co-founded the UNIA and organized women within it from the beginning [Ford-Smith 1987:11; Garvey 1976]. The full story of the Garvey movement, and especially of women's mobilization and of gender relations, has only begun to be told.

The weakness of Garveyism was its all-class nationalism which focused exclusively on race. In Jamaica in August 1929 Garvey held a convention of UNIA where he countered a revolutionary class analysis by black communist, Otto Huiswoud with Garveyite pro-capitalist black nationalism and its attendant male deal. For Garvey, the "fundamental issue of life was the appeal of tribe to tribe, of observing the rule that self preservation was the first law of nature." These were the fundamental divisions of humanity, not that between capital and labour, for the latter could not exist without the former. "There was an appeal closer to man than the appeal of labour. It was the appeal of one unto his own family and clan" [Daily Gleaner 19 August 1929:17 cited in Post 1987:3].

28

The Gavreyist male deal derived from a colonial idealization of the family promoted during the abolition of slavery in order to increase birth rates in the Caribbean, but re-emphasized in the early twentieth century when capital was drawing male workers out of Jamaica. Women were supposed to stay at home and promote 'proper family life' while the "ideal of the male breadwinner justified male migration, which also acted as a brake on male unemployment locally" [Ford-Smith 1987:5]. British constructions of manhood may be illustrated by an English doctor's 1915 definition of a likely opium addict as a man who "fails to identify with normal adult goals such as financial independence, stable employment and the establishment of his own home and family" [Uglow 1992:30].

As in East Africa where by the 1930s, British Christianity produced African men who forced the Nyabingi women's defence of peasant freedom underground; Garveyism forged a link between capitalist men, black and white, at the expense of black women's historical solidarity with black men in the Free Village movement against white capital. The male deal in both East Africa and the Caribbean emphasized race consciousness but the anti-racism insisted on a place for black men alongside white men in the capitalist system. It promised black men new precedence over women whose consequent subordination was essential to the preservation of capital's ascendency. The rise of a black nationalist male deal set the stage for struggles emanating from the global crisis of capitalism in the 1930s.

Rastafari and Mau Mau: 1930s-1960s

Rastafari in Jamaica

In the 1930s social conditions led some of Jamaica's rural poor to reject British overlordship by identifying positively with the Ethiopian monarch, Haile Selassie. Rastafari, and others in the Caribbean and worldwide supported Ethiopian resistance to the Italian invasion of 1935. Leonard Howell developed Rastafari through the Ethiopian World Federation's paper, the *Voice of Ethiopia* [Hill 1983]. Rastafari contributed to the organization and consciousness of the 1938 Jamaica labour rebellion. Jamaica's leftist paper *Plain Talk*, in February 1937, reprinted a pro-racist article which claimed that "the blacks are flocking to the standard of an organisation which dwarfs all similar federations." The organization was 'Nya-Binghi,' led by

Emperor Haile Selassie [Post 1978:173]. Thereafter some Rasta began to call themselves Nyabingi or 'Nya-men,' while Rasta forums of solidarity and the drums played at them were also called Nyabingi or simply 'Bingi [Campbell 1987:160].

Jamaican Rasta may have believed that the spirit of Nyabingi possessed Selassie and strengthened his fight against the Babylon of Mussolini's fascism. But the women-centred character of Nyabingi in East Africa was lost in its transfer to the new world. At Nyabingi gatherings in Jamaica, women were marginalized and subordinated, at least since the 1960s. Rasta 'queens' could not cook if menstruating, women could not 'reason' with the 'kingmen' nor partake of the chalice (smoke marijuana). Biblical support was found for limiting Rasta women's access to knowledge except through the guidance of their 'kingmen' [Ilaloo 1981:6; Makeda 1982:15; Silvera 1983, Yawney 1983, 1987, 1989]. What interventions transformed the independent Jamaican woman of the Free Villages into a domesticated and idealized queen? The explanation suggested here is that some Rasta men were inducted into a colonial male deal which privileged men at the expense of subordinated women.

Thousands of men returned to Jamaica in the 1930s when the recession ended migrant work. They demanded jobs and land from the major agricultural estates. In 1938 a rebellion started in the countryside with women and men demanding "land for the landless," and striking for higher wages in agricultural work. Police fired on the rioters, and a few days later the uprising reached Kingston. The Jamaica rebellion was part of a massive global uprising in the late 1930s which swept through the British and French empires. While little is known about gender relations in this international mobilization which was arrested by the launching of WWII in 1939 [Hyam 1990], we know that in the case of Trinidad, "a strong following of predominantly lower-middle and working-class women was the base of support of both the [1920s] Cipriani and [1930s] Butler movements" [Reddock 1988:496]. To buy social peace, women in Jamaica were pushed out of agricultural jobs and into domestic work. Although women such at Satira Earle and Adina Spencer worked to organize women in the early labour movement, the numbers of women in waged jobs outside the household were rapidly shrinking under the boot of the male deal [Ford-Smith 1987:11]. Between 1921 and 1943 the number of women agricultural workers fell by almost two-thirds. At the same time the number of domestic workers, including maids and garment homeworkers, increased more than fourfold [French 1987:21].

The colonial government's strategy for containment centred on women who, according to Jamaican historian, Joan French [1987:9] were to "(1) Marry a man to mind them. That way one wage would have to stretch for two or more, and jobs would not have to be found for women. (2) Stay at home to rear and service more workers for the big men to exploit - at no cost to them. (3) Accept that men should get first choice in paid work, and that women should be dependent. (4) Work for little or nothing to make big profits for the big man, since work for women was regarded as a 'privilege' not a 'right.' Yet women were forced to work because their man's wage was usually too small to 'stretch.'" In the competition for wages, men "came to see women more and more as a threat to "their" jobs. Many joined the big men in fighting against women's right to wages" [French 1987:9].

Throughout the British Empire, colonial policy during the 1939-1945 war years repressed dissent through imprisonment and exile, while war demand generated unprecedented income for the poor and especially for women. But with the demobilization of soldiers, colonial authorities launched a drive to push women out of remunerative work through the Women's Institute movement which was developed as part of the British social welfare policy for women in the colonies [Reddock 1988:496]. The Jamaica Federation of Women with a membership of 30,000 in the 1940s, was "a structure designed to contain women's resistance and control the poor black population as a whole" [French 1987:Introduction]. Through the Federation middle and upper class women organised 150 mass weddings. These echo 1915 state policy in Britain which urged men "to forego no opportunity of paternity," and pressed women into "hasty mass marriages with iron wedding rings to soldiers leaving for the front" [Royden and Wentworth Craig 1915 cited in Kamester and Vellacott 1987:33]. In Jamaica, wedding rings, acquired in bulk, were sold for ten shillings "to bring them within the reach of the ordinary people" [French 1987:29]. Through the churches, media and national and local organisations, a propaganda campaign encouraged poor women "to accept the 'dignity' of marriage as a solution to their economic problems" [French 1987:29]. However, during the 1940s militant women collected the 'mass' wedding rings and sold them to support women workers on strike for a democratic union [French and Ford-Smith 1987].

There was a resurgence of Rastafari in the 1950s with the bauxite enclosures. After the war US and Canadian capital eclipsed British capital. Alcan, Reynolds, Kaiser Bauxite, Alpart, Revere and Alcoa made Jamaica the world's largest producer of bauxite. The bauxite industry displaced thousands from rural areas and intensified unemployment. "Most of the land was purchased from small farmers, to the point where the activities of the transnationals displaced 560,000 rural Jamaicans from the countryside between 1943 and 1970" [NACLA Jan-Feb. 1981:2-8 cited in Campbell 1987:86]. Some 163,000 Jamaicans migrated to the UK and an equal number to the US and Canada between 1950 and 1968. While men went from the Caribbean abroad, women went from the countryside to the city. Jamaican rural women brought the core ideas of Rastafari with them to the urban slums. The Rasta upsurge, in addition to being a grassroots male class expression, was a rural women's urban survival network built on the organizations of Ethiopianism, Bedward and Garvey. The beginnings of the new Rastafari was a woman-identified, revolutionary peasant ideology shaped to serve new urban demands.

In the 1953 Kenya's Mau Mau revolt was covered in the world media with newsreels showing dreadlocked forest fighters. Jamaican Rasta adopted dreadlocks. In 1954 the main Rasta paper, *African Opinion* (New York) carried stories of the Mau Mau struggle, Burning Spear (Kenyatta) and Dedan Waciuri Kimathi. By 1963 Jamaican Rasta were under serious attack with eight being killed by police in the Coral Gardens rebellion. Militant reggae music and Rasta art fostered anti-imperialism and solidarity with liberation struggles. Rastafari, through Bob Marley's reggae, was poised to explode onto the world stage. Just as in the 1920s the British colonial state banned Garvey's UNIA paper, *Negro World*, because of its incendiary international affirmation of black independence, in the 1970s reggae and Rasta were targeted for repression. British counterinsurgency against Nyabingi in the 1920s included the encouragement of anti-nya movements in Uganda. The same policy was applied in Kenya in the 1950s when British intelligence formed Mau Mau 'pseudos.' In the 1970s this timeworn tactic was aimed at Rastafari: the CIA organized a pseudo Rasta body, the Ethiopian Zion Coptic Church, to divide the Rasta culture through drug deals and thuggery [Campbell 1987:116].

Mau Mau women

Kenyan women's involvement in the Mau Mau revolt of the 1950s is an important heritage of contemporary Rastafari. Essentially the struggle was for land which had been seized by white settlers on the completion in 1903 of the railroad through the rich highlands of the Rift Valley to Uganda. Here, largely with African women's labour, coffee, tea and pyrethrum produced profits for British multinationals and white settlers. By the end of WWII African 'squatters' lived on European farms providing wage labour while women cultivated small land allotments for food to feed their families and sell in the local markets [Kanogo 1987a]. Other Africans had been removed by the British to 'native reserves' where they were prevented by law from producing coffee or tea in competition with the whites. On the reserves, African men who had acted as proxies for British power owned large farms. A growing African and Indian working class had unionized in Mombasa, Nairobi and other cities. Its move to link up with agricultural workers on European farms was feared by whites whose profits depended on paying very low wages or obtaining labour in exchange for allowing 'squatters' to carry on their own cultivation [Singh 1969, Stichter 1982]. In urban areas women practised prostitution and marketed farm produce [White 1990]. A large contingent of demobilized African soldiers were unemployed, landless, militarily experienced and politicized by radical black US and Caribbean soldiers alongside whom Kenyans had fought in WWII [Shiroya 1985:164-177].

Mau Mau started in 1948 when women at Olenguruone agricultural settlement scheme went on strike. African women refused to participate in this terracing of the land to prevent erosion unless they first received title to the land. Their strike galvanized urban support from unions. Colonial reactions included repression which escalated until in 1952 the British imposed a state of emergency and launched the anti-Mau Mau war [Kanogo 1987a:105-120]. Women fought for land in many capacities within Mau Mau. Freedom fighters in the forests included women. Typically a woman 'seer' of the future worked directly with platoon commanders. Kimathi, the forest fighters' general, recommended the admission of literate women into the forest fighting force [Kimathi in Kinyatti 1986:76]. Other women joined Mau Mau fighters to avoid being sold off by their fathers as wives to pro-British 'homeguards' or 'loyalists.' Women in squatter villages on European estates provided intelligence, runners, food, refuge, medical supplies and care, and at crucial seasons, refused to pick tea and coffee. Furedi reports that "During the years 1952-56, European farmers were faced with a serious shortage of agricultural labour. In 1955, there was a shortage of 10,000 agricultural workers in Nakuru and Naivasha alone. The Labour Commissioner noted that 'the difficulty in obtaining labour, coupled with a general dissatisfaction over its quality, resulted in a growing demand for the return of Kikuyu workers'" [Labour Department Annual Report, 1955:5 cited in Furedi 1989:156]. Women on the 'native reserves' were an integral part of the Mau Mau military wing. In the cities prostitutes used their establishments as safe houses, and provided the Mau Mau Land Freedom Army with money, intelligence and especially with weapons. Women were the main arms dealers [Likimani 1993:2]. Women traders used the railroad and markets as networks of communication. Mau Mau women worked as ambassadors to mobilize solidarity in London, Cairo and in other international capitals.

The British, recognizing that success in counterinsurgency depended on cutting the supply link between villages and forest fighters, razed hundreds of communities and imprisoned women with their children in concentration camps. In Githunguri, the most repressive prison, women were divided into four categories depending on their degree of defiance. Most militant were the 'hardcore' women who were detailed to bury the bodies of freedom fighters hung by the British [Gakaara 1988]. Women in concentration camps were pressed into forced labour gangs. The British introduced a women's organization to counter the influence of Mau Mau: women who joined could be excused from forced labour. This women's organization was run by middle and upper class European women committed to enforcing Christian nuclear family values and practices on Kikuyu and other African women. Called Maendeleo ya Wanawake (progress among women) it was a vital agency in the British counterrevolution, and was fostered after independence in 1963 as the state party's semi-official and official woman's organ [Wipper 1975:330; Likimani 1993:1-4].

The Mau Mau armed phase of Kenyans' struggle for land and freedom was crushed by massive military repression in the late

1950s. However the overt, national struggle for land continued actively until October 1969 when Kenyatta banned the radical Kenya People's Union: "its demise marks the end of the era initiated by the Mau Mau revolt" [Furedi 1989:152]. While Kimathi and other men in Mau Mau worked for egalitarian gender relations, the force was weakened by sexism [White 1990a]. This polarization among men within Mau Mau divided those aspirant exploiters who sought to control women's labour from other men who affirmed women's autonomy. Decolonization was organized so as to entrench capitalist production relations and British allies to enforce them. Loyalist torturers in the concentration or 'screening' camps were made into chiefs and by April 1956 six Nakuru camps had become Chief's Centres [Furedi 1989:156]. In May 1960 a labour officer reported that agricultural workers in Eldoret and Nakuru had organized, listed grievances and "as a result are extremely truculent when returning to their employers and very often refuse to leave the farms" [NLO, C21, Labour Unrest, no. 13, SLO.RVP to Labour Commissioner, 13 May 1960 cited in Furedi 1989:164]. Women persisted throughout the 1960s in seizing land, especially from farms formerly owned by white settlers. Furedi reported that in 1960, "a number of farmers, especially those from the Afrikaner community, decided to abandon their farms and leave Kenya. A special committee on this matter received information to the effect that by November 1960, 38 farmers in the Uasin Gishu, 28 in Trans Nzoia and 20 in the Ol Kalou area "were either intending to leave after harvesting or had already left'" [Furedi 1989:166].

On the farms, the Kikuyu women and their families sought to re-establish the way of life that they had known before the Emergency. Many ex-squatters returned to the areas in which they had resided before they were evicted from the Highlands. Many unemployed, landless Kikuyu, were taken in and assisted by their ex-neighbours and relatives. The senior labour officer, in his report for 1960 noted that "the unemployment situation in the Province would have been more serious but for the custom of the Africans in providing hospitality to unemployed friends and relatives" [Furedi 1989:166]. Women organized the provision of hospitality and efforts to re-establish the way of life which Kikuyu had known before the armed Mau Mau phase.

Grassroots women and youth organized in affiliation with Kenyatta's nationalist party KANU (Kenya African National Union) which at this point "managed to convey the impression that it stood for free land for all" [Furedi 1989:168]. Meetings would be held outside the towns, and singing would take place. The administration delayed licenses for such meetings and for collecting money. Police who were stoned, raided a social dance of the Women and Youth League in November 1960, maintaining that "political singing took place without a licence." The other side of this mobilization was land seizure. As workers were given notice they told white farmers that "This will be our land soon and we will not go" [Furedi 1989:169]. The Labour Commissioner informed the Council of Ministers that in 1960 there were 171 cases of mass illegal squatting in the White Highlands" [KNA, Lab 9/305, Resident Labourers. 18 December 1960 cited in Furedi 1989:169].

The British envisaged allowing only a token few "exceptional non-European farmers" such as "Harry Thuku in the Kiambu district" to own land in the Rift Valley. A deal was struck to exclude women, children and men who had lived as squatters in the valley and who actually did the farming. By October 1959 a few African politicians, British colonial officials and white settlers introduced an ordinance removing racial barriers to land ownership in the White Highlands. 'Good husbandry' was the only criterion a new Land Control Board would recognize for inter-racial land transfers [Furedi 1989:163]. All but the very rich Africans were excluded. The male deal which accompanied this neocolonial class arrangement focused on the domestication of women. Maendeleo promoted dependence of women on husbands whom they were pressured to marry in church [Ngugi 1982:57-59]. It established a network of women's groups ostensibly for education in home economics and money-making craft work. But in practice Mandeleo extolled Christian virtues pertaining to the nuclear family and the subordination of wives to their husbands. Only through marriage could women get access to land which was registered in the names of men. Formal politics, though including token women locally, was an arena for men as was the protection of the judicial system. Medical, curative and spiritual activities of women were discredited and in some instances outlawed [Davison 1989:141-170]. In the face of this tremendous setback, Mau Mau women went underground. They kept alive their knowledge, networks and claim to the commons through indigenous women's groups, story telling and songs [Macgoye 1986, 1987]. As landlessness increased, many women were unable to find husbands through whom they could get access to land, and they migrated to the cities to work as domestics and within the expanding 'unrecorded economy.' Through selling food, domestic services, sex, changa (alcohol) and ganja the Mau Mau women bided their time and struggled to educate their children.

New Rastafari and the struggle against structural adjustment: 1980-2000

In the 1970s the International Monetary Fund (IMF) and World Bank began to impose a package of policies called structural adjustment on the third world. Structural adjustment programs may be understood as part of capital's response to the breakdown of three post war 'class deals' [Midnight Notes 1990:1-9]. Social-democratic capital at the end of WWII offered a variety of slogans to the world proletariat. These ranged from collective bargaining and racial integration in the US, to the family social wage in the USSR and eastern bloc, to colonial emancipation in Asia and Africa. A struggle ensued to determine the content of these slogans. But between 1965 and 1975, "proletarian initiatives transcended the limits of capital's historic possibilities..." [Midnight Notes 1990:3]. Profits plummeted and capital went on the attack by attempting to expand through structural adjustment programs. The debt crisis is being used in an attempt to resolve capital's productivity crisis [Federici 1990:11]. The contemporary attack involves ending communal control over the means of subsistence, seizing land for debt, weakening labour by forcing it to be more mobile, opening up the former eastern bloc and thereby intensifying competition among workers and finally, attacking self sufficient reproduction through a destruction of the earthly commons. The imposition of structural adjustment programs in the third world since the 1970s has been characterized as a war against the poor, a process of recolonization involving the enclosure of remaining commons by capital [Federici 1990, Adams 1991, George 1992, Elson 1992].

Structural adjustment is an international attempt by capital to replace the three collapsed class deals of the post WWII period with a more effective one. The third world bourgeoisie and state are enjoined to restructure economies to export cash crops, use the foreign exchange to pay debts; and give foreign capital renewed access to local resources. In this process the mechanisms of capitalist command are reorganized, beginning with the unification of metropolitan and peripheral capital. Federici argued with reference to Africa, that national and international capital together seek to implement "a wide-ranging reorganization of class relations, aimed at cheapening the cost of labour, raising social productivity, reversing 'social expectations' and opening the continent to a fuller penetration of capitalist relations, having the capitalist use of the land as its basis" [Federici 1990:12, 14]. Central to this strategy for jump starting global accumulation is land seizure or the enclosure of the commons, especially in Africa. In 1986 *The Economist* pointed out that with the exception of the white settler societies such as Kenya and Zimbabwe, "customary land-use laws prevail, which recognize ancient, communal rights to the land." These are the targets of structural adjustment. *The Economist* concludes that Africa's land "must be enclosed, and traditional rights of use, access and grazing extinguished," for everywhere "it is private ownership of the land that has made capital work" [*The Economist* May 3, 1986 cited in Federici 1990:11]. The same theme is expressed in Hardin's mainstream ideology of 'the tragedy of the commons' which advocates enclosure on the inaccurate presumption that socially held resources are not subject to indigenous custom and rules [Hardin 1968:1244; McCay 1987, Feeney 1990:15]. Land rights and squatter entitlements are the terrain of struggle.

Despite the IMF's neoliberal rhetoric about debt reduction, with structural adjustment the debt of most third world countries has increased. The deepening of the relationship of unequal exchange is fundamentally an attack on impoverished women who are being made to do more unpaid labour, the costs of which are revealed in statistics on the deteriorating health and nutritional status of such women [Elson 1989:68; 1992]. Structural adjustment seeks to make of women a 'fourth world' whose heightened exploitation is intended to subsidize the greater efficiency of capital and thereby its recovery from the current crisis of accumulation [Mies 1988]. Capital cannot expand without severing the link between people and the land. In the face of this drive toward capitalist agriculture and the universalization of a wage-dependent workforce is a growing fightback centered around the production of life and of the conditions of subsistence based on a defence of the earthly commons. The focus of structural adjustment on "the annihilation of the old African system of reproduction of labor power and struggle based upon the village and its tenure of the commons" means that women are the strategy's central target [Federici 1990:12]. This is part of the explanation for the prominence of women in resistance. The intensified resistance to feminism that women are experiencing worldwide is part of the male deal to aid capital in implementing its 'women as the last colony' strategy. The struggles of the poor, and in particular of women, at the end of the 20th century have been struggles against the class and male deals encompassed by structural adjustment [Trager and Osinulu 1991]. Popular movements including the new Rastafari may be understood in part as organizational responses to structural adjustment.

Kenya: new Rastafari and the democracy movement

Wanoi, a Mau Mau woman and oath administrator from Mutira, Kenya, reported that "When we finally got our freedom, we had something to rejoice about. There was much happiness and singing. I can remember one of the songs we were singing that day" [Davison 1989:161]:

Home guards, be praying to God
When the British go back home
you will be fed as meat to the vultures.

In 1978 a Kenyan peasant who had fought with Mau Mau observed that "The land, which we expected to be distributed free to the poor and landless, was grabbed by the former homeguards and the big politicians. ...most of the beneficiaries from our glorious struggle are the former collaborators, and not the legitimate freedom fighters. ...if the situation continues to worsen, our children will be forced to fight - to fight for the same things we fought for" [Mau Mau peasant, Nakuru District, Kenya, 5 September 1978 in Kinyatti 1986:131].

In the post independence period initial economic growth and the unusual persistence, in coup-prone Africa, of a non-military government in power, made Kenya the showcase of capitalist success and Nairobi the preferred African headquarters for multinational corporations. But the positive climate for foreign capital and local collaborators changed in the 1980s beginning with a coup attempt in 1982. In 1987, the leading corporate political risk analysts, Frost & Sullivan, reported that while the IMF in 1985 "expressed satisfaction with Kenya's economic performance, as did the World Bank to a lesser extent, ...perhaps a greater threat [than drought] in the long term is the continuing decline in confidence of the foreign business community, which is showing signs of steady disinvestment" [Frost

39

& Sullivan April 1987:3-A]. In summarizing the future prognosis for profit making, the political risk analysts concluded that "While under no immediate threat of political upheaval, despite frequent rumours of an impending coup, by the 1990s Kenya will experience more public protests and substantial guerrilla action stemming from Moi's preferential treatment of his Kalenjin tribe and his lack of concern for such problems as the high rates of urban and overall population growth" [Frost & Sullivan July 1986:U-1].

The children of Mau Mau freedom fighters have been carrying on a silent class struggle. Survival strategies of grassroots women are ingenious and sometimes heroic, as in the Nairobi Muoroto squatters' fight against removal in May 1990. Indigenous women's groups are used as a defence against the exploitative 'women and development' programs which structural adjustment seeks to implement through the state women's wing, Maendeleo. The collectivity of indigenous women's groups is founded on the continuity of the fundamental survival and resistance networks created by Mau Mau women from earlier forms during the 1950s. In the late 1980s when Maendeleo was officially incorporated into the ruling party, women voted massively with their feet. Evidence of an autonomous rising of women began to appear. Early in 1990 throughout Kenya rural women defied the law by uprooting coffee trees. Coffee, after tourism, is Kenya's major source of foreign exchange. Structural adjustment seeks to expand production and export despite a global glut and falling prices. But women who do the work have responded to the corrupt state buying monopoly's refusal to pay by destroying valuable trees. Coffee production fell sharply between 1988 and 1992 from 117,000 tons to 70,000 tons [IEU 1993:3]. In the place of coffee, they plant maize, a basic food crop and an immediate means through which to keep their children alive.

In December 1991 the Group of Seven met in Paris to organize a freeze on the disbursement of development aid funds to the Kenyan government pending improvements in payment practices by the coffee authority. As early as 1987 foreign investors were avoiding Kenya because of the misallocation of funds. Frost & Sullivan reported that "Governmental corruption and ambivalent policies toward international business remain at the core of an indifferent business climate" [April 1987:1-ex]. By 1992 the repressive single party political system was judged to be thoroughly corrupt and human rights abuses, according to OECD, had gotten out of hand.

Foreign pressure to move to a two party system increased. Ajulu contrasted this remedial, conservative intervention by capital with popular objectives: "It must also be recognised that the unmitigated looting of Kenya's resources, and the unbridled corruption, which are the hallmarks of this [embryonic bourgeois] class, has done irreparable damage to the image of capitalism as a system of production. Imperialism is therefore looking for a more *respectable* way of managing capitalism. Thus, the two issues: the peoples' cry for democracy, and imperialism's support for political pluralism, must not be confused; they are not the same thing. While the people seek an alternative, imperialism seeks to manage the crisis" [Ajulu 1992:84].

The attack by rural Kenyan women on the state's source of foreign exchange from coffee is only the most recent in a long series of direct actions which women have taken against efforts to subject them to husbands' discipline to grow cash crops rather than food. In 1980 Rogers reported that "economically successful production of pyrethrum, a women's crop, was halted because of the formation of a co-operative to market the crop to which only men could belong. The women simply lost their incentive to produce, and started to withdraw their labour" [Rogers 1980:181 citing Apthorpe 1970]. More research is needed to compare the social relations giving rise to the crucial pyrethrum strike and land invasions by Bahati women in 1963 and this pyrethrum boycott of the late 1960s.

In another case in Kenya's Nyanza Province, a colonial cotton project was stillborn because it required women's labour at the same point in time when women had to attend to food crops. "Women gave precedence to spending their time on their families' subsistence needs, and the cotton crop failed" [Rogers 1980:183 citing Fearn 1961]. The Mwea land settlement scheme is one of capitalist agricultural planning's best documented disasters for rural families [Hanger and Moris 1973, Rogers 1980:183-185, Wisner 1982, Lewis 1984:181-182, Agarwal 1985:102-105, Stamp 1986, 1989:64-67]. During the Mau Mau struggle Kikuyu who were destined to be settled in Mwea grew maize and beans for food and sale on women's plots, and coffee on men's plots (but mainly with women's labour). The colonial government dispossessed these Kikuyu of their land. In the neo-colonial government's rush to pre-empt land invasions during the early 1960s, the Mwea settlement scheme gave title to over 3,000 men who, with their families, moved onto 1.6 hectare plots with irrigation for commercial rice but with no land allocated for food crops. Women insisted on growing food and at the crucial maize planting season refused to weed the rice. Only their husbands could sell rice to the government monopoly buyer. The money was essential for food, fuel and household necessities. But women could get access to the money only by successfully begging it from their husbands. Instead women harvested rice and sold it directly onto the black market, or they allocated their labour time to wage work and kept the money. Whereas women previously had controlled their own allocation of labour time, within guidelines established by the kin group, now husbands directly controlled wives' daily use of time. Tensions abounded, nutrition deteriorated between 1966 and 1976 and a third of children under five were 20 percent underweight.

Identifying a long standing pattern and one which has only been intensified by structural adjustment programmes, Stamp argues "that women and families are subsidizing the monocropping of rice in Mwea economically, socially, and with their health" [1989:66]. Women worked harder, produced less, had less control over their own labour process and less control over family decisions. Profits which the state capitalist National Irrigation Board continued to reap through 1982, are a measure of the degree to which Kenyan men were able to impose the gender ideology of the capitalist male deal. Lewis concluded that schemes such as Mwea "are predicated on a given level of profit in a given form, obtained through a hierarchy of state, scheme management, and male household heads: women's labor is assumed to be an asset of the male head of household" [1984:182].

The Mwea scheme's capitalist hierarchy in which is embedded the capitalist male deal *replaces and opposes* the organizational bases of popular power on which people relied during the Mau Mau struggle: indigenous women's work collectives as well as community councils for decision making. Among the many contemporary forms of women's resistance were refusal to work on rice paddies and flight. Women who "found Mwea an intolerable place to live," left altogether, disrupting families and reducing the project's labour force. Reports of family breakup and women killing their children increased in the Kenyan press in 1990. A sensitive investigation of the social relations into which women were incorporated when they killed their children and fled would illuminate the extent to which such desperate actions were forms of resistance to the Mwea type of super exploitation. Some male title holders to Mwea land could not succeed in finding women "willing to marry into such an exploitative political economy" [Hanger and Moris 1973:244]. "Not surprisingly," reports Agarwal, "cases of women deserting their husbands and returning to the old settlements were not infrequent" [1985:104]. The disasterous Mwea rice project illustrates the three way struggle for control over women's fertility and productivity. The three parties to this struggle are grassroots African women themselves, African men and foreign (white male) capitalists. This fight for fertility has characterized Kenyan social struggles throughout the twentieth century [Turner *et. al.*, 1993; Turner and Ihonvbere 1993].

Kenyan women are increasingly self-reliant, in the face of increasing insecurity following upon post colonial agricultural policies which originated in the 1950s [Mackenzie 1986:397]. The Mutira Mau Mau fighter, Wanoi produces most of the food her family eats and sells any excess in the local market. She and her children harvest coffee but "it is her husband who receives the proceeds, which he may or may not share" with his wife and family. In 1985 Wanoi described her self-sufficiency to Jean Davison: "Like the granary I'm adding here at the homestead, I will not ask my husband for a cent, even though he got his coffee harvest money just the other day. If I rely on him to give me money, the day he misses I will have a problem" [Davison 1989:208]. And what is the point in working on a husband's coffee crop if a woman has taken steps to be self-reliant? An element of rebellion against husbands' labour discipline may inform the social situation in which women felt compelled to destroy coffee trees.

There is a strong thread of continuity running through twentieth century peasant women's struggles in Kenya. Women's consistent offensive to reclaim the commons is the historical context out of which arose the resurgence in the 1990s of the feminist attack on coffee capital. The actions of peasant women in ripping out coffee trees and thereby undermining an important element in the success of structural adjustment programmes, met with almost immediate response at the international level. This is a victory which builds upon earlier gains of popular resistance to IMF 'economic recovery' measures. The 1989 OECD Paris summit's decision to cancel a part of the African debt for those countries that implemented structural adjustment is a recognition of the power not only of uprisings and insurrections, but also of the "daily warfare" against IMF policies and their results [Federici 1990:17; Afshar and Dennis 1992; Elson 1991].

In cutting off external funds to the Kenya government, the Group of Seven gave a major boost to the multiclass pro-democracy mobilization. It includes a broad front of women, 3,000 of whom held a conference in Nairobi in February 1992 to plan strategies. On that day the fence enclosing a proposed construction site on Uhuru Park in the city centre was torn down, signalling the victory of the Greenbelt Movement in blocking KANU plans to build a skyscraper. The Greenbelt Movement is an internationalist, grassroots network of women which includes people described here as the new Rastafari. It brings together women in several African countries not only to plant trees but to defend the land on which they grow. Led by Kenyan feminist and professor of anatomy, Dr. Wangari Matu Maathai, the movement carries forward the ecology politics of Olenguruone women who, in the 1940s, insisted on title to land before they would reclaim it. The women, men and children of the Greenbelt Movement elaborate the stance of Bahati Transit Farm women who in 1963 refused to work for white settlers and carried out a land invasion. In the manner of a Nyabingi medium or a Mau Mau seer, Wangari Maathai invokes the ecological wisdom of African foremothers and forefathers. Direct action such as uprooting coffee trees, combines with an indigenous philosophy to make the Greenbelt Movement a vehicle for women's, men's and children's defence of the environment and their rights to resources. As such it constitutes one of the more startling responses to the dislocations of structural adjustment. As part of the pro-democracy mobilization in Kenya it mounted fundamental challenges to the capitalist class deal and the KANU regime in 1992.

The new Rasta of East Africa consists of dozens of autonomous groups which above all provide for survival. They combine study, artistic creation, childcare, economic activities, community service and politics. These are part of a larger and older Rasta network with links to London, Lagos, the Caribbean and elsewhere. In Nairobi feminist Rasta women work as maids, vegetable sellers, traders, seamstresses and prostitutes. They are influenced by Christianity, Islam, indigenous religions and many strands of spiritualism. Political reggae is of central importance. Marley's lyrics and those of other artists are studied carefully in Saturday afternoon 'reasonings' in slum yards. Marley's teachings are virtual primers for those seeking to develop their capacity to speak English. While extreme repression discourages the display of any Rasta symbolism or the Garveyite colours of red, gold and green; phrases such as "beat down Babylon

44

ghetto child," may be seen traced in the dust on a city bus. Since 1982 Kenyan Rasta have been commemorating Bob Marley each year. In 1991 the tenth anniversary of Marley's death was celebrated by an array of events in Kenya's clubs, bars, parks and other meeting places. Marley's power, one Ruandese dread disc jockey explained, is proportionate to political repression: "Marley says for us what we can't say." Concert videos of Marley and other reggae performers are accompanied by DJ narrations in Kiswahili, Kikuyu and other languages for the benefit of those who don't 'hear' Patwah or English. The tremendous popularity of Tracy Chapman is based on the revolutionary clarity of her lyrics, but also on the fact that, as in Nyabingi, she is said to be "Bob Marley come back from the dead."

In February 1992 Kenyan women demonstrated against the imprisonment of their menfolk. On their fifth day of a hunger strike to release 52 political prisoners, the women were attacked "with tear gas and gunfire and savagely beaten by baton-charging police. Several women, many of whom were mothers of the detainees, were knocked down unconscious in pools of blood" [Dadiran 1992:43-44]. One of the victims of this unprovoked attack was Wangari Maathai. In response to the police attack, several country women threw off their clothes in outrage. This traditional sexual insult, *Guturama*, which "entailed the exposure of a women's genitals to an offending party, was the ultimate recourse of those consumed by feelings of anger, frustration, humiliation or revenge" [Kanogo 1987b:82].

Despite strict censorship, the government press published photographs of the protesting women. These photos galvanized the society. They evoked memories of the 1922 insurrection when, in an attempt to release the imprisoned nationalist 'Chief of Women,' Harry Thuku, women charged armed police, exposing their bodies, and Mary Muthoni Nyanjiru and at least 55 others were shot dead [Muchuchu 1964 cited in Rosberg and Nottingham 1966:51-52, Mugo 1978:213]. The 1992 photographs evoked the courage of women under Mau Mau who stripped naked, thereby damning the police with "the worst curse one can expect" [Likimani 1985:71, Ardener 1975, Wipper 1982, Turner 1991]. In 1992 Nairobi women responded to police attacks with another hunger strike, demanding the release of political prisoners and an end to one party rule.

The new Rastafari culture has merged with the rising of Kenyan women and poor men which is the popular democratic movement

45

of the 1990s. Kenyan women are unearthing the tactics of their Mau Mau mothers and Nyabingi grandmothers. Allied with them are Rastafari, marginalized *and* organized by structural adjustment programs. Together they constitute the new Rasta which nevertheless is opposed by sexist, fundamentalist elements within such groups as the Tent of the Living God. This movement's leader lays at the feet of women most of the ills of society. Using Mau Mau and indigenous Kikuyu imagery, and wearing dreadlocks, he advocates the reintroduction of clitoridectomy as a means of reimposing the pre-capitalist male deal [Turner August 1991, Dawit 1993]. Imbued with an ideological mix of Mau Mau, Marley, Chapman, anti-apartheid, liberation theology and environmentalism; Kenya's new Rastafari are contending with these contradictions.

Like the democracy movements elsewhere, including in the former eastern bloc, the Kenya pro-democracy movement is multi-class, bringing together those who want merely political change with those who aspire to social transformation. In August 1991 Kenya's Forum for Restoration of democracy (FORD) was launched to embrace "the classes of property and capital, the professional classes, and sections of the clergy...[who] have won popular acceptance in the urban and rural areas, and above all, have convinced the working class and the peasantry that they are the champions of their democratic aspirations. ... Under the banner of multi-party democracy, this class hopes to mobilise the urban working class and rural peasantry against Moi's dictatorial regime and establish its own class rule" [Ajulu 1992:86]. Marx made clear the classical pattern of bourgeois betrayal in multiclass mobilizations: "It is self-evident that in the impending bloody conflicts, as in all earlier ones, it is the workers who, in the main will have to win the victory by their courage, determination and self-sacrifice. As previously so also in this struggle, the mass of the petty bourgeois will as long as possible remain hesitant, undecided and inactive, and then, as soon as the issue has been decided, will seize the victory for themselves, will call upon the workers to maintain tranquillity and return to their work, will guard against so-called excesses and bar the proletariat from the fruits of victory [Marx and Engels 1978:282].

This pattern was played out in the Kenyan decolonization process in the 1950s and 1960s. The British shaped the neo-colonial ruling party, KANU. It embraced loyalists in an imperial male deal which, in particular, deprived peasant women of land. The post-colonial economic restructuring of Kenya gave rise to a massive unrecorded economy and a more proletarianized agricultural workforce, both dominated by women who are most directly targeted by structural adjustment. These women are at the core and forefront of the exercise of social power which has halted Kenyan economic transactions and drawn world attention to the pro-democracy movement. As is the Mau Mau mobilization, the mobilization of the 1990s in Kenya encompasses two classes and within each, both genders. It embraces the bourgeoisie and the exploited classes. It also embraces women's and men's initiatives based on gender-specific histories, motivations and methods of struggle. Country women and city women initiated the contemporary uprising, drawing on deep historical and organization roots. They are sustaining it, through refusal to produce for export and through control of the 'informal' economy especially with regard to food supply to the cities. New Rastafari daughters of Mau Mau are demanding not the impotence of a vote by queuing every five years but 'land and freedom,' to control the means of production necessary to sustain life. Against these feminist politics of transformation are negotiations between international and Kenyan businessmen to update the capitalist male deal the terms of which are detailed in structural adjustment's conditionalities.

New Rasta: from the Caribbean to the world

Third world feminisms have emerged from the simultaneous limitations of male controlled state policy and liberation movement policy on the one hand, and expanding internationalism on the other. This historical trajectory roots women's movements of today in Nyabingi and Mau Mau, and it traces the trans-globalization of Rastafari.

This internationalization was fostered by women reggae artists especially after Bob Marley's death in 1981 and the continuation of his work by members of the I-Threes, Marcia Griffith, Judy Mowatt (*Black Woman*) and Rita Marley. By the late 1980s, feminist reggae was exploding forth from third world capitals and from the metropoles to be joined by a veritable flood of black feminist and womanist expression in the full range of media [Cooper 1986; Hernton 1987]. The magnitude of this power is illustrated by the April 1990 Mandela concert broadcast live from Wembley in London by CNN. The largest ever television audience saw Tracy Chapman in dreads singing "*Let us all be free! Poor people gonna rise up and take their share, Talkin' 'bout a revolution.*" In seeking to explain Chapman's popularity, Brownhill observed that because she is a black woman, "at the bottom of the worldwide hierarchy of power," Chapman speaks for all exploited people: "She is the oppressed singing about oppression. She is poor singing about poverty, she is black singing about racism, she is a woman singing about battering, she is a lesbian singing about love, and most poignant, she is an ordinary person singing about revolution. ... And herein lies the unprecedented revolutionary popularity of Tracy Chapman" [Brownhill 1989:36, 44].

In 1992 Chapman told *Sparerib* that "So many people feel like they don't count. They feel frustrated that their needs aren't being considered, and certainly aren't being met by a government that is supposed to be accountable to them. I think one of the things stopping us from getting together and challenging all this is that we are very afraid of difference. And we allow that to affect the way we live and the way we treat other people. It's a matter of being able to respect each other, of losing some of the fear that we have and realising that despite our differences, there are so many ways in which we're very similar. We need to realise that we're not benefitting anyone, not even ourselves, by holding on to this fear, hatred and anger, and by misdirecting our anger and our energies towards each other instead of towards the people who have the power. Of course, the powers that be encourage us to fight amongst ourselves, so that we forget to focus on them and their actions. Sometimes it seems like such a simple thing, to try and get people to realise that there's the possibility for consensus and for community; to realise the power we have in numbers to make changes; to realise that by working together, by putting ourselves on the line, by making our opinions known, we can actually challenge what's happening" [Chapman 1992:8-9].

Transformational women's networks which gathered strength in the 1980s include WAND (Women and Development Unit of the Extra-Mural Department, University of the West Indies), the Arab Women's Solidarity Association in Cairo, DAWN (Development Alternatives with Women for a New Era), the Greenbelt Movement in Africa [Sen and Grown 1984, Antrobus 1989, 1991]; the Self-Employed Women's Association (SEWA) and the Chipko movement in India, along with similar initiatives in virtually every region of the world [Shiva 1987, 1991, Elson 1992, Braidotte *et al* 1993, Kelkar 1992]. Women are defending the environment and their lives by saying no to ecological destruction by capitalist firms locked into a 'grow or die' dynamic. The fissures enforced by capital between first world women 'breeders' and consumers and third world women 'informal sector' unwaged producers are being bridged by the insistence on women as conscious, diverse human actors, and not the natural resources of others. Mies suggests that if this insistence on the human essence of women is recognized as the deepest dimension and motive force of struggles against intensified exploitation of women, neo-colonies and nature, then "...it would no longer be possible for one exploited and oppressed group to expect its 'humanization' at the expense of another exploited and oppressed group, class or people. For instance, white women could not expect their humanization or liberation at the expense of black men and women; oppressed First and Third World middle-class women at the expense of poor rural and urban women, oppressed men (black or white workers and peasants) at the expense of 'their' women. The struggle for the human essence, for human dignity, cannot be divided and cannot be won unless all these colonizing divisions, created by and capitalism, are rejected and transcended" [1986:230].

Transformational feminist movements are by no means limited to Rastafari. But the new Rasta includes detailed philosophies and practices founded in the defense of land, self-sufficiency, markets and women's autonomy. It transcends capital's definitions of the protected, domesticated woman, the dependent 'housewife,' whether she be in the first or the third world. This history catapults the new Rasta to the forefront to today's global resource defence movements. The material basis for true global solidarity among women is approximated in the actual processes of daily life as lived by the new Rastafari. The growing internationalist practice of the new Rasta is akin to Mies' imaginative perspective on how real solidarity among women worldwide might be forged: "If women are ready to transcend the boundaries set by the international and sexual division of labour, and by commodity production and marketing, both in the overdeveloped and underdeveloped worlds; if they accept the principles of a self-sufficient, more or less autarkic, economy; if they are ready, in Third World countries, to replace export-oriented production by production for the needs of the people, then it will be possible to combine women's struggles at both ends of the globe in such a way that the victory of one group of women will not be the defeat of another group of women. This could happen, for instance, if the struggle of Third World women for the control over their own land and their subsistence production - often fought against the combined interests of international or national corporations and of their own men - was supported by a consumer boycott in the overdeveloped countries" [1986:232-233]. We see this prescription played out by new Rastafari. While Kenyan women are ripping out coffee trees and planting maize, first world women are refusing to consume caffeine which is widely recognized by I-tal (pure or healthy food) conscious Rastafari as an addictive and dangerous drug.

Gender relations, as they have been shaped by the struggles against the new international division of labour that is structural adjustment, are most obviously marked by women's efforts to establish economic autonomy. Mies suggests that "if we no longer accept the capitalist separation between 'productive' and 'non-productive' work, we will see that, in fact, more men depend on women's work than do women on a male 'breadwinner'" [1986:160]. The struggle for economic autonomy involves women seeking their own form of financial independence instead of seeking to construct themselves so as to be well placed in a competition with other women for marriage and the 'protection' of a man. A Jamaican woman in Sistren says "I want to be free to have di relaxation I missed as a child.... I don't want to have anodder struggle again fi get dat freedom at home. Das why I stay a single woman" [Sistren 1987:128]. Another member of the theatre group reports that "Me never waan live wid no man. Mama used to warn me seh me no fi live wid no man. She used to be concerned bout how man ill-treat woman. Me used to see plenty example round di place and me never used to like it" [1987:182]. A third Sistren actor's mother made her own money but was brutalized by a rum-drinking, whoring husband: "From me know Mama she a work. She never depend pon no man. ... Mama always say, 'Yuh see how me batter? If me never married to yuh faada, me wouldn't haffi batter so. Is a mistake ah mek and tie up meself. Else ah could a look anodder man.' A mama first change me mind from marriage" [1987:221-222].

Economic autonomy for women is inseparable from sexual autonomy. The politics of new Rastafari contend with the politics of male dominance in 1990s dancehall music and styling in Jamaica and its diaspora. Feminist dub poets such as Jamaica's Cherry Natural organize women to protest by getting off the dance floor at the sound of anti-women lyrics or rap. This refusal of sexism is combined by an affirmation of sexual autonomy evident in dancehall fashion.

Young women are dancing in what amounts to beach wear. This is only one of the move visible expressions of what Cooper has called 'a celebration of female sexuality and women's power.' British artist Carmen Tunde is concerned with "the re-emergence" of black women's "ancient, woman- and earth-centred spiritualities." In her poem "Dreadlocks Lesbian," Tunde writes of teaching Rasta men [1987:206]:

Dreadlocks lesbian
is a powerful woman
because she listen to reason
no matter where it come from
and she no need
to preach 'pon you
Yet she will teach dreadlocks man
a thing or two
coz him still a fight
and show off
like cockatoo
But she know sistalove
from time
And peace is not a sign
of weakness
I tell you
dreadlocks lesbian
is one powerful woman

In Trinidad and Tobago, East Indian women are transforming stereotypes of domestication: "Thus subservience becomes discipline, submissiveness passion and sacrifice diligence. ... Several [of the people interviewed] felt that the phenomenon of a relatively large proportion of professional Indian women who were unmarried today was a result of their increasing outspokenness and assertiveness" [Mohammed 1988:395-396]. Trinidadian women "of all age groups, ethnic origins and religious persuasions," succeeded in July 1986 in partially reinstating a clause in the Sexual Offenses Bill which recognized marital rape as a crime for the first time. Women's groups and Trinidad's National Commission on the Status of Women had demanded improved legislation against sexual abuse and sexual violence. Their success against "the negative reactions of men in general including men in the governing and opposing political parties," was "the result of the united action of women of this country of an unprecedented scale. ... It marked the recognition by the majority of women that marriage did not make them the property of their men and that their personal autonomy should never be surrendered" [1988:501].

In East Africa, as in the Caribbean, women and especially Rasta women, are avoiding marriage in order to channel into their own and their mother's families the fruits of their labour [Wairimu 1991, Berman and Lonsdale 1992:462]. According to one Kikuyu country woman, "most women do not rely on their husbands today. They try to get money for themselves selling vegetables, clothes, or making handicrafts and selling them. They have an obligation to make sure that children do not sleep hungry or go without clothes" [Kariuki 1985:224 cited in Davison 1989:208-209]. According to Davison this woman speaks for "an increasing number of Gikuyu women who find their husbands coming and going as wage earners, but whose husbands' physical and economic presence in terms of labor and income are unpredictable" [1989:209]. Increasingly, women want children but not live-in husbands who rarely can offer any access to farm land yet are more driven to domestic violence by the crisis of manhood precipitated by landlessness and no income. Women's tendency to refuse the 'housewife' relationship in Kenya is paralleled by a rejection of clitoridectomy which prospective Kikuyu husbands used to require of wives "in order to channel our sexual energies into agricultural labour where we were little more than slaves" [Wairimu 1991, Hosken 1980, Dualeh Abdalla 1982]. New Rasta's economic autonomy for women also involves the refusal by women to be coerced into supporting men [Sistren 1987:296]. For example, among new Rasta women are those 'baby mothers' who, though under threat of violence, resist pressures to support their children's fathers financially and through the provision of domestic and sexual services. Contemporary dub poetry, reggae and calypso include lyrics which celebrate women's insistence on such autonomy. This change undermines capital's male deal in favour of egalitarian relations among women and men.

Of utmost importance is the fact that in the Caribbean and other ex-slave societies of the new world, indigenous male deals did not exist because the total population was uprooted from their indigenous traditional political economies. The experience of slavery further broke up the functioning of old world precapitalist male deals [Reddock 1985]. The newness of Caribbean society has fostered that region's tremendous creativity. Many elements of social relations had to be created anew from the ultra-advanced capitalist factory system, the sugar plantation and the sharp black-white division between the classes of African slave and European master. Much has been written about how this history gave rise to the new world's creativity with regard to class struggle [James 1984:218]. The astonishing universalism of the Caribbean's contributions to art and to resolving race and class contradictions is rooted in the absence of indigenous pre-capitalist social relations in a highly modern region. We are only now beginning to appreciate the implications of the absence of pre-capitalist male deals for gender relations. Among these are the relative autonomy of Caribbean women and the evolution of a revolutionary alternative to the capitalist male deal which we see now in the new Rasta.

Conclusion

The new capitalist deal embodied in structural adjustment programs requires a new male deal whereby men agree to extract more unpaid work from women under conditions less costly to capital. The difficulty faced by capital is that the prerequisites required by exploited men in order to realize this male deal - jobs, a 'family wage,' a positive future for their children, a liveable environment - are not there. They cannot be delivered as is demonstrated by the breakdown of the post WWII capitalist deals. Consequently, the male deal is based increasingly on rhetoric and symbolism which construct manhood on models akin to the machine, especially the war machine, devoid of human feeling and expressing unprecedented misogyny, racism and competitive violence. This symbolic male deal tends toward ever greater extremes of racism, sexism and the dehumanization of women, and inevitably, also of men.

The state in both the first world and the third is the central instrument in enforcing this dispensation. In January 1992 Canadian Labour Congress president Shirley Carr said that "racial and sexual discrimination have increased in the workplace...[and yet governments and employers] use the recession to quash the push for human rights" [*Toronto Globe & Mail*, 25 January 1992]. In the late 1980s Reddock criticized the Trinidadian government for privatizing social services under pressure from the IMF just as it had become apparent that the demand for the services of rape crisis centres surpassed the capacities of voluntary women's organisations and urgently required financial support from the state [Reddock 1988:502]. According to Mies, "It is now known that violence against women is increasing in the West" as well as in the third world and the then eastern bloc [1986:159]. One expression of this is sex tourism and the flesh trade of third world women to industrialized countries which is expanding as are "the more open sexist, racist and sadistic tendencies in this market" [Mies 1986:141]. In West Germany in the mid-1980s fully 52 percent of the home video market consisted of horror, war and pornography films. "Violence against women itself becomes a new commodity" and firms trafficking in women openly advertise 'submissive, non-emancipated, docile' Asian women as wives for European men [Mies 1986:139,137; Truong 1990].

Pornography and militarism have contributed to deracinating a generation of lumpen male youth. But they have also provoked a search for alternative constructions of manhood [Kimmel 1991, Davies 1993]. This search by men is motivated, in part "by the desire to restore to themselves a sense of human dignity and respect" [Mies 1986:223]. Dauda argues that analyses and practices which leave out gender relations in fact analyze and pursue the struggle between male collectives. "It is also evident that without gender consciousness, class consciousness remains an illusion. Rather than being informed by a genuine class consciousness, men and women are too often organized only by the dynamics of the sex/gender system; men struggle for their share of the male deal while women are lost in the struggle for or against protection" [Dauda 1992:144]. New Rastafari involves women who accept neither but rather seek their own independence. New Rastafari includes an in-formation contingent of men who have 'committed gender suicide,' and rejected the capitalist male deal in favour of feminist solidarity and transformational, egalitarian women-men relations.

The male deal is no longer universal. Independent men are breaking away and expressing solidarity with women's struggles against the new capitalist deal that is structural adjustment. There have always been individual men acting in solidarity with women. But now there is a groundswell of mobilization. In a movement which is growing with astonishing rapidity, men are consciously deciding to "forego building up their ego and identity on the exploitation and violent subordination of women, and to accept their share of the unpaid work for the creation and preservation of life...." [Mies 1986:223]. This fissure in the cross-class, cross-race male alliance plus the objective impossibility of realizing the structural adjustment linked male deal constitute a serious crisis for capital. How, other than through the sexist discipline of men, can structural adjustment programs extract more profits from women? As some men in the exploited classes refuse to strike downward at women, substituting power over women for power over their own lives, the beliefs and behaviours of other men caught up in the male deal come under sharper scrutiny. Capital's monolithic definition of manhood is fractured. The protection which capital has hitherto enjoyed is dissolving. With this continuing dissolution of the male deal, the unity of exploited women and men of all races can only increase at the expense of the power of capital. Sharper polarization between the exploited, so united, and the exploiters must characterize the emergence of the new society of which the new Rastafari is but one expression.

The new Rastafari has emerged through a process whereby black feminisms have garnered the weight and media access necessary to enable them to appropriate Rastafari and redefine its content. This has also been a process of rediscovery of the history of women in struggle and an excavation of global gender, class and race relations. While the theories and practices of struggle for the new society are much broader than the new Rastafari, and exist separate from it, they are to a remarkable extent expressed globally through the cultural movement of Rastafari, making it a fertile social force for the 21st century.

Chapter 3

Selected Historical Events in the Evolution of Rastafari

Bryan J. Ferguson

1492: Columbus discovers the new world signalling the dawn of the Atlantic slave trade. The trade continues for four centuries, displacing an estimated 15 million Africans and killing countless others.

1655: Britain captures the island of Jamaica and inherits Spanish slaves known as Maroons, many of whom flee to form isolated mountain communities. Because of the profitability of its sugar plantations, Jamaica quickly becomes the gem in Britain's West Indian possessions and a centre for the reexport of slaves to other British colonies.

1664: Jamaica's first elections are held. As the right to vote is restricted to the property owning class, the House of Assembly represents only a fraction of the Jamaican people.

1673: Large slave revolts on many Jamaican plantations increase the number of free slaves.

1729: The first Maroon War escalates into an island wide conflict. The Maroons demand autonomy and an end to British harassment.

1739: Unable to defeat the Maroons, British authorities accept Maroon autonomy and sue for peace.

1760: The Tacky rebellion spreads throughout the island. The British succeed in putting down the revolt and 600 slaves are executed.

1795: Two Maroons are beaten by British planters and the 2nd Maroon War begins. A total of 556 Maroons are deported to Nova Scotia where they are called upon to fight in the Napoleonic Wars.

Following the war, the Maroons are returned to Africa, the first new world slaves to be repatriated.

1800s: The revival of African customs and the Cumina religion challenges the British ban on African ceremonies. Literate black preachers, skilled in interpreting the European debate over abolition, emerge as powerful Caribbean leaders. Numerous plots are revealed, and many open revolts occur throughout the West Indies.

Industrial capitalism replaces mercantilism. The industrialists, realizing that waged labour would increase productivity and enlarge the international market for their goods, lobby for the abolition of the slave trade.

1804: The first black independent state in the new world is formed in the French colony of Santa Dominigo (Haiti). Led by an African slave, Toussaint L'Ouverture, the Haitian Revolution permanently destroys the myth of the docile slave and inspires slaves world wide to challenge the colonial order.

1807: The slave trade is abolished by the British legislature, but Africans already enslaved in the new world remain in bondage.

1815: The first of 15,000 American slaves are repatriated to Liberia.

1831: Led by Sam Sharpe, 20,000 slaves in western Jamaica free slaves and seize plantations. Within two weeks, the rebellion spreads to Montego Bay and property valued at over 1 million pounds sterling is destroyed. Sharpe and thousands of others agree to surrender when promised amnesty. The promise is quickly retracted and all are executed.

1834: The British parliament legislates the abolition of slavery in all British dominions. The Emancipation Proclamation is delivered to Jamaica but blacks remain politically disfranchised and economically impoverished.

1865: Paul Bogle refuses to pay taxes to the Magistrates in Morant Bay. Chanting 'Cleave to the black,' thousands march on Morant Bay, set fire to the court house and free prisoners. Martial law is imposed and thousands of blacks, including Bogle, are hanged. In the wake of the rebellion the House of Assembly votes in favour of its dissolution and accepts direct colonial rule from Britain.

1885: The emergence of multinational corporations leads to intensified capitalist competition and the advent of direct exploitation of African resources and labour. At the 1885 Berlin Conference, European powers agree on the partitioning of Africa.

1887: Marcus Garvey is born in Jamaica.

1896: In what is today Ethiopia, the Abyssinians, under Emperor Menelik II, defeat the Italians at Adowa. The redemption of Africa seems near with the defeat of a European power by an African king. Ethiopianism emerges as a brand of radical black nationalism throughout the African continent and the diaspora.

1900: The 1st Pan African Conference is convened by W.E.B. Du Bois and Dr. Robert Love.

1906: Members of the Ethiopian Movement lead the Bambata revolt against white rule and exploitation in South Africa.

The first Pan-African Association branches are established by Dr. Love in Jamaica.

1912: Marcus Garvey begins to organize the Universal Negro Improvement Association (UNIA) in Jamaica. His efforts are largely frustrated by the colonial authorities.

1914: WWI, a war fought by European powers for control of the third world, especially the Middle East and North Africa, begins.

1916: Garvey emigrates to the United States to raise funds for the UNIA. The organization is formally founded along with the African Communities League. While in the United States, Garvey launches the Black Star Line Shipping Company as visible proof of Negro self-reliance.

1919: Black arts and culture flourish in the Harlem Renaissance.

1920: The 1st International Convention of the Negro Peoples of the World is held in Harlem.

1921: Threatened by Garvey's brief return to the island, British authorities station battleships in Jamaican harbours. Despite constant state harassment Garvey draws widespread popular support and forms the People's Progressive Party.

1927: On his return to the USA, Garvey is arrested on charges of having defrauded black investors in the Black Star Line Shipping Company and is deported to Jamaica. Garvey continues to preach 'Africa for the Africans' and, according to current belief, prophesizes the emergence of a black ruler who will lead Africans to redemption.

1930: Prince Ras Tafari is crowned Emperor Haile Selassie I in Addis Ababa, Ethiopia. There is tremendous international media coverage of the event and many Jamaicans begin to take seriously Garvey's promise of redemption.
At the 1930 Moscow Conference, Haile Selassie is elected head of the Nyahbinghi Order. He is recognized as the saviour of the black people and the returned Messiah.

1931: Joseph Hibbert returns to Jamaica from Costa Rica and begins preaching the divinity of Haile Selassie.

1932: Leonard Howell returns to Jamaica. He argues that black loyalty should be to Haile Selassie and not to the King of England. Joseph Hibbert organizes the Ethiopian Coptic Faith.

1933: Howell sells over 5,000 photographs of Haile Selassie, representing them as both passports and passage by ship to Africa. The British colonial authorities in Jamaica arrest him and sentence him to two years for sedition.

H. Archibald Dunkley forms the Kings of Kings Mission in Kingston.

An article which appears in the *Jamaican Daily Gleaner* details the growing Rastafarian movement. It is the first known published account of Rasatafari.

1935: Italian facists under Mussolini invade Ethiopia. The failure of the League of Nations to respond causes many blacks to view the League as an instrument of European imperialism.

The Kingston chapter of the UNIA demands that members be allowed to serve as volunteers in Ethiopia.

1936: Marcus Garvey meets Haile Selassie in London. Although he publicly criticizes the Emperor for presiding over a feudal society, Garvey, he supports the Emperor's defence of Abyssinia against Italian incursion.

1937: The Ethiopian World Federation (EWF) is formed by Dr. Malaku Bayen.

1938: The first EWF local is established in Jamaica. A national revolt engulfs Jamaica. Starting among rural workers but involving all poor and exploited Jamaicans, the uprising challenges the colonial order. Similar rebellions were mounted in many other colonies in Africa, the Caribbean and the Middle East in the late 1930s.

1939: World War II begins. The conflict spreads to include much of East and North Africa.
Under the leadership of Norman Washington Manley, the People's National Party is founded in Jamaica.

1940: Howell buys the Pinnacle estate in the Jamaican parish of St. Catherines. The House of Youth Black Faith is founded by Ras Boanerges, Philip Panhandle and Breda Arthur.

1941: Haile Selassie returns to Ethiopia after the defeat of the Italians.

Hibbert establishes a local branch of the Ethiopian Mystic Masons. Howell and other members of the Pinnacle commune are arrested on charges of disorderly conduct and cultivation of cannibis or ganja.

1943: Howell returns to Pinnacle.

1944: Jamaica receives a new constitution which leads to the provision of universal adult suffrage and full internal self-government. In the country's first democratic elections, William Alexander Bustamante's Jamaica Labour Party wins a majority in the House of Representatives.

1953: Professor G. E. Simpson conducts the first academic study of the Rastafarian movement in Jamaica. His 'top down' establishment findings distort Rastafari philosophy and undermine the movement's legitimacy. His research coincides with sharpening class struggle in Jamaica as the prospect of independence looms and contributes to justifying police attacks on Rastafari.

To demonstrate their support for the Mau Mau freedom fighters of Kenya and their own African identity, many Rastas begin to grow their hair in locks.

1954: After many unsuccessful attempts, the police finally succeed in disbanding the Pinnacle commune.

1955: The Rev. Claudius Henry visits Ethiopia and returns to establish the African Reform Church in Jamaica.

1958: The House of Youth Black Faith Rasta Commune Convention is held in Kingston. The public meeting is called to disseminate information on the Rasta movement and attracts thousands.

1959: A clash between a Rastafarian and a policeman at Coronation Market results in the market vendors siding with the Rastaman. The confrontation sparks a wider conflict with the authorities. The police react by destroying the Rasta commune of Back-o-wall and forcibly shaving many Rastas' dreadlocks.

1960: More sensitive researchers from Jamaica conduct another study which recognizes that Rastafari are creating an alternative culture and survival system. The University College of the West Indies' "Report on the Rastafarian Movement in Kingston, Jamaica" supports the repatriation of the Rastafarians to Africa.

Rev. Henri is imprisoned when a police raid reveals a large store of guns and a letter to Fidel Castro.

1961: Norman Manley's PNP government sends a mission to Africa to explore the possibility of repatriation. The mission visits five African states, including Ethiopia, all of which agree in principle to the repatriation of the Rastafarians.

1962: Jamaica is granted independence.

1963: A killing at Coral Garden is blamed on a Rastafarian. The Prime Minister orders the round up, dead or alive, of all Rastafarians resulting in open conflicts between Rastas and the police.

1966: Haile Selassi visits Jamaica. Police destroy the Rasta commune of Back-o-wall in CIA sponsored 'Operation Shanty Town'.

1968: Walter Rodney, a Guyanese revolutionary historian, is deported from Jamaica. He had been teaching African history to young people in the shantytowns of Kingston.

1969: The Rasta movement association is formed.

1970s: A particularly revolutionary strain of Rastafari spreads throughout the Eastern Caribbean islands. The politicized reggae of Bob Marley and the Wailers gains popularity worldwide.

In Jamaica, Vernon Carrington founds the Twelve Tribes of Israel. This organization is more hierarchal and less democratic than are the groups of orthodox Rastafari. The Twelve Tribes of Israel relaxes gender and racial barriers and is implicated in large scale drug trading with the USA.

1974: Emperor Haile Selassi is overthrown and detained.

1975: Haile Selassie dies. Some Rasta deny that the death occurred.

1978: Thousands turn out at a Rasta convention held by Rastafarian patriarchs. The meeting lasts for thirty days, finally being broken up by the authorities after the patriarchs call for the removal of the Jamaican cabinet.
A Universal Negro Improvement Association (UNIA) conference is held in Kingston to discuss the question of repatriation. Bob Marley visits the Rasta settlement at Shashamane, Ethiopia.

1979: Rasta patriarchs Jah Lloyd and Ras Makonren cut down the British flag at the British High Commission in Kingston, Jamaica in protest against British slavery, colonialism, capitalism and domination of blacks.

1980: Rastafarian Stephen McDonald runs for office in Jamaica. Bob Marley performs at the national independence celebration in Zimbabwe.

1981: Black youths, many of them Rastafarians, launch spontaneous revolts in many British cities in opposition to growing police brutality and repression.

1982: Bob Marley dies and is remembered both as a national hero and a Rastafarian spokesperson.

The "First International Rastafari Conference" is held in Toronto, Canada. The discussion includes the changing relations between men and women and the power of women within the movement.

1984: Three Rastafari elders travel to Canada on a four week cultural education mission. The programme, "Voices of Thunder: Dialogue with Nyahbinghi Elders" is aimed at dispelling many of the misconceptions surrounding the movement and increasing public awareness of Rastafari.

1986: An international Rastafari conference is held in London, England. Discussion of gender relations is on the agenda. In the two weeks following the conference, Rastafari elders promote their culture throughout much of the United Kingdom.

1987: Horace Campbell's book *Rasta and resistance from Marcus Garvey to Walter Rodney*, is published in Trenton, New Jersey by Africa World Press. It is the first book to trace the cultural, political and spiritual sources of this movement of resistance and to break the intellectual traditions which placed the stamp of millenarianism on Rastafari.

Sources:

McPherson, E.S.P. and L.T. Semaj, "Rasta Chronology," *Caribbean Quarterly Monograph*, 26:4 (December 1980):97-98.

Campbell, Horace, *Rasta and Resistance: From Marcus Garvey to Walter Rodney*, Africa World Press, Trenton, New Jersey, 1987.

Chapter 4

Moving with the dawtas of Rastafari: from myth to reality

Carole D. Yawney

Carole Yawney's "Moving with the dawtas of Rastafari..." considers why there has been such a long silence about women in the literature on Rastafari. Ethnocentrism, with its male bias, has colluded with the patriarchal quality of the Rasta movement to bracket discussion of women's experiences. The struggles against cultural misperception, racism and imperialism have seemed to some more pressing. But in the 1980s the silence was broken as internal discussion of relations between women and men burst forth into public discussion and media expressions. In considering who should do research on gender relations, Yawney notes the progress made by those in the movement. But false consciousness characterizes analysis from within and without. Feminist scholars do have a part to play in this exploration, but exactly what part has yet to be determined. Yawney concludes by affirming that the theoretical framework essential for understanding gender relations among Rastafari must embrace gender, race and class.

The discussion of the role of Rastafari sistren raises important methodological and conceptual questions. In the first place, we have to ask why the subject of Rastafari women is only of recent concern, and in fact, has hardly been researched at all, except as part of a larger study. Given the number of writings on Rastafari, this is a critical omission. Second, if as researchers we decide to examine the situation of Rastafari sistren, or other sensitive issues within the movement, how do we go about it? What are our motives? Do we simply describe and report, or do we analyze and evaluate in a way that directly challenges the status quo? This concern raises the issue of the social responsibility of the researcher. Thirdly, who is best equipped to appreciate the experience of women in Rastafari? Or should both outside researchers and researchers who are themselves Rastafari leave this discussion to Rastafari sistren themselves? And

Carole D. Yawney

if as ethnographers we choose to undertake this work, what kind of fieldwork strategies are most appropriate? Do we network with the women thereby alienating the men, or do we talk about "family studies" instead of female-male relations? Finally, given that we have collected sufficient data, how do we design a theoretical framework which can incorporate the factors of class, race, and gender? While in the context of Caribbean studies the relationship between the first two factors has often been the subject of scholarly concern, gender relations per se have not been considered problematic enough for incorporation into the political ideologies of the region. In this chapter I propose to deal with the four concerns in terms of my own experiences in this regard during the 15 or so years that I have been involved in Rastafari works.

Let us consider first the silence concerning Rastafari women. Why is the growing volume of literature on Rastafari, which is produced largely by male researchers, so limited when it comes to the subject of women? Here we need to examine the possibility of ethnocentrism on the part of most academics (myself included) who, having been socialized in sexist societies and into professions with largely unexamined male biases, do not generally consider women's experiences to be serious and independent subjects of study. This orientation would be reinforced in societies such as Rastafari where its patriarchal ideology would confirm western ethnocentrism and encourage us to identify with the male definition of what is culturally significant. It is only since the late 1970s that accounts dealing primarily with the subject of Rastafari gender relations have started to appear. With a couple of exceptions most of these articles are by Rastafari brethren and sistren themselves and are to be found in cultural publications. Furthermore, with the exception of Blake [1983], Ilaloo [1981], and Silvera [1983], these materials tend to support the traditional role of Rastafari women. However, it at least appears as if female-male relations are something no longer simply taken for granted by the Rastafari community but represent an issue which needs to be addressed.

The clearest statement of the traditional role of Rastafari women in the Jamaican context is written by a Rastafari sistren as part of a 1985 special issue of *Caribbean Quarterly* devoted to the subject of Rastafari. According to Rowe, "There can be no denying the fact that Rastafari is a patriarchal movement. The male is at the head, having responsibility for conducting rituals, interpreting events of sig-

66

nificance to the community. Rastafari is based on the Bible, it therefore follows that its structure and philosophy would pattern that which unfolds in the Bible [Rowe 1985:13-14]."

Rowe describes in some detail the Rastafari gender ideology about women (who she calls females), emphasizing that since women's way to God is through man, then women cannot be leaders in any ritual. Rowe acknowledges the double standard of behaviour regarding sistren: their exclusion from sharing the chalice and reasoning with the brethren; their modest dress code which includes covering their heads at all times; and restrictions such as not cooking during menstruation when women are considered unclean [Rowe 1985:15]. On the other hand, Rowe notes the idealized conception that Rastafari hold of women as "Queens, Madonnas, and Earth Mothers," arguing though that this should not be regarded as contradictory [Rowe 1985:16]. She goes on to show that in the 1970s a trend developed towards more independent and individual behaviour on the part of sistren, although this usually occurred only conditionally with the approval of their male partners [Rowe 1985:19]. However, while demonstrating that Rastafari sistren have become increasingly active outside their traditional roles (although still oriented towards service work), Rowe ultimately takes the point of view that "The concept of male dominance can have no validity where the female understands, accepts, and operates within the parameters of a prescribed role. It is only when the female resists this role that the concept acquires significance [1985:16]."

On the other hand, I have argued elsewhere that male dominance is built into the basic nature of Rastafari in such a way as to constitute its central contradiction. If Rastafari shares with the social system to which it is so opposed a fundamental oppression of women, how can it represent in the final analysis a genuine alternative social form [Yawney 1983:120]? I have even suggested that perhaps in some ways brethren have co-opted the strengths of traditional Jamaican women's culture and redefined the social context so as to support patriarchal privilege [Yawney 1983:141]. While the matrifocal family pattern in Jamaica confers upon women a certain degree of independence, it also means that ultimately women have to assume responsibility for their children. A man who has more than one "baby mother" may not be economically capable of supporting all his children. Many Rastafari brethren advocate the adoption of a polygamous household arrangement on the grounds that this is an

Carole D. Yawney

African cultural practice. But in situations with which I am familiar this has in effect served to centralize the baby mothers under one roof where sharing child rearing can be somewhat advantageous in economically precarious Jamaica.

In fact a short article written in 1978 by two Rastafari sistren acknowledges and defends these very consequences. Sister P. and Sister Bernie write:

> Most Rasta man like to have more than one queen, so as to enable him to have the best of both worlds (using the sisters at their convenience), it may even be to boast to his idrens...You will find a man who will show one of his queens that there is another queen and eventually he will introduce them and after that who knows, they may well see eye to eye. In that way all the queens can associate more fully with each other, give each other guidance and understanding, therefore helping their children to grow up the rightful way. At the same time the man will not need to play such an active part in the first few years of the children's life-cycle...Polygamy has its advantages and disadvantages, for example a dread can be with all his youths and queens at the same time, and also there would be less unmarried mothers about. A dread should not only be concerned with the queen and youths he dwells with but he should be concerned with all the others he has out there...The white man tell I that polygamy is wrong and that I and I should practice monogamy, but at the same time take other women outside their marriage and call them sweethearts, then this leads to broken marriages and no-one suffers but the youths, why not dwell with all of them in peace and love like the days I and I know before slavery [P. and Bernie 1978:7]?

Clearly we need to understand more about women's experience of Rastafari. While these two sistren support the practice of polygamy on cultural grounds, another set of three sistren became temporarily involved in such an arrangement simply because they felt it would be easier than struggling to raise their six children by the one father on their own. While they ran a small business their Kingman (from whom they were all emotionally alienated) skuffled unsuccessfully and continued to make the social rounds of his brethren. These sistren had no illusions about their circumstances and in fact the household finally broke up when the brother tried to incorporate yet another (and younger) woman into the scene.

This discussion leads directly to my second point. As researchers how do we deal responsibly with this kind of complex social issue? While most Rastafari sistren apparently accept what to outsiders appears to be a double standard of behaviour, relations between men and women are increasingly the subject of concern and ongoing dialogue within the movement. While a well-rounded ethnography would have to deal with the subject, in my own case I was able to postpone addressing the problem for several years because I recognized that there were other, more pressing research priorities. The Rastafari movement has been the object of continuous criticism and even persecution from several sources. It seemed to me more important to clarify popular misconceptions about Rastafari first, rather than to stir up further controversy that would cause still more ideologues and authorities to jump on the anti-Rasta bandwagon. Consequently, I became somewhat of an advocate for the movement - speaking widely, doing court cases as an expert witness for the defence, writing in the popular press, and even sponsoring visits by leading Rastafari from Jamaica to give talks in Toronto. One experience in this regard was co-organizing with a Rastafari sister a cultural and educational programme entitled "Voice of Thunder: Dialogue with Nyahbinghi Elders". In September, 1984 three Nyahbinghi Elders from Jamaica spent a month in Toronto putting on workshops in schools, at the university, and in local community centres. In all these different efforts I emphasized the more progressive cultural dynamics of Rastafari.

It would probably help to set this discussion within the context of the sociology of knowledge. The atmosphere in Toronto in the 1970s was characterized by racism and hostility towards non-white minorities. Not surprisingly, the media, police, and immigration officials came in for considerable criticism for what was perceived as their part in perpetuating stereotypes. Rastafarians were not only Black, but they were engaged in "deviant" cultural practices from which even some members of the upwardly mobile black community wished to disassociate themselves. One of the first pieces I wrote dealt with the Rastafari use of cannabis or herbs, in which I tried to combat anti-drug prejudices [Yawney 1972]. Another work analyzed Rastafari attitudes to race and nationality in order to demonstrate that Rastafari, despite their image as exclusive black nationalists, treat individual outsiders with respect and dignity [Yawney 1976].

Then, in June 1975 just after an extremely successful concert by Bob Marley and the Wailers in Toronto, the *Globe and Mail*, one of the city's leading newspapers, ran an article on the front page with the headline: "Rasta, the bizarre cult suspected of violent crimes in Metro." The entire third page of the edition was dedicated to the problem, including an article reprinted from the US press which conveyed an image of Rastafarians as violent drug-using criminals. During this period several trials involving Rastafari were underway. One case was a sentencing hearing of a Rastafarian who had been found guilty of assaulting a police officer. I was prepared to testify on the basis that the Crown intended to argue that the maximum prison sentence should be handed down because Rastafarians belong to some kind of "cult" that practices a form of revenge. Here the defence lawyer was concerned that Rastafarians were being seen in the same light as members of the Kung Lok branch of the Triad Society of Hong Kong or an Italian Mafia secret society, groups which are alleged to be committed to assisting each other and practising violence respectively. In this instance, when the defence lawyer was ready to call me, the judge stated that he had decided not to make an issue of the Rastafarian culture in this case.

During another court case for which I gave expert testimony three Jamaican youths, whose association with Rastafari was not entirely clear, were on trial for murder. This attracted a great deal of publicity in the media. You could telephone the number of the Western Guard, a "white power" organization for their weekly recorded message and obtain something like the following:

> Once again this reporter has to say we told you so. And this time it's about those blacks who were charged and cleared of the murder of cabby Gordon Stoddard while attempting to rob him. Now of course, these nice gentlemen are being sought by the Metro police after pistol whipping and robbing some guests at a party last Sunday. During the Stoddard trial these punks were described by their humanitarian lawyers as poor misunderstood Black immigrant youths high on marijuana who are accustomed to playing with guns coming from their Jamaican society. Well, they're playing with guns again folks and let's hope they don't kill any more people as they import their Jamaican culture to Canada...[Bob Smith for the White Power Message Service:1976].

In 1979 I published a paper on rituals of Rastafari who lived in a notorious part of West Kingston. I tried to show how brethren struggled continuously to maintain an open and peace-affirming environment in the midst of corruption and gang warfare. I explicitly made the point that these Rastafari did not tolerate weapons in their sacred space [Yawney 1979]. These and other works were intended to disabuse the public of misconceptions about Rastafari.

At the same time I continued to collect data about the experience of Rastafari sistren. Then, during the First International Rastafari Conference which was held in Toronto in July 1982, the problem seemed to come to a head, as evidenced by the degree of conflict over the weekend between brethren and sistren about the role of women in the movement. After all, Toronto is outside the range of social control exerted by traditional Elders in Jamaica, so dialogue could take place in a way that was not possible there. It seemed like an appropriate point to raise this subject in a more serious way.

This leads to the third problem I raised in the introduction to this paper. Who is qualified to undertake this kind of research and what are its possible consequences? Here I am referring to the kind of feedback effect researching such a sensitive topic may have on the movement. As more Rastafari scholars emerge they maintain that only Rastafari possesses the credentials to do this kind of work. However, I would argue that while as outsiders we have to come to terms with our own ethnocentrism, Rastafari researchers need to examine their own ideological biases. I have already quoted above Maureen Rowe's argument that the concept of dominance can have no significance if people accept their condition. The problem of false consciousness it seems is a universal one. It is significant that the three Rastafari sistren who have spoken out about the inequality of women in the movement have all published outside of the Caribbean. One of them, Makeda Silvera, states that "For as long as there is misogyny and sexism in the movement there will continue to be this inner turmoil, and with this inner turmoil, there can be no unity. Where there's oppression and domination there can be no unity - inequality breeds discontent [1983:120]."

Feminist scholars undoubtedly have a role to play but the precise nature of their contribution remains to be determined. Obviously we need to devise fieldwork strategies to make it possible to work with women without exposing them to the possibility of harassment from their menfolk. There were times during my own research when I was intimidated and discouraged from pursuing this line of inquiry. Nevertheless we need to know why women continue to participate actively in Rastafari within the gender framework prescribed for them. Many sistren I know emphasize the significance for them and their children of the Pan-African and black consciousness dimensions of Rastafari, and the sense of dignity and pride it generates in them as black women.

My fourth point is that we need a theoretical model capable of incorporating the factors of class, race, and gender. When we pay attention to writings by black feminists on the subject, we find viewpoints that are helpful in appreciating the situation of Rastafari sistren. When we take into account this critique of cultural imperialism and racism in the women's movement, we cannot make simple assumptions about women's priorities in underdeveloped and post-colonial societies. Urdang makes this clear in her discussion of both the class and gender struggle Guinea Bissau in "Fighting two colonialisms" [1979]. There is also another literature which deals with the politics of race, class and gender, such as the special 1984 edition of *Critical Perspectives* on "Women, Race, and Class in a Cultural Context." In this regard Amos and Parmar have argued that "True feminist theory and practice entails an understanding of imperialism and a critical engagement with challenging racism - elements which the current women's movement significantly lacks, but which are intrinsic to black feminism [1984:17]."

And they suggest that due to a lack of appreciation of these factors at least two aspects of black women's experience - family dynamics and sexuality - have been poorly understood. Scott also has made a similar case, arguing that "there must be more examinations of the black and female experience that are sensitive to the ways in which racism and sexism bear upon black women[1982:90]." According to Parmar, the failure to recognize this triple oppression of class, gender, and race results in the inability "to accommodate the specificity of the black women's experiences of racism, which have been structured by racially constructed gender roles [1982:237]." Carby develops this idea further by arguing that "racist theory and practice is frequently gender-specific" resulting in the fact that "the gender of black women...differs from constructions of white femininity because it is also subject to racism [1982:214]." She goes on to ask if, given the factors of colonial history and continuing underdevelopment, "can it be argued that black male dominance exists in the same forms as white male dominance [1984:215]?" Bourne has observed that this tendency to consider cultural practices (such as female circumcision or arranged marriages) outside their socioeconomic context of colonialism leads more to racial stereotyping than to the recognition that these behaviours may be representative only of a particular historical phase [1983:20]. In this regard Green has insisted that while "Third World Women have to be understood in their totality as oppressed-national/racial, class, ethnic and gendered subjects," there are priorities in the struggle to resolve these contradictions [1985:59]. As members of the Combahee River Collective put it, "We struggle together with black men against racism, while we also struggle with black men about sexism [1983:275]."

Chapter 5

Rasta mek a trod: symbolic ambiguity in a globalizing religion

Carole D. Yawney

In "Rasta mek a trod..." Carole Yawney offers insights into the internationalization of Rastafari. A core of "master symbols," along with other
imagery and music have been important. While devotional and didactic
Rasta art has been globalized, most international is Rasta mystical art. It
"welcomes evocative imagery from other traditions," and reflects struggles
of all people. The range of symbolic ambiguities "encourages oppressed
people everywhere to articulate and resolve their grievances with redemptive imagery." The result is consensus which is part of the groundwork for
moving toward power to use in regaining an "Eden" where all things are
possible. Yawney recounts the excursions of Rasta elders from Jamaica to
North America and Europe in the 1980s. They offered cultural performan-
ces, the Nyahbinghi experience, much attenuated for being outside the
rural Jamaican milieu. Nevertheless these encounters between Nyahbinghi
and nihilism awaken the participants to "eternal verities" and "brings us to
our senses." It is healing work, says Yawney, and offers us the possibility
of experiencing communitas and rectitude. She concludes by pointing to a
core theme in Rastafari: the sistren and brethren are exiles from Eden, from
Africa, cast out by slavery into the diaspora. This chapter argues that the
globalization of Rastafari is fundamentally due to the promise it contains
to all of us who experience exile or alienation.

Although it has its roots in an island culture on the capitalist
periphery, and although it has always appealed expressly to
Africans and the diaspora, Rastafari nevertheless has acquired the
status of a global religion over the last two decades. "Global" is used
here rather than "universal," in order to stress the movement's
distribution in space more than the transcendental appeal of its
creed. To some extent the dissemination of Rastafari can be explained sociologically by the fact that Jamaicans themselves have
had to go into the diaspora, whether for political or economic

reasons, and some of them accordingly have carried with them the Word/Sound/Power of Rastafari abroad - to Africa itself, but also to the Americas, to Britain, northern Europe, Japan, New Zealand, and elsewhere in the Caribbean. Yet to cram Rastafari's global spread into the baggage of emigration is to ignore the fact that Jamaicans - not to mention Rastafari - are socially enclaved if not outrightly persecuted in most of the countries where they have settled. How then can they exert any real cultural influence in these places? The alternative explanation treats Rastafari mainly as a media phenomenon, borne along on a wave of enthusiasm for reggae as it is heard worldwide in broadcasts, recordings, and live concerts. But here again, in this explanation there is a lack of appreciation for the depth of commitment to Rastafari outside of Jamaica, for this clearly exceeds the aesthetic dimension alone.

In this chapter we will seek to go beyond both positions by approaching the vision of Rastafari as a constellation of ambiguous symbols, which today has the power to focalize and even mediate certain socio-cultural tensions that have developed on a global scale. Theoretically this is an important line of investigation, for it promises to shed light on the ways in which sacred imagery passes across an ethnic boundary. But it is also worthwhile to reason along these lines if only to neutralize ethnocentrism, for there is a pronounced tendency among those not in the spirit of Rastafari to ridicule its sacred imagery as reactionary, anachronistic, or merely eccentric. More than present-day, text-centred Christianity, Rastafari puts great emphasis upon the practice of contemplation, which employs visual imagery as a focus for concentrated thought. Orthodox Rastafari contemplation draws upon a small lexicon of "master symbols" which allude to a realm that is pure, righteous and potent. In Rastafari sacred art these symbols are assembled with typical iconographic rigor, so that their spiritual and/or historical message might be "read" without risk of heresy or confusion.

Foremost among these master symbols are images stemming from the political dynasty of Ethiopia, as this was portrayed in the press of the 1930s. Time and again in the yards of West Kingston we see represented the austere visage of Emperor Haile Selassie I; or profiles of the Emperor's power totem, the Lion of Judah; or trinitarian figures, including the Star of David, which derive from the Emperor's throne name, "Power of the Trinity;" or pictures of the Empress Menon in the company of her husband; or epigraphs in

Amheric script, an official language of Ethiopia; or reproductions of the Ethiopian flag, sometimes rippled and sometimes flattened. And everywhere prominent use is made of red, gold and green; the colour symbolism which bands the Ethiopian flag. Apart from these specifically Ethiopian motifs there are four other master symbols which have a more general African origin, these being dreadlocks, the herb chalice, the standing drums, and finally, the continent of Africa itself.

Nowadays, however, Rastafari iconography employs a number of what may be called "adjunct symbols", whose sacredness is not beyond dispute. Most of these elements originate in the Jamaican experience; thus palm trees and outline maps of Jamaica appear frequently, as do images of Marcus Garvey and Bob Marley. Still, we must recognize that the leading edge of Rastafari has not yet been rendered in visual imagery. Around such matters as Ital livity, Nyahbinghi culture, African liberation struggles, and converging New Age spiritual traditions some consensus may already have emerged, but there is no final agreement as to how they should be visualized symbolically.

Those Rastafari Elders and craftspeople who make use of visual imagery have the opportunity to work in any of three iconographic genres, which vary according to the complexity and lability of the symbolism. In the observer's own terms these may be characterized as the devotional, the didactic, and the mystical genres, though within Rastafari itself such distinctions are not made.

Of these three genres the simplest and most orthodox is the devotional one, since this often consists only of a single master symbol accompanied by an empowering slogan. Intended as a guide for contemplation, but sometimes also as a call to action, the Rastafari devotional icon has been reproduced in a wide range of media, including postcards, framed photographs, tabloid covers, and lapel buttons. Since its message is unambiguous, the devotional genre does not inspire commentary, nor does it need decoding.

More complex and idiosyncratic is the didactic genre, which combines both sacred and secular elements in order to represent the suffering of black people in a white ruled world. Ranging from ephemeral cartoons to paintings in oil, works in this genre may portray in simultaneous tableaux a number of historical characters who may actually have lived at very different points in time. Such works beg for commentary for this reason, and in fact they may become meaningful only through the narration of the artist who in this case teaches with the aid of iconic images rather than abstract symbols. Partisans of Rastafari who have not yet reasoned in the Elders' yards are apt to be unfamiliar with didactic art, for this is a genre that does not travel well, except in those rare instances when the Elders themselves accompany their works abroad.

But the most complex and labile of all Rastafari works are those of a mystical cast. These can range from pencilled sketches to technically sophisticated album jackets. In this genre the artist seeks to provide visual keys to ineffable states of mind, which by nature are beyond verbal commentary. He or she does this by arraying sacred symbols in such a way that these unfold or mutually reinforce one another along ordained visual pathways. The mystical art of Rastafari most clearly reflects the movement's global connections, since it welcomes evocative imagery from other traditions, then goes on to organize this by means of a cosmopolitan 'syntax.'

When cast in the mystical mode, Rastafari imagery is furthermore liable to lose its oppositional character as reflecting the struggles of black people solely. Here there is a tendency for it to become 'universal' and not merely 'global'.

This is possible in the first place, because certain master symbols by themselves can be interpreted ambiguously. The features of the Emperor, for example, do not conform to black stereotypes, while Ethiopian culture can be regarded as either Coptic or pagan. Again, one may chose to emphasize Ethiopia's theocratic hierarchialism, or the simple egalitarianism of its dread warriors and ascetic monks. There is also room for ambiguity over the contention that Amharic is the Pure Language of pre-slavery, or an esoteric script with universal relevance. Finally, there is an ambiguous element about the Emperor's historical mission, for on the one hand until 1935 he led the only free state in Africa, yet on the other hand he fulfilled the immigrant's secret wish-dream by prophesying the European's doom on their own home ground at the League of Nations.

Ambiguity is also generated when certain master symbols are juxtaposed with other adjunct ones. Currently this possibility has arisen over the matter of the canonization of Marcus Garvey, which in iconographic terms involves placing the Jamaican leader visually on par with the Ethiopian Emperor. In ways that are richly suggestive, Garvey represents a type that is the polar opposite of Selassie I. In contrast to the austerity, the lean physique and the personal isolation of the Emperor, Garvey is typically portrayed as genial, ample in girth and charismatic.

An ambiguous mix of adjunct and master symbols is also created by the common practice of printing outline maps of Jamaica with the Ethiopian colours superimposed. To some this may suggest that the island has become saturated with the vision of continental repatriation, but to others it may imply, in Garvey's phrase, that a continent has been exchanged for an island.

Overall, the range of symbolic ambiguities in Rastafari imagery encourages oppressed people everywhere to articulate and resolve their grievances with redemptive imagery. Although this falls short of a political solution, it assists in bringing about a consensual community. This in itself is empowering. Why such symbolic resolutions can be achieved on a global scale has to do with the kinds of common issues faced by people of all countries: the ecological crisis stands over against Ital livity; the corruption of secular leaders is counterposed by the theme of theocratic morality; engulfing materialism is challenged by the vision of pre-industrial Ethiopia; and disenchanted youth are awakened by the words of the elder.

However, by becoming virtually a global currency, the Rastafari vision has been threatened with dispersion and trivialization. In response, a number of Jamaican Theocratic Elders are counselling a return to orthodoxy. Through their efforts a new symbolic complex has come before the public, both in Jamaica and abroad. Known as Nyahbinghi, which has roots in the 1930s in Jamaica, this complex is embedded in a ritual process consisting of extended drumming, chanting, reasoning, and testimony, all of which are meant to release spiritual energies that will vanquish Babylon. Nyahbinghi is adamantly opposed to reggae runnins and the dance hall style, and at the very least it is ambivalent about the universalizing trends in the works of Bob Marley. Rather than simply disseminating a symbolism divorced from everyday life, the Nyahbinghi Elders insist on teaching the actual practice of Rastafari since this alone can generate true understanding and foster inspiration. As an effort at counter-missionization, Nyahbinghi is currently striving to rectify a visionary impulse that is imperiled by its very triumphs.

Carole D. Yawney

Nyahbinghi, however, cannot be marketed like reggae, for if reggae is essentially a musical phenomenon sometimes with a political message, Nyahbinghi is a cultural performance (and not a media event) consisting of a complex integration of chanting praises, drumming, reasoning, proper conduct, dancing, clothing, symbolism, and devotional discourse. Springing from a primarily oral culture, Nyahbinghi Rastafari are not comfortable with the radical separation of artist and audience. When binghis are convened in Jamaica it is assumed that all are participants, that all are in a state of devotional awareness, that all will strive to observe certain ritual injunctions.

It is customary in Jamaica to establish a Nyahbinghi compound, one that is clearly separated from the ordinary world, by the fact that it is in isolated rural parts, with a main entrance monitored by self-appointed gate keepers who take it upon themselves to reason with strangers as to their purpose in being there.

The central focus of Nyahbinghi activity is the Tabernacle, a roofed-over open-air structure, usually containing an Alter, around which participants dance and chant praises, and near which a large fire is maintained for the duration of the celebration. By the fact that both food and fuel are generally provided by those convening the Assembly there is no need for the participants to leave before the end of the event, which could last for several days. Binghis differ from the rural folk festival by the fact that there are no ordained performers upon whom audience attention is focused. While it is true that between women and men there is an assignment of background and foreground roles, it cannot be said that there is a distinction between performer and audience. Antiphonal chanting, interactive reasoning, collective dancing, and communal cuisine all serve to forestall this polarity. Brethren phase one another in playing the drums, and can exercise their virtuoso talents only within strictly ordained rhythmic parameters. And last but not least, their sounds go unamplified in these places where there is no electricity.

In 1984 a group of three Jamaican Nyahbinghi Elders travelled outside the Caribbean for the first time on a four week cultural educational mission to Toronto. This programme, known as "Voice of Thunder: Dialogue with Nyahbinghi Elders," was co-organized by the author and Sister Charmaine Montague. It involved at least a dozen public events in different venues. In 1986 this same group of brethren as well as the author participated in a two week long international Rastafari conference in London, England, called "Rastafari Focus." In the weeks following this conference these Nyahbinghi brethren visited different scenes in the UK to promote their culture. In the follow up to this conference a group of local Rastafari initiated in the UK a series of reasonings and cultural activities known as "The Nyahbinghi Project." Finally, in 1988 a group of a dozen Nyahbinghi Elders from Jamaica, including for the first time three sistren, spent several weeks chanting Nyahbinghi from Washington to New York City. This programme was called "The Rainbow Circle Throne Room of Jah Rastafari: the musical and oral traditions of the Nyahbinghi order." At the same time several Nyahbinghi Elders travelled to California on a similar mission.

Now, when Nyahbinghi Elders decide to make a trod beyond the Caribbean they are faced with all the contradictions implicit in moving from an oral to an electronic context. This results in another set of symbolic ambiguities which may stimulate further cultural creativity on the part of Rastafari.

Outside Jamaica Nyahbinghi Elders find their movements restricted. Unlike reggae stars they need a special social and cultural milieu to be authentically themselves. Travelling always as a group, as brethren, they insist that the standards of ital livity be upheld wherever they take lodging. This means that they expect to be sustained by a community of Rastafari. Obviously such communities must attain a certain critical density before they can perform this service for the Nyahbinghi Elders. And what this means in practical terms is that Nyahbinghi pathways are restricted to those countries where there is a substantial host community. Currently this means Canada, United States, and Britain, but in the near future may well include Zimbabwe, Nigeria, and Ethiopia.

In the second place, even though Nyahbinghi Elders nowadays can rest assured that their livity will be upheld in a few countries beyond the Caribbean, they nevertheless face substantial contradictions when it comes to celebrating Nyahbinghi in such places. It must be remembered that here we are referring to public Nyahbinghi activities organized in the context of a "tour." For years Rastafari in the diaspora have held Nyahbinghi celebrations in the United States or Britain privately.

Apart from the difficulties of sponsorship and the responsibility of the Elders to those who have organized the venues, neither they nor their hosts feel comfortable in rural circumstances where the majority of the population is white. First World Nyahbinghis therefore are staged, not held, in auditoria. This not only limits the length of the occasion but is also makes available amplification devices which enhance the sounds of the performers at the expense of the rest of the gathering. With a stage at their disposal the drummers assume an unnatural prominence over the Rastafari arranged in tiers of chairs before them. Sensible fire regulations prohibit ital cooking in charcoal braziers and invariably disallow firepits which in Jamaica are a non-personal focus of ecstatic energy. And it goes without saying that the chalice cannot be in view, that instead of being a public sacrament it becomes a secret. In all these respects the full expression of Nyahbinghi is hobbled in the First World.

On the other hand there is a much broader exposure to Nyahbinghi than would ever be possible in Jamaica. Apart from local Nyahbinghi Rastafari attendance, who may even be in the minority, there will doubtless be Rastafari who have never visited Jamaica, Third World sympathizers of Rastafari, and whites who may be politicized or who may simply be there for the music. Here then is a symbolically potent situation where a pure but parochial culture is radiated onto an audience sure to provide a mixed response.

Still, in this dialectic between stern parochialism and jaded postmodernism there is none of the hysteria or hilarity that one might suppose. Even though this polarity of performer and audience is largely maintained, one discerns in these gatherings a kind of quizzicality. Far from ridiculing the performance, members of the audience typically make (and are encouraged to make) hesitant, even timid attempts to bridge the gulf between their emptiness and the performer's fullness. There is a poignancy in this, an instability, for we can see beneath the post-modern addiction to pastiche and self-reference a profound yearning for a simpler way. Having been alerted to the abuses of dogma people in the audience hold themselves back with exemplary finesse, but they suffer at the same time from a paralysis of cynicism. And you can see their hearts warm to a level of the performance that is deeper than dogma. In these first few encounters between Nyahbinghi and nihilism can we see emerging a new way of being together where orthodoxy is simultaneously bracketed and reversed?

If such an attitude is emerging it is certainly not rooted primarily in nostalgia. There can be no sepia-toned sentiment where Nyahbinghi is concerned for in their reasoning the Elders channel pure Word/Sound/Power. Perhaps what we harken to in these gatherings is the possibility of experiencing communitas and rectitude in a situation of symbolic ambiguity: while we feel no commitment to the symbols as such, it is nevertheless this very provincialism that provides us privileged access to the Cosmic. Rastafari have chose to speak in the metaphors of the Judaic heritage, the deepest tradition they could trace, given the disruption of slavery. And this radical simplification of things - call it fundamentalism - awakens us. It brings us to our senses. We see the world from the point of view of eternal verities. This is healing work, even though it uses symbols for which we feel only the echo of allegiance.

Let us return to the basic dualism that links together the hierarchical and egalitarian, the theocratic and the anarchic, the vertical and the horizontal, Elder and youth. Underlying these, what is the basic contradiction that when reconciled creates a rich panoply of symbolic ambiguities? To keep the faith with Rastafari we would have to pay only nodding attention to all these no doubt profound Western perplexities and then assert in their place the view that the innermost or fundamental contradiction involves Africa in relation to the diaspora. Cast anew from the Garden which was a paradise not because everything was fulfilled, but because all was possible, Rastafari articulates the dignified sadness of passionate exile to the point where it evokes such primordial imagery and sentiments that it becomes one with the mind and ways of all exiles, including ourselves.

Chapter 6

The history of America and Tompkins Square Park

Seth Tobocman

Seth Tobocman is a comic book artist and the son of a nuclear physicist and a social worker who grew up in Cleveland Ohio and moved to the Lower East Side, New York City in 1977 where he has lived ever since. He founded the World War 3 Illustrated collective with Peter Kuper in 1979. He has worked in both mainstream media and the underground press and has been a partisan of the squatters' movement and the homeless movement on New York's Lower East Side.

Commentary by artist and author, Seth Tobocman

I did this piece in 1988 shortly after the Tompkins Park riot which was sparked by the attempt to curfew Tompkins Square Park. The area around Tompkins Square Park is a kind of a multi racial multi cultural ghetto with alot of different groups of people living in it and alot of abandoned buildings in which people have been squatting. And the curfew was directed against two groups of people, one being young people who used the park as a place to socialize and the other being people who lived in the park. By curfewing all the parks in New York, the authorities are in essence trying to keep people from living in the parks. The riot in 1988 happened when people protesting the curfewing of the park were attacked by the police, and in retaliation people attacked condominiums which are expensive housing. The city responded within several days by lifting the curfew on the park because the politicians were embarrassed by the media coverage of the behaviour of the police. The police had been photographed with their badge numbers covered beating up, without discrimination, not only participants in the protest but also anyone who was on the streets that night.

I had been travelling that summer with a multi media show all across the United States by car. I got back into New York City the week of the riot which was late July early August. The trip had been my first experience of the south western United States where you can see alot of what is basically desert and mountains, and pretty much undeveloped land which is fenced in. And so I came back to New York, prepared to do a piece about ecology and the exploitation of land and I was immediately confronted with this riot. And so the two things kind of came together in this piece. And I also tried maybe less successfully, to bring together the issue of exploitation of land and the exploitation of women. I see these as two of the most basic issues that underlay all the struggles going on in the world right now. I am not entirely happy with the piece. I have found that some people really liked it and some people had criticisms of it. But it was my first real attempt to put these things together, that is, the exploitation of land and the exploitation of women and then the specific situation around the park. I think that maybe it romanticizes or glorifies our movement more than I would do now, although that is possibly a problem with alot of my early work. I think it contains some things that are very feminist and I also think it might contain some things that are sexist as well. And that's because I was and am still working out these issues.

The situation as of mid 1991 in Tompkins Park is that the entire park has been surrounded by a chain link fence to keep people from using it and to keep people from sleeping there. And a virtual police state exists in the immediate vicinity of the park. That is, hundreds of police are on duty there at all times and will arrest you at any time for no reason except that you are against closing the park. I have been told a number of times that if I did not leave the corner of Avenue A and 7th Street immediately I would be arrested for being there. I have also been arrested two times for going into the park and once for hanging a painting on the fence. Police have installed cameras on the rooftops all around the park and there is no longer such a thing as a private conversation between two people on Avenue A.

So after four years, the movement which developed around Tompkins Square Park is either in retreat or at a turning point. Some criticisms have to be made of that movement and while I would never want to blame us for the actions of the state, I think the current situation does have to do with the poor decisions coming from male leadership and macho posturing among the people most publically associated with the defence of the park. I view this as particularly tragic because the issue that this movement has raised, that is, the right of the public to use public land is so important and universal. The macho posturing is also tragic because those pursuing the issues around Tompkins Square have access to media and it is a high visibility issue. Consequently, this closing of Tompkins Square Park will have an impact on similar struggles all over the world.

July 19, 1991
New York, New York

The following comic strip was originally published in WW3 Illustrated, #11, (The Riot Issue). Fall 1988.

Seth Tobocman

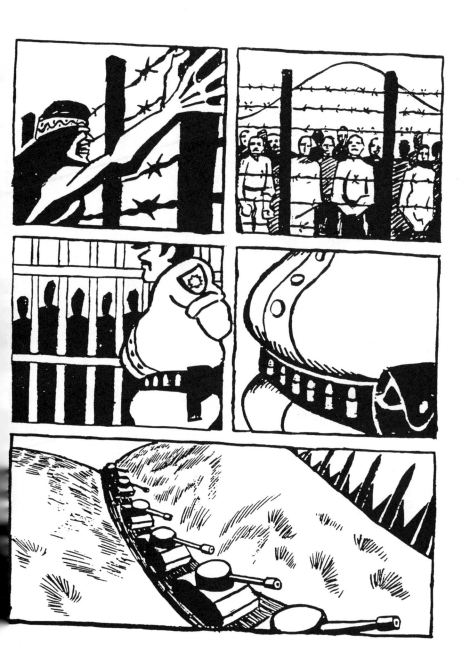

Seth Tobocman

Chapter 7

Message to intellectuals from the grass roots

Brother Book

I, is a grass root man
a born Triniagonian.
Is love and pain
That produce me
In this wicked society
So the grass root
Send a message through me,
Dey say.

Young intellectuals,
Of this society
Men and women
Of great mental faculty
You are being trained
To lead we.

Young intellectuals
Indian and African
You are part of
The Trinago population.

Young intellectuals
I know you could see
Is less food, food
Growing in the country
And more being imported
From the imperialist countries.

Young intellectuals
Within the society
Is more Youths
Being driven crazy
And don't talk 'bout
police brutality.

Young intellectuals
Don't try to stand aside
Is either you decide
To let exploitation
Continue peacefully
Or you stand up for
The oppressed in society.
Young intellectuals
What will your glory be?
A big fat salary
And just touch glasses
In cocktail parties.

Young intellectuals
Don't be no armchair revolutionary.
Just write a book
To be published internationally.
With the language heavy, heavy
Some of we can't read.
Remember, is we you come out to lead.

Young Intellectuals
You have to come out
Put brains and muscles together
And rub shoulder to shoulder
With your brother and sister.

Young Intellectuals
Don't just tell we
Come out and show we
Because, history tell we
Beware of the man
With the Ph.D.
'cause one of them
Done fool we already
Just keep promising we.

Young intellectuals
The grass root send me
To deliver their story,
They say without you
The job go be more hard
So when victory come
Dey go deal with you
Sad, sad, sad, sad.

Young Intellectuals
Come out and learn from we
Is we make the latest
Contribution to the world musically.
So Young Intellectuals
When you come out with yuh theory
and join us
With we creativity
There'll be no way stopping we
In carving out a most beautiful
history
Transforming the society.
Dat is the message
The grass root send
Through me.

Chapter 8

Rise!
in solidarity
with the people of Kenya

Sophie Striker

Come to Nairobi
"City in the Sun"
Welcome to Kenya
a country of fun.
Tourism's booming
see our animals and trees
when you leave, take home
Grade A coffee and teas.
But know that the hotels
are all a disguise
to keep you from seeing
how reality lies.
Just look behind
the mask and see
the people who run
the industry.
Just beyond your vision
ask and you'll hear
of the lives of the PEOPLE
who are living so near,
of their works and loves
of their hurts and joys
too much of their sweat
going to boys
who sit on their bottoms
directing the might
of more boys whose sole purpose
to crush and to fight
any uprising

that comes from the people
threatening power
of money or steeple.
The world must change,
the world must conform
democratic dictators
exporting the norm.
The Global Policeman
raiding the till
free elections for all
even against their free will
so Mr. Policeman
can grab up the land
the people - exploit
the army - command
The colony's freed!
Independence at last!
but corruption's bred leaders
whose loyalty's fast
to IMF scams
and World Bank loans
the upkeep relying
on continuing moans
of kids' empty stomachs
poor health care, poor schools
tribes selling customs
to smooth-talking fools
who've themselves bought the line
that capitalist gain
is good for everyone
especially them.
And true, a few
get rich and fat
tasting the good life
and forgetting that
the people they're building their empires on,
their brothers and sisters
up before dawn
work through the day
and into the night
all the time thinking
"For this did we fight?

through mountain and river,
through bush and through tree,
is this what it meant
when we fought to be free?"
As I pass through these places
feel conflict, read books,
I'm hearing the sighs
and seeing the looks
that tell me contentment
is not all too high
though quiet the whispers
to keep from the spy
information to damage
the quiet formations
of resistance groups of
denominations
as varied in tactics
and varied in scope
a representation
of all one would hope
could form in the spaces
confined underground
condemned to the dungeon
if ever were found
by special branch spies
paid to take notes
on any activity
that possibly denotes
disrespect for the rulers
disregard for the law
irresponsible statements
the ultimate flaw.
To be found and reported
as unpatriotic
you're dangerous indeed
to a government neurotic.
"Bow down to me,
your lord and your master,
have kids, do more work,
do it well, do it faster!"
You play dog to the west,
play God to your own,

you lap up their milk
and return to your throne.
Bedazzle the people,
big words, silent threats
increase their production
compounding your debts.
Now look what's happened
MP missing, found dead
Minister of Foreign Affairs[1]
shot through the head
Did he criticize the system?
Did he uncover your lies?
Don't think the people
don't see the ties.
Last person he's seen with
the President himself
and investigations
are put on a shelf.
But the people are restless
some of them mad
taking the same stick
that earlier had
fought off the exploiter
the white man last time.
Look what you're doing
repeating the crime -
detaining the students
lawyers and writers,
the same way the British
detained freedom fighters.[2]
Unjust and deceitful
your time's running thin
and when it collapses
crushing you in,
you'll blame someone else
you'll run for your life
but will you escape
the organized strife?
of all those hushed critics
whose time has come
revolution will happen
regretting that some

will be lost in the fight
you're top of the list
yourself to be blamed
that you won't be missed.
These harsh words a warning
from strength underground
'cause when it comes off
you won't hear a sound
too busy with pettiness
your theft and your greed,
ignoring the voices
of those who're in need.
"One Party, One System
unites us all!
Without Nyayo philosophy[3]
the country will fall
along tribal lines,
wars will break out!
You know those Luos[4]
ready to shout!
They'll crush the Tugens[5]
don't you see?
You need this repression
so you can be free."
Wananchi hear, tho you[6]
wear two different hats
"Multi-party advocates?
I'll hunt them like rats!"[7]
And so more detentions
riots and shooting
Kangemi erupts[8]
in frustrated looting.
But what about all the
investments from the West?
You get rid of the people
who have not acquiesced.
"Come in, line up
take some land, it's o.k.
The people won't protest
No worry, don't delay.
'Cause I think I need
a new Mercedes

or maybe a Rolls
to entertain ladies.
There are many, you know.
They come to the city
but can't find a job
unemployed, what a pity.
Oh, prostitution's
not so bad
it brings in those sailors
uniform-clad.
They spend so much money
those dollars so green!
prostitution's not bad,
you see what I mean?"
So listen now
you who steal from the poor,
look who you're doing
the dirty work for.
And the people know
what they will do,
fight the power
of neo-colonial rule.
They have risen before
and they will rise again
and I think you know
that it won't be the men
not them alone
who'll succeed in the fight
WOMEN are the threat
you try to keep out of sight.
A pretence of power
you've put in their hand
without giving them say
over their money or land.
You push Women's Groups,
there are thousands around,
but in court or a bank
they have no legal ground.
It's easy to see
and common to know
the more defense you build up
the stronger they'll grow.

Inevitably, soon,
an uprising will succeed,
it's a matter of time
before the people are freed
from the tyranny of your words
and the scorch of your threats
and to look at history
you can place your bets
on the women of Kenya
as the first to shake
the foundations of the system
that's designed to break
their spirit and strength,
but you will see
the women will move
and the people will break free.

Endnotes

[1] Member of Parliament, Mr. Ouko, known for his criticism of government corruption, was assassinated near his home in February 1990.

[2] Rebels such as Dedan Kimathi who fought for independence from British colonialism were arrested and killed.

[3] Nyayo means 'footsteps' in Kiswahili and is the key word in the slogans of the President of Kenya, Daniel T. arap Moi. Although he uses the term to imply following the footsteps of Kenya's first President Mzee Jomo Kenyatta, many understand it as a command for Kenyan's to follow in Moi's footsteps, without question or complaint.

[4] From the Luo tribe of western Kenya have come many powerful anti-government people. Several Luo politicians have been assassinated, including Mr. Ouko in February, 1990.

[5] President Moi comes from the Tugen tribe of the Rift Valley of Kenya.

[6] Wananchi is the Kiswahili word for inhabitants of Kenya.

[7] Quote by President Moi during the uprisings in July 1990 in Kenya by pro-democracy Kenyans. The Kenyan government describes itself as a single-party democracy.

[8] Kangemi is a slum area outside of the city of Nairobi.

Chapter 9

response - ability

Susan Ward

struggling now for days

days, days

days to come to terms

terms, terms

term-inology to
those seriously dead ends

you know the One - the ones

broadcasting no exit warnings
making of lively mistakes and accidents
cornered cul de sacs

beautiful ones not yet born

prancing yet and still

about the sidebelly dangers

lonrho shell esso agip

total

those signs of dis-entry

peddlers along the way

made treacherous with

those hags and brats and cripples
those ruts and bumps and ditches

rivets of the mind

with certainty closing the gates

making of you and me

strangers to our land

disembodied knowledges

and yet, after all,
murder is not irio or ugali

ever so organically

these fragments lie

stark deeds
deeds without a name

ha, ha rejoins abdullah

veritable mountains of shit
conspirial voices of abuse
inscriptions upon the rag and bone shop
of the heart
scratches upon the earth

before dramatic exits are made to other grounds

vultures, hawks, yarning theories
picking clean those petals of blood
those song lines, dream lines
cross-cutting, shadowing
the routine paths of on-the-record
statements of truth

they play their own games

these *Fragments* do

they analyse
    theorize
   define

oh, mwalimu, interpretation too

they spin their tops

whirlwind voices

sun and dust and drought

walking thoughts

squelching long and sticky trails

across the arteries of my face

decisions made in tight corners

sifting words, storing phrases

women winnowing beans in the wind
clearing off the chaff
looking for a line
    a key
    a thread
    a connection
    an image
that would tie everything together

explain, summarize, conclude

and yet, but, still

with none of these

do i touch the petals' blood

nor handle the cracked and tea-stained

cups of the heart

fragmented beginnings
lying undiscovered
in the falsity of The Start

walk not on the grass

do not pick the flowers

do not open the petals' touch

people - the people - are to be protected

from their art:

"All the principal museums in New York, for example, are associated with the names of the fabulously rich: Carnegie, Frick, Rockefeller, Guggenheim, Whitney, Morgan, Lehman. Such museums are not designed to protect art from the people, but to protect the people from art [James P. Carse, Finite and Infinite Games, A Vision of Life as Play and Possibility. The Free Press, New York, 1986, page 54]."

meanwhile - in the meanest of times -

outside his hovel abdullah sits
an open-air keeper of shop

perhaps it is april in new jerusalem

abdullah - a mere twist of fate -

merely, justly, pettily

a small cash item of receipt or expenditure
sitting in all his unimportance and minority

abdullah - is of the streets again -

houseboy cum roadboy

the cugini/mburaki of oranges and
                        mushrooms and
            skins

he pays no attention to the parrot's catalogue of ills

itemizing, costing, indexing

commoditized sufferings of today

for the Revolution's second coming tomorrow

slogan's bottling experience -

for vacancy come tomorrow -

joseph chatters on, talking like karega

abdullah's mind is elsewhere

yes, the may bes
let the maybes be

karega is being visionary again

seeing nought again

thrashing about in the agitation of images

waves of a manifesto so very purifying that

in fact his look quite passes

the woman beside him

even though she, in her quiet affirmation,

has been spectator to

these three hundred and forty four

leaves of his life

115

he, quite forgetting in his heroine's list

wanja - creature of the ineffable

that new kind of power

too great for the dominating Word -

sketches with the charcoal and cardboard

of forgotten places

her poetry of belonging

voicing with the texts of her hands -

textures of hands cracked, nails broken, hearts
bleeding -

the laughter re-reading, re-visioning

those inscriptions of crime
                    and treachery
                    and greed

scarring the face of the land

those demarcations, those corridors of separate
rooms
                The River Between
those statements of facts
juke-box truths
recorded melodies of the Big Ones

we are indeed the small people

the forgotten ones
the forgetting ones

forgetting that we have forgotten to re-member

dwarfs, lining-banking the way of the road

whose tarmac burns the souls of our feet

and scorches the petals of blood

we become One - Twin to the land

sons of sand, daughters of dust

this land is my face
my face is now your land

occupied terror stories

I am a Flag - rainbow dreams of green black and
red
a Myriad on the ridge,
the verging and merging of ruin

my distance is a guarantee of neutrality

touch me not/remember me not

keep your petals of blood

those leaves of your lives

those pages in your book

        inconsistent
        contradictory

ever so non-sequential

        in-consequential
        in-significant

do not unroll those images

do not make of my mind

a fluidity of tides

of rhythms

of dances of

possibility - possible dreams dancing

ever more complicated
ever more inventive
ever more uncertifiable

in this bifurcated mind

this motionless movement that is the logic
of my equilibrium

I insist - absolutely insist -

upon my way of your world

or, better yet, your world of my way

"Poets can make it impossible to have a war ... The danger of the poets, for Plato, is that they can imitate so well that it is difficult to see what is true and what is merely invented ... all poets must be put into the service of reason [James P. Carse, ibid, pages 62-63]."

ayi kwei armah knew better

'poets are bandleaders who have failed'

With our feet we walk the goat's earth.
With our hands we touch God's sky.
Some future day in the heat of noon,
I shall be carried shoulder high
through the village of the dead.
When I die, don't bury me under forest trees,
I fear their thorns.
When I die, don't bury me under forest trees,
I fear the dripping water.
Bury me under the great shade trees in the market,
I want to hear the drums beating

I want to feel the dancers' feet
(extract from a poem of the Kuba people)

feet drumming the land

hands drumming the earth

poets drumming the mind

swaying
moving
crashing down, burning up

those brothels of separate rooms

"Your attention is always focused somewhere else, beyond what is in front
of you. You fail to hear the questions put to you, you fail to respond. The
dialogue is interrupted.

By striving for what is furthest, you abandon that which is nearest. For the
sake of humanity, you leave your brother, your sister. But where, except
with them, shall, you meet up with your humanity? [John Friedmann, The
Good Society, MIT Press, Cambridge, Massachusetts, 1979, page 173]."

but he was glad that he had saved a life

when he was on a mission of taking one

and he would be happy to know

that wanja was happy

and that, sometimes she remembered him

i offer apologies Mr. Ngugi

or, is that Mr. Wa
or yet again
Mr. Thiong'o

(How much easier it was when you were simply,
purely

just a James

proud of our endowment of an ancestry)

for I am not, phallocentrically speaking,

quite up to it

I can't - or maybe I'm refusing

to be your interpreter, your critic,

to name your deed
to plant a flag on your mountain of Truth

in Truth, I did think about mapping you

you could, you know, fit quite nicely into
some prettily fancy schemas of post-modernism

or, I could have made a plot for you in the
annals of post-colonial literature
tears of the white man
tears of the White He/She
you know, the contempt as compassion exercise of
those
who tell me you have invested
(whose investment may I ask?)
this book, these petals of blood
'with a stature comparable to
the very best of the world's literature,
past and present.'

stature, statute, statue

a monumental African

there you are, frozen

safely canonized, benevolently colonized

a giant - a Bwana Mbenzi, Mtumbo, Mkubwa
of Literature, or, at least, of African Literature

somehow, seeing you, hearing you

talking with you

i did not feel a stoney presence

our conversation continues

a luta continua

this gift of talk - the talking voices

walking near the stand pipe, the music is talking

"and it would be saying the same everywhere: 'Is Anancy is a spider is Hope
is a green thing is politics is Anancy is Anancy is Anancy!' [Andrew Salkey,
Political Spider, in Political Spider: Stories from Black Orpheus, edited by
Ulli Beier, Heinemann Educational Books, London, 1969, page 30]."

we know that no lie can live forever

i think that laugh you may

a real belly load of tidy affirmation

to know that i have stripped you of

your canonization

they think you wrote a novel, a narrative

author that you are, you have been authorized

a literary piece 'ranging back and forth between

satire, metaphor and stark realism'

what a feast for academia they think you have
prepared

what a wealth of literary dexterity

you lay before the systematic mind

shall we catalogue and recount

images, stories, parallelisms
cosmic coincidences and prophecies come true

shall I determine your meaningfulness
shall I explain how red the *petals of blood* really are?

what do i do to, or should that be with
these petals of blood?

the conversation turns a page

new leaves

new petals

the voices are talking

Chapter 10

Women's uprisings against the Nigerian oil industry in the 1980s

Terisa E. Turner and M.O. Oshare

In the 1980s women attacked oil industry installations and personnel throughout Nigeria. This chapter considers two revolts: the 1984 Ogharefe women's uprising and the 1986 Ekpan women's uprising. In the oil centre of Warri where both took place, women do most of the peasant farming but land is controlled by men. The study argues that oil-based industrialization superimposed on this local political economy a new regime which dispossessed women of access to farm land. Women responded by attacking the oil industry with varying degrees of success. In the 1984 uprising women seized control of a US oil corporation's production site, threw off their clothes and with this curse won their demands. These had to do with financial compensation for pollution and alienation of land. In the 1986 uprising women shut down the core of the whole region's oil industry. They were less successful in winning their demands for land compensation and oil industry jobs.

The different levels of success are explained by reference to class formation and gender relations in the uprisings themselves. The success of the 1984 struggle derived from it being a relatively straight forward peasant initiative against a foreign oil company. In addition, women had the support of young men against the old men who had bargained away land rights to the state. In contrast, the 1986 uprising was less successful because of its complexity, combining as it did women's peasant and proletarian demands. Furthermore, in the 1986 uprising, women lacked significant support from men who for the most part, aligned themselves with the state against the women. The study concludes by noting the prominent place of women's initiatives linked to gender solidarity in the success of the exploited classes in struggles with big business and the state.

Research for this chapter was carried out in Nigeria in the 1970s and 1980s, supported in part by the Canadian Social Science and Humanities Research Council.

Introduction

This chapter considers two Nigerian women's protests against the oil industry: the Ogharefe women's uprising of 1984 and the Ekpan women's uprising of 1986. These clashes were explosive moments in an on-going movement of resistance brought on by the operation of big capital in the oil industry. First a civil war largely about oil and ethnicity was fought in the late 1960s [Turner 1976, Nnoli 1978]. This war brought social disruption and over a million deaths in a population of about 100 million. It left an economically and ecologically traumatized society saddled with a massive military state. The oil boom of the 1970s and bust of the 1980s brought on further dislocations [Turner 1987]. The uprisings reveal the oppositions between men and women, between citizens and state. They hark back to Nigerian women's struggles against colonial exploitation, to the tax riots, market closures and cocoa holdups, to the unseating of kings and the kidnapping of officials. The uprisings return to the historical theme of women warring against men who sell out the interests of the community and become allies of the exploiters. This study examines the conditions impelling contemporary resistance. It tells the story of the women's uprisings, showing them to be expressions of what could be termed 'gendered resistance,' shaped by the world oil industry.

Two objectives here are to set down information about the women's uprisings and to consider the alignment of social forces in those confrontations. This second objective involves a class analysis which embodies the analysis of gender and ethnic relations. Three arguments are made: (1) the uprisings were clashes resulting from class formation spurred by oil based capitalist development; (2) the gender character of the uprisings, the fact that they involved particular class factions of women against specific class factions of men, followed from changes in gender relations that took place in the process of capitalist development; and (3) the degree of success enjoyed by women in their struggles reflects both the extent to which peasant relations persisted or were eroded by proletarianization and the degree to which men acted in solidarity with women.

Feminism in Marxism

The uprisings of Nigerian women are social experiences against which certain orthodoxies and innovations in social theory may be tested. These theoretical elements of contending paradigms include perspectives on issues such as feminism and the third world state, women and transnational corporations, women in development, gender relations and gender analysis, the party and revolution, national versus international socialism, privatization and the market, and democracy and egalitarianism.

Social analysis has been transformed in the last century and a half as the historical stage has been captured successively by new world slave revolts, proletarian revolution, colonial uprisings and women's mobilization. Two distinct paradigms, the reformist and the revolutionary, inform most analysis; but their outlines are blurred. The disarray stems in part from the collapse of stalinism embodied in the dictatorships of the communist party governments of the Soviet bloc. For many who thought stalinism was marxism and centrally planned state capitalism was socialism or communism, this collapse was cause for despair, theoretical bankruptcy and de facto subscription to the end of ideology camp.

The extraction of the revolutionary paradigm from this confusion over what constitutes marxist theory and practice is complicated by the stance of those claiming to be marxists who persist in discounting peasants, the unemployed, women, the poor and others as social forces. On the other hand, feminists and analysts of those on the margins (and frontiers) too frequently labour under the misconception that stalinism equals marxism. The ignorance and misogyny of self styled marxists who at best, observe as a convention the practice of 'adding on' women to their analyses, drive deeper the wedge between feminists and a revolutionary paradigm. The overall result of this confusion is the dominance of a reformist paradigm, in versions ranging from world systems theory to neo-liberal modern-ization theory.

While the present analysis of Nigerian women's uprisings does little to solve this crisis of theory, it does draw upon a revolutionary paradigm. The paradigm's revolutionary character derives from its source in orthodox marxism as extended by CLR James to embrace colonial revolts and feminism [Grimshaw 1991a, 1991b, 1992, James 1970, 1973, 1977, 1980, 1984, 1986a, 1986b]. Features of the revolutionary paradigm which are important in this chapter are its emphasis on capital's simultaneously destructive and constructive power, its recognition of the vital part played by intensified sexism and racism in the history of capital accumulation, its global and historical scope and finally, its appreciation of the capacity and imperative which capital has given all exploited peoples to use the organizations of capitalism to establish a global, egalitarian successor system. The revolutionary paradigm suggests that the central question about Nigerian women's uprisings has to do with how these uprisings demonstrate the emergence of a new society from the debris of the old [Turner 1989, 1991].

This study is informed by Boserup's [1970] major insight, that the expansion of capitalism marginalizes and disempowers women. But the political consequences which Boserup understands to follow from her analysis - 'help' for poor, marginalized women to ameliorate their hardships [Beneria and Sen 1981:284] - are different from the political consequences of this analysis of capital's expansion in Nigeria. In fact, in Nigeria not only did capitalism break up women's social order but it also created or strengthened the conditions for resistance. The uprisings are products of capitalist development just as much as is women's marginalization. This suggests, counter to Boserup's reformist and ameliorative stance, that support for the objectives of the uprisings, and the organizations and alliances that facilitated them, would contribute to the empowerment of women and of all exploited people. In short, it is suggested that it is through uprisings and the successful consolidation of the social power marshalled through them that women can be empowered.

The conceptualization of capital as the social dynamic impelling its own transformation provides analytical power that is absent from the one dimensional emphasis in Boserup's conceptualization of capitalist development. First, a transformational conceptualization requires that attention be focused on social struggle. Clashes such as the anti-oil uprisings examined here assume great importance. Instances of fightback yield lessons about people's organizational capacities. They reveal fundamental social alliances and conflicts, especially with regard to class and gender. Second, it gives the highest priority to historical analysis, particularly for those interested in policy and in the political potentials of the future. Analysis of the history of a social group reveals, for instance, whether a development aid project such as a water supply is embedded in defeat or victory for residents of a community. This is to restate the dictum that technology such as a water pump is far from neutral, but rather takes its meaning from the social relations and historical process of which it is a part. It can be a means of class domination or popular empowerment. The importance of historical analysis is too that it offers a way of understanding project failures (the neglect or sabotage of wells, for example). It illuminates the systemic and subsurface meanings of state 'women and development' policies [World Bank 1992, St-Hilaire 1993:57].

For people seeking to resolve social problems, historical analysis identifies the groups which have been shaped and empowered by capitalist development to be the carriers of the transformational impulse. Such groups are obvious candidates for partnership in projects to resolve social crises. The distinction between a conceptualization of capitalist development as only destructive and one which sees it as simultaneously destructive and constructive, is also a distinction between reformist versus revolutionary social forces and their respective strategies.

In sum, a dimension of the method used here is the perspective that capital generates its own demise and succession. Nothing is destroyed until it is replaced. A second dimension of this method is gender analysis as an integral part of class analysis. This means that as we examine how the process of capitalist development creates social forces capable of transforming exploitative into collective relationships, we specifically examine relations between and among men and women [Meillassoux 1964, Coquery-Vidrovitch 1975]. Some key questions are how does capitalist development change the ways in which women are exploited? What do these changes mean for the types of social power at women's disposal? How does capitalist development change relations among men and change relations between categories of men and women?

Capitalist development, at least in most of Africa, superimposes upon pre-existing gender relations, a new set of relations which facilitate the realization of state and capitalist objectives: order and profits. Capitalism marginalizes women through the redirection of existing gender inequality, for instance, in the realm of control over land, into new capitalist projects. In what could be described as a 'male deal,' class formation is effected in part through cross-class (and frequently cross-race) alliances among men to the disadvantage of most women [Turner 1991, Dauda 1992]. Indigenous men collaborate with capital to meet its imperatives at a particular historical period, and as a consequence gender relations are altered. For example, some men, rather than allocate land for food production, may alienate it to foreign oil companies in exchange for some personal gain. A type of reciprocity is overridden by market relations which might, for example, result in the employment in waged work of some landless women in businesses established by indigenous men using money from land sales. The change in gender relations with the development of capitalism pits women against those men who have become powerful through allying with the purveyors of capital.

The most important change in gender relations, attendant upon the development of capitalism, results from the new significance which capitalism gives to women's work of producing people [Cox and Federici 1973, Mies 1986]. This significance resides in the necessary nexus between the production of human beings as labourers and capital's profits. A central, defining feature of capitalism is its commodification of labour power. The capacity to work is bought and sold on a global market. Capitalism is fundamentally a system which allows a few to profit from the labour of many, and it is women who produce and service this labour, including their own. State policies have, since the rise of capitalism in the 16th century, been geared to provide capital with cheap labour. This necessitated the development of policies to make particular groups of women in specific geographical locations bear, socialize, service and nurse people of a particular nature - labourers - in conditions least expensive to the state and to capital [Mies 1985]. The IMF structural adjustment programs of the late 20th century are geared in part to cutting the costs of labour power production [Elson 1991, Beneria and Feldman 1992, Afshar and Dennis 1992].

The change in gender relations which aids capital in harnessing women to household production of labour is the instituting of men as the disciplinarians over women's work. Men in the state, capitalist men themselves, but most significantly, proletarian men are encouraged to define themselves as men with reference to their control over women. They do so through supervising labour power production by women. The proletarian man, bound to his exploiter through new bonds of shared masculinity, serves this exploiter by rendering up to him in a reliable fashion, cheap wage goods and fresh labour power, the products of the work of female kin. However, to the extent that proletarianization is successfully resisted by peasant and other subsistence producers, the degree of division between the interests of women and men may be reduced.

Resistance by women to this type of capitalist exploitation takes many forms including struggles for better work conditions (electricity, water, schools), the fight for control over fertility including the refusal to bear or nurture children or a fight to keep them (contraception, abortion, retaining custody), and efforts to get or keep means of survival independent of men (land, crafts, marketing, women's collectivities). Because capitalism changes gender relations to place men in supervisory positions over their wives (and other women); women's resistance is directed against male discipline, against poor work conditions and against reducing people to cheap labour power.

Women's resistance is indivisibly both a class and a gender conflict. It has two foci of empowerment for women. First, social power may be exercised by women against exploiting men and second, men who have not aligned with capital but instead are, like women, marginalized by capitalist development, may align with women. Both foci are charged with ideological constraints. Miller's six country study, including Nigeria, showed that with industrialization the ideology of male dominance within the family persisted to the detriment of women's rights within the home [Miller 1984]. It is characteristic of all societies that there is a gendered division of labour. Illich [1982] and Leacock [1981] showed that in pre capitalist societies this gendered division of labour does not necessarily point to male dominance, but rather that there can exist a reciprocity between women and men, with each in charge of different tasks and areas of knowledge. With the development of capitalism there continue to be specific areas of gendered experience, resource control and knowledge, that a can either be used by men against women or used by women to reunify the class.

Among women's strengths is that their struggles and resistance start with a politics of mothering and by extension, a politics of fertility and creativity which includes, in many societies, the employment of collective nudity as a compelling tactic [Fiske 1992, Turner, Brownhill and Neal 1993]. In addition, men may be bonded in many ways to each other, while being divided from women through highly formalized processes which engender all work and social activity. For some men to break away from other men and pledge solidarity with women engaged in confrontation with exploiting men bespeaks a fundamental change in social relations and how they are conceived. Given the way in which capitalism pits husband against wife, a strong alliance between them requires a leap in consciousness. Where solidarity is expressed between women and men, it may, in specific societies, most readily draw upon kin relations such as sister/brother or mother/son. However, the advance of class formation combined with women's organizational sophistication fosters solidarity based on shared objectives which cut across kin relations [Dennis 1984].

Such alliances are necessary conditions for revolutionary change. Alliances of solidarity between women and men are prerequisites for overcoming the power of capital and for organizing an egalitarian, cooperative society. The need for such alliances follows directly from capital's reliance on men to discipline women in a daily process of producing labour power embodied in those very men, the women themselves and in a new generation. A revolutionary change involves the breaking of this conduit or intermediary practice into which certain men are structured. Note that an alliance is necessary: the connection cannot be between a men's movement and women 'auxiliaries' who service and support the program of men. Why is a specific quality of alliance a condition for revolution? The notion of class solidarity or of alliance implies that particular women have stated their own demands and are acting through their own organizations in their own interests. Men who ally with women must do so on women's terms or there is no alliance. Women's social power can be marshalled by no one but themselves. The use of this power is essential if a challenge to capital is to succeed. A revolutionary clash is one in which women take the initiative and have the solidarity of some men. A struggle only among men (for instance, male workers and male capitalists) cannot produce fundamental change because absent from the struggle are women with their social power to produce and reproduce. A struggle which is restricted to men is likely to be limited to an attempted revision of the relations of exploitation and not go more deeply into eliminating the relations through which women are exploited. In addition, the joint collaboration between exploited women and men provides the strength in unity required in order to mount a fundamental challenge to capital.

In sum, this study employs a theoretical perspective which emphasizes capitalism's revolutionary power to transform class relations and in so doing, to transform gender relations. The key point is that revolutionary power to transcend capitalist relations derives from the splitting (by capital) of the male gender into classes, and the alignment of exploited men with women. The thesis in this chapter is that capitalist development promotes such a gender realignment and hence the basis for both the transcendence of capitalist relations and the creation of an egalitarian society free from gender exploitation as a condition of freedom from class exploitation. The women's uprisings of the 1980s against oil companies in Nigeria reveal, if only in faint outline, these patterns and this direction of movement.

The first section has considered some theoretical dimensions of feminist marxism. The second section turns to some instances of women's mobilization in Nigeria's colonial history; and the third, to the political economy of the Warri community in which the 1980s women's uprisings occurred. The fourth section examines the 1984 Ugharefe women's uprising against Pan Ocean; and the fifth outlines the political context of the 1986 uprising. The sixth section describes the 1986 Ekpan women's uprising and section seven compares it with the earlier uprising in 1984. The conclusion returns to the questions about class and gender relations raised in the introduction.

Nigerian women's mobilization in the past

Throughout the twentieth century, Nigerian women have exercised the social power under their control in their own interests, and in the interests of the community [Amadiume 1987, Mba 1982]. The Aba women's war of 1928-1929, the Egba women's movement of the early 1930s to the 1950s, the Ogharefe women's uprising of 1984, the Ughelli women's anti-tax protests of 1985-1986, and the Ekpan women's uprising of 1986 are some examples.

In 1928-1930, Aba women rose in mass protest against the oppressive rule of the colonial government. These Igbo women of eastern Nigeria feared that the head-count being carried out by the British was a prelude to women being taxed. The women were unhappy about the over-taxation of their husbands and sons which they felt was pauperizing them and causing economic hardship for the entire community [Van Allen 1972]. They also resented the British imposition on the community of warrant chiefs, many of whom carried out what the women considered to be abusive and extortionist actions such as obtaining wives without paying the full bride wealth and seizure of property. Previously, new village leaders or heads had been chosen and removed by the people themselves. Power had been diffuse; decisions were reached informally or through village assemblies of all adults who chose to attend. While they had less influence than men generally in society, women did control local trade and specific crops. Women protected their interests through the village assemblies. This balance of power had been changed by the colonial government which appointed its agents as warrant chiefs to rule over the people.

The abuses of the British appointed native judges and tax enumerators impelled the women to stage a protest on 24 November 1929. They danced and sang all night around the house of a particularly offensive tax enumerator. The women censored the man through ridicule expressed in lyrics and dance. This ridicule is a deeply rooted Igbo women's practice called 'sitting on a man.' When this 'sitting' treatment was ignored, the women rioted and the rampages spread. Late in December 1929 they forced the Umuahia warrant chiefs to surrender their caps thus launching the women's successful campaign to destroy the warrant chief system. In Aba, women sang and danced against the chiefs and then "proceeded to attack and loot the European trading stores and Barclays Bank and to break into the prison and release the prisoners [Perham 1937:208]." Some 25,000 Igbo women faced colonial repression and over a two month period of insurrection, December 1929 to January 1930, at least 50 were killed [Hanna 1990:338-340, Nwabara 1965, Gailey 1970].

Similarly, between the 1930s and 1950s the women of Egba in western Nigeria pressed for and subsequently secured the abdication of the Alake or king of Egbaland from his throne. He was forced to abdicate on the grounds that he was collaborating with the exploitative colonial government. The Egba women also claimed that the king was hiding under the cover and protection of the colonial government to perpetrate misrule, hardships and oppression on Egba people, and especially on the women.

These instances of women's political intervention during the colonial epoch demonstrate the use of market power and the expression of gendered resistance [James (1938) 1986]. Rapid and massive mobilization was possible because of women's strong societal organizations and effective communication networks based on concentration in the markets and dispersal along the trade routes [Hanna 1990:340, Callaway 1988]. Nigerian women's actions have to do with market control and with women's dual focus on both the state and those among their own menfolk who were instruments of the state. First, women engaged in the business of long and short distance marketing took the initiative in mounting mobilizations. But peasant women and townswomen joined the market women to constitute a mass movement. The social power marshalled by this amalgam centred on the women's ability to withhold food from the cities. They paralysed the trading system within which they exercised considerable power. Not only was food denied the cities, but cash crops were denied the colonial authorities and their merchant allies in repeated confrontations over who should determine prices (in the western Nigeria cocoa holdups during the second world war, for example).

Second, women mobilized not only against the British state directly but also against collaborating indigenous men whose power was underpinned by a male deal with men in the colonial regime. In so doing, women stood against class formation which distorted popular control over indigenous political institutions. The women manifested their distress at the deterioration of their own circumstances with the intensification of capitalist relations. In mobilizing against the colonizer-chief alliance among men, women were acting simultaneously on behalf of women and on behalf of both men and women in the peasant and trading classes. We see here the coincidence and indivisibility of feminist and class politics in the history of Nigerian women's uprisings. To what extent have these qualities persisted in women's uprisings in the post colonial era?

Since independence in 1960 Nigeria has been characterized by political instability and a series of coups which degenerated into the genocidal civil war of 1967-1970. The oil boom of the 1970s profoundly transformed Nigerian society from one based on agricultural exports to one based on exports of crude oil. The state received dollars from oil sales and hence relaxed the exploitation of alternative revenue sources such as export crops and agricultural development. A massive class of middlemen flourished on the basis of state connections [Turner 1976, 1980, Graf 1988]. Oil money was appropriated by indigenous capitalists who tended to invest abroad rather than locally [Turner 1978]. Much theft was geared toward conspicuous consumption and land acquisition.

The state sector expanded dramatically as oil wealth financed infrastructure and some industrialization. Imported fish, chicken, wheat, cloth and other consumer goods undermined indigenous production. This rapid extension of market relations throughout Nigeria encroached on women's spheres of economic and social power. Land alienation, pollution and disturbance of fishing grounds, the absence of men who answered the call of the construction boom, labour shortages and high cost of labour, lack of credit and the need for cash in an import dependent market were factors which contributed to most women's heightened insecurity and marginalization.

The negative impact of these forces was felt most intensely with the collapse of the international oil market in the early 1980s [Turner 1985:7-10]. By 1984 Nigerian women were mobilizing again against the state and indigenous menfolk on whom the state relied to enforce its authority in the localities. Protests were particularly numerous in the petroleum exporting regions around the oil towns of Warri and Port Harcourt on Nigeria's Atlantic seaboard [Turner 1987; Turner and Ihonvbere 1993]. The two uprisings considered below occurred near Warri in Ethiope and Ukpe Local Government Area (LGA).

The political economy of the Warri oil communities

Both the 1984 and the 1986 women's uprisings can be better understood against a background sketch of the political economy of the community. The two Local Government Areas (LGAs) in which the uprisings occurred are Ethiope LGA with its headquarters at Ogharefe and adjacent to the south, Ukpe LGA, where the major towns of Ekpan and Effurun are located. The LGAs are located in Bendel (now Delta) State on the Atlantic coast in mid western Nigeria. Bendel state is the site of Nigeria's second most important oil production, refining and export complex at the port city of Warri. The largest complex is at Port Harcourt, 100 kilometers east in the Niger River delta. Some 100 kilometres north of the Warri coastal oil complex is the Bendel state capital, Benin. The region encompasses a patrilocal, patrilineal peasant agricultural society producing food crops for consumption and trade. While Ogharefe, site of the 1984 uprising, is more rural and characterized by peasant production; Ekpan, cite of the 1986 uprising, is a more urban village of some 14,000 people located very near major petroleum industry complexes sited within Okpe Local Government Area.

The population consists mainly of the Urhrobo community which itself is broken up into clans. Two clans of relevance here are the Ugharefe clan which mounted the 1984 uprising and the Uvwie clan, which organized the 1986 women's revolt. The Uvwie community consists of several clusters of hamlets and villages with its head-quarters in the town of Effurun, adjacent to the oil city, Warri. While the largest number of people from the Uvwie clan live in Effurun, the second largest concentration is four kilometres away in the town of Ekpan.

Effurun is a modern Nigerian town that is as large as the oil centre, Warri. The towns of Effurun and Warri have grown together as they share a contiguous boundary. Nearby Ekpan is now a suburban centre as a result of the vast housing developments and oil industry installations constructed by the state oil corporation. It has a medical dispensary and a hospital, both underequipped. There is no electricity in the town and a single borehole provides water. Ekpan also has one primary and one comprehensive secondary school. The communities of Effurun and Ekpan are marked by the lack of basic infrastructure in shart contrast to the relative wealth of services available to the oil industry housing estates and facilities built on community land.

Land Rights

Land allocation and permission to use land or fishing areas are the focus of the most intense political struggles. These struggles reflect the presence of several competing and overlapping systems governing allocation of land. Land has historically been controlled by men, not women. The Uvwie clan was ruled, since the late 19th century, by a royal king or Ovie. However, prior to 1977 certain senior men had the power to allow members of clans to use parcels of land and fishing grounds. This system of permission was itself complex and disputed. While the king claimed full control, in fact elders and chiefs participated with private owners in parcelling out land for use.

After 1977 all land not privately owned was appropriated by the federal government through the 1977-1978 Land Use Decree (and later Act). While this momentous revolution in land ownership occurred through the stroke of a pen, in practice it was disputed and rejected by those peasant communities whose very existence depends on communal control over land. The state simultaneously recognized certain chiefs as having special status with the federal government. These chiefs tended to support the new order under which the state owned and controlled all communal land in Nigeria. Taking this position pitted the chiefs against ordinary peasants among whom the state takeover of communal land was not recognized. Nevertheless, through the operation of the British legal system, and with the cooperation of certain chiefs, land was legally leased or sold. The direct beneficiaries in the oil producing territories were companies; state and private, local and foreign, which were connected with the largely foreign oil industry.

For at least the last hundred years, Uvwie Urhrobo people have been, in the main, peasant farmers with the women doing most of the farming. Women also do important marketing work. The work of the men is generally restricted to bush clearing. Uvwie agricultural production consists mainly of food crops such as cassava which provides the people's staple food. In addition yam, sweet potato, plantain, banana, cocoyam, and other food crops are cultivated. The people of Uvwie also engage in intensive fishing. Surpluses of fish and food crops are exchanged for money and other products in local markets or in nearby markets such as those in Warri, Sapele, Jeddoh, Adeje, Agbarho, and Enerhen.

Indigenous governing councils

Another feature of the political economy of Ethiope Local Government Area is the indigenous decision making apparatus which consists of councils. There are four councils: married women, male youth, male chiefs and male elders. The council of chiefs has been decreed by the federal government as the most powerful.

Government in Uvwie society has historically been based on geron-tocracy. This system also prevails in the larger Urhrobo society of which Uvwie is part. As in other Urhobo clans, the Uvwie clan's women's council is, in practice, made up only of wives, since unmar-ried women, divorcees and widows who live in their parents' homesteads are not members. Uvwie is not politically centralised. The Council of Chiefs shares power with the Council of Elders. However, the Council of Chiefs has become increasingly powerful under colonial and post colonial federal rule. This growing power was accelerated by the government's recognition of the Ovie of Uvwie as one of the First Class Traditional Rulers in Bendel state. This recognition has made the Ovie and his Council of Chiefs the most prominent and thus most powerful organ of administration in contemporary Uvwie society.

The only council that is powerful enough to resist the Ovie and his Council of Chiefs is the Eghweya or Council of Women. The Council of Youth exercises differing degrees of power, depending on the community in question. In 1984 the Ugharefe Council of Youth was active in exercising power. In contrast, among the Ovwie, the Coun-cil of Youths (known as the Ighele or Emoha) has not featured prominently in political matters since the civil war (1967-1970) al-though it continues to exist.

Part of the difference may have to do with the fact that the youth of Ekpan were more profoundly unsettled by the oil industry than were their more rural counterparts. Because industrial development was more intense around Ekpan, more of the youth of the generation of the 1980s were faced with economic dislocation and crisis. The cash nexus in contemporary neocolonial Nigeria has driven a majority of the members of the Ekpan Council of Youth into national and international diaspora. Those left at home have been dominated by the pressure to obtain means of subsistence in nearby industrial and commercial activities. In this context communal political matters had low priority for most Ovwie clan Council of Youth members in the 1980s.

The oil industry and land alienation

In the 1970s and 1980s much of Ethiope Local Governme virtually swallowed up by oil developments of two ki. petroleum exploration and production on the one hanc building of many major oil processing facilities on the other. Peasant agriculture and fishing came under tremendous pressure as a result of this incursion [Hutchful 1985:51, Turner and Badru 1985].

The headquarters of the Ovwie clan, Effurun, became a commercial and semi-industrial city. Industries established under the abundant revenue regime of the oil boom include the Delta Steel Company at nearby Ovwian-Aladja, a refinery, a petrochemicals plant, and sub-sidiaries of multinational oil companies including Shell, Gulf, Elf and Pan Ocean. Other industries auxiliary to oil production, have sprung up in the nearby cities of Warri and Ughelli thus changing the socio-economic landscape of Uvwie. In addition several small-scale and service industries as well as commercial ventures sprang up in Effurun and Warri. In 1978 a multimillion naira (one US dollar was officially equal to 29 naira in 1993) refinery owned by the Nigerian National Petroleum Corporation was commissioned two kilometres away from Ekpan. Adjacent to the Warri refinery is another NNPC multimillion naira project, the Petrochemicals Plant, which went on stream in the late 1970s.

The refinery and petrochemicals plant, along with the NNPC staff housing estate, occupy several hectares of fertile agricultural land and fishing grounds of the Uvwie people in and near Ekpan. In addition, the Delta Steel Plant at Ovwian-Aladja and its gigantic staff housing estate (10 kilometres from Effurun) have taken over large portions of Uvwie farmlands for a dual-carriage access road. Finally a well funded but under utilized Petroleum Training Institute was built at Effurun on a large tract of arable land.

The construction and operation of these mega projects led to in-creased economic activities in Warri, Effurun and their environs. Part of this expansion was a rapid increase in population. Most of the population growth was accounted for by people who were not indigenous to the area. This influx resulted in a great demand for land on which to build housing. The Uvwie people had more land than their neighbours in Warri, and therefore bore the brunt of this land alienation. The consequence was a rapid and marked reduction in the amount of farmland available in the community. Despite these major developments in the 1970s and 1980s, most of the Uvwie people continued to depend largely on the land and fishing areas for their subsistence.

The oil industry at Warri swallowed the people's land, and made the federal government extremely rich. Through Urhobo land pipelines carry up to a million barrels of oil a day. Warri is one of Africa's largest oil export terminals. Crude oil flowing out of the dozens of tanks through a single point buoy and onto supertankers brings in a third of the government's yearly revenue. From Warri comes half of Nigeria's own petroleum product needs. Each day, kerosene, petrol, diesel and other oil products are loaded onto dozens of road tanker trucks. Warri is the source of fuel for Lagos and major cities in the west including Ife, Ilorun, Ibadan and Benin. This is the source for the oil supplies to the west coast of Africa, and to the continent's port cities to the south.

Offshore Warri, US oil companies exploit some of the world's most prolific and profitable oilfields. Shutting down this Warri nerve centre brings to a standstill billions in investment. Losses amount to millions of dollars a day. International energy prices respond to the least hiccup in the global system [Turner 1990:24]. World oil and national oil were wired into the social crises simmering in the Warri oilfields in the 1980s.

Ethiope and Okpe LGAs constitute a region which is two realities: for the oil industry, nationally and globally, it is the site of a major resource concentration with immense financial and strategic import. For the indigenous people it is land, fishing areas, markets, religious sites and homes which continue to underpin an essentially peasant existence. The contradictory relationship between these two realities were expressed by women's uprisings against men. Farming women confronted bourgeois men. And the division between collaborating men and those men in solidarity with embattled women echoed the fact that oil industrialization was choking out the community's farming roots.

The 1984 Ogharefe Women's Uprising

The Ogharefe women's uprising was a portent of more massive mobilizations to come. It paved the way for the August 1986 Ekpan women's uprising, and offers significant contrasts. The 1984 revolt took place before political mobilization had reached a national level in post oil boom Nigeria. The uprising aligned the indigenous Council of Youth with the Council of Women to produce a decisive power bloc.

The curse of nakedness against the US oil company

The women demanded that the oil company pay them for lands seized, and for pollution damage. This oil company is a subsidiary of the United States multinational, Pan Ocean. The women demanded the drilling of a reliable water well and the provision of electricity. Ogharefe has suffered from oil pollution and other effects of oil exploration and exploitation over the years. The Ogharefe community along with villagers throughout Nigeria's oil belt suffered acutely from skin rashes, stomach ailments and other health problems associated with hundreds of 24-hour a day natural gas flares and the discharge of 'oil production water' into the environment. Hunting had deteriorated as a result of the gas fires and heavy oil traffic. Corrugated iron roofs dissolved under the impact of ash from gas flares. Productive fishing ponds and agricultural land had been reduced sharply by oil company expansion [Hutchful 1985:53-55]. The people of Ogharefe had been denied compensation payments for land acquired as oilfields. On the one hand, the oil company had rejected community evaluations of the amounts of compensation necessary to replace the losses people calculated they bore as a result of petroleum development. On the other hand, the company refused to pay out to claimants the sums which it had determined were adequate compensation. The people had been denied the provision of social amenities by the main oil company operating on their land. By early 1984, "all peaceful efforts to make Pan Ocean listen to the community's protests and demands had fallen on deaf ears [Oshare 1986]."

An important feature of the grassroots political constellation in Ogharefe which was not present in the Ekpan uprising of 1986 was the high level of political organization of Ogharefe youth. In fact, there was widespread community agreement that "only the youths could effectively represent the interests of the community. The youths claim that the elders are selfish, too easily satisfied and ignorant of the realities of modern times [Oshare 1986]." And the Council of Youths had the backing of the Eghweya or Council of Women.

In 1984 the women of Ogharefe decided to call Pan Ocean's bluff. One early dawn saw the entire womenfolk of the community laying siege to the company's Ogharefe Production Station. The mass protest of several thousand women was aimed at preventing workers from coming into the station to relieve their colleagues who were already held 'in captivity' by the women. The personnel locked in the station made frantic radio contacts with Pan Ocean's offices in Warri and Lagos. Several hours later the higher authorities responded: the company's managing director himself was coming with his team to appeal to the women to come to the negotiation table. When the women heard this they threatened to strip naked to drive the point home that what they needed was compliance with their demands and not new negotiations. They had negotiated enough already. Disrobing by women in public is considered a serious and permanent curse on those to whom the women expose themselves. The curse is related to mothering, agricultural productivity and fertility in general. It is used by women in Kenya, Trinidad, South Africa and probably internationally [Kanogo 1987, Rosberg and Nottingham 1966:51-52, Globe and Mail (Toronto) 13 July 1990:A10]. No man would wish to bear the lifetime curse organized by the throng of naked Nigerian women. Any foreign man subjected to this curse would lose his credibility (potency) in Nigeria and would be effectively neutralized.

When Pan Ocean's managing director approached the site the women had in fact made good their threat. Before the arrival of the company's officials, the women had removed all their clothes. The sight of thousands of naked women of all ages was not one that these officials nor the police could withstand. They all fled without hesitation. The women's demands were met almost immediately.

Reasons for the 1984 uprising's victory

The Ugharefe women's uprising was a dramatic success. The US oil company paid compensation for land taken for oil operations. It paid small amounts against pollution claims. And Pan Ocean began to install water and electricity for the villagers. The women's revolt made a major impression on all parties, not least the women of neighbouring communities who experienced hardships similar to those challenged by the Ugharefe women.

Features of the uprising which contributed to its decisiveness include first, the alliance between women and youth. Probably the single most important way in which young men strengthened the women's case was by publically stating their opposition to the secret deals which senior men had struck with the oil company. The concrete result of this stance was the expectation that young men would join with women in shutting down Pan Ocean's operations should the women require such assistance. Amongst the youth were articulate graduates ready to provide the services of documentation and advocacy. Not only was the male Council of Youth active, but it had community status as a defender of the Ugharefe people. In contrast the Ovie and his Council of Chiefs had been discredited. The Council of Women was supported in the uprising by this dynamic and popular Council of Youth.

Second, the Ugharefe women used a combination of well orchestrated tactics. They kidnapped and held hostage a shift of US oil company workers. They took over the production buildings. They blocked the access roads, and thereby enforced the work stoppage which had already been imposed by the women's securing of Pan Ocean's production site. And most seriously, the women refused to negotiate and used the ultimate weapon at their collective disposal: exposing their naked bodies enmass to curse the oil company management.

Third, the Nigerian government was not involved in the clash. It was a confrontation between women farmers and traders on the one hand and US oil company management on the other. There was no state mediation between these third world women and the representatives of the US oil company. The US company rushed to settle or ameliorate the dispute possibly because it recognized the danger of allowing the conflict to escalate. Pan Ocean may also have recognized that backroom deals struck between the local king and the Nigerian state on behalf of the US company had been exposed. Prolonging the crisis could create a demand for damaging disclosures.

A direct settlement was beneficial for Pan Ocean because it allowed oil to flow from the Production Station after the short interruption, thus minimizing financial losses. The incendiary naked women curse guaranteed Pan Ocean a massive public relations loss if the conflict hit the media and was not settled immediately. And Pan

Ocean itself was contending with the government over payments for oil. Pan Ocean was refusing to pay the Nigerian National Petroleum Corporation for many millions of dollars worth of crude oil that it had extracted from the Ogharefe oilfield years earlier. Consequently the US firm could not rely on the Nigerian state for support in quelling the Ugharefe women's uprising. Under these circumstances the Ugharefe women scored a decisive public victory. They dramatized for the larger community women's power to right injustice for the benefit of the whole society.

The political context of the Ekpan Women's Uprising

Nigerians against the IMF

In 1986 Nigerian women of the Uvwie clan in Ethiope Local Government Area organized to shut down the international and state oil industries. This confrontation took place in a charged political atmosphere. The military coups of 1983 and 1985 unleashed anti-women rampages by soldiers along with official measures to discipline and limit women. For example, the Nigerian Labour Congress attempted to halt an initiative by women to establish their own network within the union organization. Head of State, General Buhari's 'War Against Indiscipline' targeted women with charges of over spending in the household, failure to supervise children, inadequate service to husbands and kin and neglect of farming [Dennis 1984, Mba 1989]. International Women's Day was changed to 'Family Day,' on which women were enjoined by the state to change their wayward behaviour and become more disciplined. In the Muslim north unmarried women living alone or together in rented accommodation were turned out of their rooms, allegedly to combat prostitution. In the south women wearing trousers were pulled off buses by soldiers and stripped of their western clothing.

Nigeria had, in July 1985, experienced yet another military coup. Buhari, who seized power by the gun on December 31st, 1983, was out and Babangida was in. The people, sorely pressed by an economic downturn because of the fall in oil prices, expected improvements from the new government. This expectant and militant demeanour was evident in the popular campaign against the International Monetary Fund.

In the last half of 1985 Nigerians from all walks of life made known their opposition to the government's taking an IMF loan. The conditions of structural adjustment were rejected. In distant villages and in the urban cores ordinary people attributed all manner of hardship to the machinations of the IMF. Babangida's military regime had little choice but to pay rhetorical tribute to what amounted to a near unanimous popular rejection of a deal with the IMF [Turner 1985, Ihonvbere 1993].

The 1986 Ughelli women's tax revolt

The loans would not be taken, announced the military government in late 1985. But in practice the 'conditionalities' were imposed. There was resistance. Women were hit especially hard by price hikes, increased petrol and transport prices and cuts in social services. They were at the forefront of the fightback. One vivid illustration is the 1986 Ughelli women's tax revolt. This uprising established the immediate atmosphere of popular, woman-centered mobilization within which the Ekpan women were moved to act. A key element in IMF structural adjustment packages is higher taxes. African colonial history is replete with instances of women leading tax revolts. Carrying on this tradition, in 1986 the women of Ughelli community laid siege on the Ovie's palace. The mass protest accused the king of supporting the Bendel state government's efforts (under the military regime) to make women pay income tax in the state.

The women stated that "it was ridiculous" for the Ovie, "who ought to know better than anyone else in the community," to support the taxation of women. They demanded that the Ovie should show them the tax receipts of his mother and grandmother, dating back to when the colonialists introduced taxation into Nigerian society. Of course no such receipts existed. Had not these women, the kin of the king, participated in the historical refusal of Nigerian women to be taxed? The fury of the Ughelli women moved the Ovie to flee to Benin, the state capital, probably to seek the protection of the military governor [Oshare 1986].

Within three days women in other parts of Ughelli Local Government Area joined the protest. This anti-tax protest also spread to other Local Government Areas in Bendel state including Isoko, Okpe and Oredo. Notably the women of Ethiope Local Government Area also mobilized against the proposed tax on women. Market women in Benin City closed their stalls, threatening to deprive the metropolis of food. Benin market women were against taxing women. But they also refused to pay school fees. The Ughelli women's tax revolt was highly successful. The state government withdrew its directive to tax women.

Multiclass mobilization

The political setting for the Ekpan women's actions involved women's mobilizations. But it also involved a broad based political intervention by the community of dispossessed. A crucial development in the early 1980s was the return to their villages of thousands of unemployed high school and college graduates capable of assisting peasants in organizing against the oil companies. Graduates and their families expected jobs, especially in the state. But recession meant unemployment, retrenchment, dashed expectations and a pressing need to find alternative means of livlihood [Shettima 1993:84-89]. Youth were encouraged by the government to 'return to the land.' But when they did, young graduates encountered the effects of oil pollution, land alienation and a general lack of both infrastructure and credit which were required for successful agricultural ventures. By the mid-1980s farmers, fishing people, market women, urban workers and the unemployed, men and women were resisting land grabs and power plays by big oil and the state. In the southern oil regions, the politicization stimulated by the oil bust brought together many sections of the community to demand compensation for pollution and land use [Turner 1986:44-45].

On March 29th and 30th, 1986 some 400 Bonny Island residents including oilworkers, shut down Africa's largest oil export terminal, claiming that the operator, Shell, had disrupted their lives and contributed nothing. Some 100 women sat on the Shell helipad to prevent any helicopter from landing at the tank farm base. Their placards read "Shell's 28 years in Finima is a curse to us," "Our means of livelihood has been destroyed by Shell," and "No light, no water for us after 28 years of Shell [*The Vanguard* (Lagos), April 4, 1986:1]." Among the specific grievances were that "all bush roads linking the terminal with the village have been sealed up by the company thus locking Bonny Island residents in and out; and that villagers passing through the terminal roads are often subjected to rigorous interrogation and search by Shell's security agents." Further north in Imo state, villagers protested the police murder of an oilworker by demonstrating in front of the military governor's office. In April 1986 the villagers of Egbema in Imo state, numbering more than 5,000, held hostage for two days over 40 staff of Shell at the Anglo-Dutch subsidiary's office building. The occupation protested "the company's neglect of the community since it came there 28 years ago [*Nigerian Tide*, April 18, 1986]."

Nigerians living near production or exploration sites consider themselves entitled to employment by the companies. They engaged in covert forms of class struggle such as sabotage, theft, road blockage and harassment of company activities if a specified number of jobs were not awarded. Such incidents appear to have increased since 1983 with the economic downturn. Despite the government's decree that pipeline sabotage was punishable by death; explosions, puncturing and pipe theft persisted. The difference after the government decree was that peasants refused to report oil gushes or leaks to avoid the police practice of arresting on suspicion of sabotage any bearer of such news. One theme informing the general mobilization was insistence that the government or foreign firms pay compensation for land taken over for oil pipelines, facilities and roads. A related but more radical theme was the refusal to accept land alienation and an insistence that no amount of money could compensate a community for the destruction of its way of life.

The Ekpan women's uprising was fuelled by militant political currents stemming from the anti-IMF campaign, the women's successful anti-tax revolt and protests against the oil companies. Women in Nigeria, and especially in oil rich Bendel state mobilized themselves when their expectations of some relief from the new military government were dashed. Instead of getting better, after the 1985 Babangida coup, things got worse. When living became even more precarious, women moved to secure what they considered their rights. In so doing they confronted not only the government, but also US oil companies and a faction of their own menfolk.

The 1986 Ekpan Women's Uprising

Ten thousand women demonstrate

At 5 a.m. on Monday, August 25, 1986, a large crowd of demonstrating women from the Uvwie community besieged the premises of the

NNPC Refinery, Petrochemicals Plant and the Pipelines and Products Marketing Pumpstation, all located at Ekpan. The demonstrating women were estimated to be about 10,000 strong. The throng was made up of all age groups of women, including the very old [*Daily Times* (Nigeria), August 28, 1986:3 and *Sunday Telegraph* (Nigeria), August 31, 1986:1].

The demonstrators chanted war songs and carried placards some of which read: "Give us Social Amenities," "Review all forms of employment within the Petrochemical," and "Our sons, daughters and husbands are qualified for key posts within the Petrochemical." These demands were similar to those of the women of Finima Community in Bonny Local Government Area who had protested against Shell at the Bonny terminal only weeks earlier.

The Uvwie women were shouting, angry and riotous. They chanted demands for preferential employment opportunities for their people. They threatened to go naked if they did not get satisfaction. In the early morning, thousands of women surged forward in a determined attempt to break into the premises of the Petrochemicals Plant. While the women blockaded the access route to the three gigantic projects, their supporting menfolk laid ambush armed with "dangerous" weapons, with "possible attack in mind just in case their women were tampered with [*Sunday Telegraph* (Warri), August 31, 1986]." The Ekpan women successfully blockaded the access road. All activities at the sites of the three projects were halted. Workers could not reach their offices. Large oil tanker trucks could not go in to load fuel for distribution to petrol stations. A team of men from the Nigerian Police Force led by CSP G.A. Olatunbosun could not disperse the angry women.

It was not until about 2:30 p.m. that the women agreed to hold discussions with a management team from the government's Nigerian National Petroleum Corporation (NNPC). This team of state oil officials was comprised of the refinery's General Manager, Refinery Manager, Administration Manager, Zonal Manager and the Inspectorate Manager. The women on the other hand were represented by three of their leaders. They insisted that no man from their community should be at the meeting. This insistence reflects the suspicions which some of the throng held that women's interests had been sold out by senior men in the community who were closely connected to the government and oil industry [Oshare 1986].

The negotiation meeting was a marathon, lasting for over four and one half hours. While the meeting continued inside the Refinery's board room, thousands of women remained at their demonstration posts. They continued to cripple the central core of the midwest's oil industry for the whole of that day. At about 7 p.m. the meeting adjourned to enable the NNPC management team to communicate with its headquarters in Lagos. The oil administrators agreed to convey the women's grievances and demands to top management. This level of top management included the Managing Director of Nigeria's 'state within a state,' the Nigerian National Petroleum Corporation along with the powerful federal Minister of Petroleum and probably General Babangida, the military head of state. The women demanded feedback and positive response within two weeks failing which they would resume their action.

Demands made at the first meeting

At the meeting the women stated their case as follows [Oshare 1986]:

(i) The indigenous people of Uvwie were not given a fair share of the recruitments made for the Petrochemical Plant in line with the catchment policy of the Federal Government as regards low cadre staff. The immediate development precipitating that day's protest march was the recruitment of seven drivers the week before. Of these, four were from Anambra state, one from Imo and the remaining two from Ethiope Local Government Area. Not one was from the Uvwie clan within Ethiope Local Government Area. The women said that they had tolerated this kind of discrimination in recruitment in the NNPC establishments located on their land for too long. They said it was only happening because all the top positions were held by non-indigenous people. These senior officials hired people from outside. For example, the Petrochemical Plant's Project Manager is from Anambra State, the Refinery General Manager is Yoruba and the Pipeline and Products Marketing Sector's Manager is from Anambra. All the officers immediately subordinant to them are also from states other than Bendel. This ethnic and regional composition of top management makes it possible for them to fill employment positions with people from their respective home states at the expense of the indigenous people. This, the women demanded, must stop.

(ii) Compensations had not been paid for farm lands acquired as long ago as 1973 for the refinery and petrochemicals projects. When the NNPC acquired the land for the refinery in 1973, it claimed that the land was donated to it by the Bendel (then Midwest) State Government. The Uvwie Community went to court to dispute this claim. The community won their case against the federal state oil company. But as of the August 1986 action, the NNPC had failed to pay the community compensation for alienated land. The community demanded seven million naira (in 1986 about US$14 million). The Nigerian National Petroleum Corporation claimed that the land was not worth so much but did not say how much it is worth. The dispute was unresolved a full 13 years after the land was acquired and was being utilised. The NNPC Estate Officer involved in the matter said that the compensation was still being worked out by the Corporation. On the Petrochemical Site which is adjoining the Refinery the NNPC was not paying any compensation for land. It paid only for one season's worth of crops being cultivated on the land when it was alienated. The NNPC justified this non-compensation for land takeovers with reference to the 1977 Land Use Decree (now Act). The federal government is not recognizing communal land rights under the Land Use Act.

(iii) With regard to the award of petty contracts, the women claimed discrimination against people indigenous to the community. They charged that contractors from the home states of the NNPC top management staff have the lion's share of small contracts. This, they demanded, must also be rectified in their favour.

(iv) The women asked for the provision of pipe-borne water and electricity at Ekpan. They pointed out that although the NNPC Staff Housing Estate which enjoys a constant supply of electricity and an abundance of potable water is a mere stone's throw away from Ekpan, the people of Ekpan remain totally without electricity and lack potable water. The contrast with their NNPC neighbour, occupying their land, was stark. The women likened this situation to that in apartheid South Africa.

(v) The Ekpan women also demanded scholarships for their children in secondary and post secondary institutions of higher learning. The state oil corporation should provide scholarships, they argued, referring to precedents established by Gulf Oil Company of Nigeria (GOCON) and other oil companies in the country.

Men take over the second meeting

The next meeting between the NNPC and the Uvwie community took place two weeks later on Monday, September 8, 1986 at the Palace of the Ovie of Uvwie in Effurun. The NNPC was represented by the Warri Zonal Manager, the Project Manager of the Petrochemicals, the Manager of the Petroleum Inspectorate, the Pipeline and Product Marketing Manager, the Refinery's Administration Manager and the Zonal Head of Public Affairs.

The Uvwie Community on its part was represented by seven chiefs, one evangelist and two women. Unlike the first meeting of August 8, 1986, at the second meeting the community presented a proposed agenda which stated the objective of the meeting and its modalities. Also unlike the first meeting the Uvwie delegation was no longer an all-women body. Instead there were only two women in the ten person delegation. According to one view "this male encapsulation of women's struggles means in fact that corruption takes over and the political content of women's struggles is lost to the economic interests of chiefs and elites [Ihonvbere 1991]."

In a written statement signed by the ten members who comprised the Uvwie delegation on behalf of the Community and entitled "Why Our Women Folk Demonstrated on Monday 25th August, 1986: A Case of Displacement, Neglect and Non-Rehabilitation By NNPC," the community once again restated their grievances and demands in unequivocal language. They stated *inter alia* that

> "Land as commonly known and accepted is the most impor-
> tant as well as the most precious asset and implement for the
> realization of real wealth by both state and individual. ... Be it
> known that together with the NNPC, the State and Federal
> Governments are already occupying (over) 65% of Uvwie
> farm lands while others, including major and minor private
> companies are occupying yet another (over) 30% leaving the
> Uvwie people with barely 5% of their arable farmland. Based
> on this, therefore, the community does not see why it should
> suffer non-provision of potable water and electricity at Ekpan,
> scholarships, job employment and petty contract awards for
> their sons and daughters, and worst of all non-payment of
> compensations for land acquired by the NNPC since 1973
> [Uvwie Community 1986]."

They found it highly objectionable that all the NNPC establishments on their land failed, for no good reasons, to implement the catchment area policy of the federal government. This policy committed the state oil company to hire people indigenous to the site on which oil operations were located, at least for lower level, unskilled and semi skilled work. The lack of job recruitments was intolerable because jobs were viewed by the indigenous people as one way to compensate them for land seizures by the state for NNPC. When the NNPC officials tried to refute this by saying that Ethiope Local Government Area to which Uvwie belongs was fully considered on the basis of "Catchment Area," the people replied that Ethiope Local Government Area is comprised of many autonomous clans or communities to which Uvwie has no obligation beyond linguistic ties. They then pointed out that of the Refinery's staff strength of 1,600 only 40 are from Uvwie while only 22 sons and daughters of Uvwie are in the Petrochemical Plant. None of these Uvwie people, employed by the government owned refinery or petrochemical plants are in management positions.

However, in the course of the meeting "it was discovered that certain things were being done for the community from which only the Ovie and his chiefs were benefitting without the knowledge of the people. For example the Ovie had recently submitted the names of four persons to the Petrochemicals' Project Manager to be employed without telling his people. When this and other revelations were made at the meeting, the people felt cheated and queried this action of the Ovie and his Chiefs [Oshare 1986]."

The meeting ended with the NNPC promising to implement the catchment area policy with more discretion, to service the only water borehole in Ekpan, to reactivate the faulty generator at the Ekpan Hospital and to speed up efforts at effecting the long delayed payment of compensations for land acquired in 1973. Both parties agreed to work in close collaboration to avoid confrontational tendencies in future.

An assessment of the Ekpan Uprising

The Ekpan women's uprising was characterized by complex gender relations, a reformist outcome and multiclass demands. First, with regard to gender relations, most notably, Ekpan women were placed under male control soon after the start of their uprising. The August

25, 1986 shutdown of the heart of Warri's oil industry was an all woman action. In contrast to the 1984 uprising, the Ekpan women decided to negotiate and this meant that they had to select representatives. Only women negotiated that day with state oil managers. Women explicitly excluded men from representing them. But in the two week interval before the next negotiation, men including chiefs and a Christian evangelist, assumed the right to settle the issues. The second meeting's agenda and a written brief were prepared by Ekpan men. Ten thousand women rose up. Then elite men moved in to explain the actions of "our women folk." In the men's version, women were not challengers of power but victims of it. The reconceptualization of power relations to construe women as objects rather than subjects is evident in the male standpoint embodied in the negotiation document's title: "Why our women folk demonstrated on Monday 25th August, 1986: a case of displacement, neglect and non-rehabilitation by NNPC."

One view suggests that Ekpan women originally took action "because they may have felt that the men were slow in pursuing the grievances of the community. They may have felt that the male community leaders were benefitting secretly from the NNPC jobs, contracts and pay-offs and therefore showing little or inadequate concern for the community's grievances. The revelations at the second meeting held at the Ovie's palace buttress this argument Oshare [1986]."

Women engaged in a peaceful but militant shutdown of the oil industry after years of frustration. Their rights were not secured through existing channels nor through the efforts of more powerful male community representatives. Any suspicions which women may have had about chiefs selling out to the government and oil companies were confirmed at the second negotiation meeting. Women discovered that the indigenous leaders had betrayed the clan, could not be trusted, and were part of the problem. This group of indigenous men had taken charge of the negotiations and were targeted in the second meeting as sellouts. The task confronting Ekpan women was revealed as doubly complicated: the government had to be forced to do justice, but a prior battle against indigenous men aligned with the government had first to be won.

A second feature of the uprising - its reformist outcome - follows directly from its takeover by establishment men. The immediate settlement included a condemnation of Ekpan women's tactics and a denunciation of confrontation. Members of the Chief's Council, in alliance with the oil industry, sought to impose limits on the women's action. Consequently the Ekpan uprising was in effect reformist and incremental rather than transformational. The results were palliatives, vaguely defined and subject to no implementation timetable. At best Ekpan and Uvwie women secured a partial victory. Probably more important than the tokenism of some compensation and amenities is the leap in consciousness made by those engaged in the uprising and its denouement.

A third feature of the Ekpan women's protest was the multiclass character of its focus. The demands addressed the concerns of peasant farmers, traders and marketers, artisans, craftspeople and wage workers. Ekpan women demanded land compensation, jobs, scholarships, electricity and running water as well as a range of social services, including health and education.

The Ekpan demands were complex, involving who was employed in new oil industry jobs and who in government made those decisions. Ekpan women were posing policy issues on several fronts. Their demands around employment questioned the ethnicity of the industrial establishment's management who make hiring decisions. Ekpan women posed micro-local hiring priorities against the national and even international scope of NNPC's personnel recruitment pool. The Ekpan uprising questioned the alleged ethnic and regional (state of origin) bias according to which managers awarded small contracts.

The women challenged compensation policy and the very concept of compensation for land taken by the state for the oil industry. How, they asked, can a way of life be destroyed and 'compensated' through the payment of a small sum of money? The women objected to lack of amenities, comparing the privileged western style housing across the fence to their own poverty. Using the analogy of apartheid, displaced peasant women pointed to their poor domestic working conditions with no electricity, water or functioning medical system. They raised the fundamental issue of who benefits from the oil wealth. This tremendous national treasure from their own communal lands was being used to benefit others and in the process their own lives were being destroyed. The Ekpan women failed to settle these complex, multiclass issues. However, they took an important step forward through the organization of an uprising which put the issues on the agenda.

A comparison of the two uprisings

There were important differences between the successful 1984 Ugharefe women's uprising and the less decisive 1986 Ekpan women's uprising. The difference in scale is relevant in making comparisons. The 1984 protest was small and localized. It focused on a single oil production station. It cost one US oil company some financial loss. In contrast, the 1986 uprising shut down a major section of the national oil industry. It threatened not only the government's oil revenues and international exports, but also the flow of oil products to road tankers to supply Nigeria and West Africa. The state had to contemplate the possibility that the 1986 uprising would spark solidarity strikes by road tanker drivers. In the 1980s these road tanker drivers were very militant and frequently acted on threats to shut down Nigeria by halting the delivery of fuel. All sections of the population were resisting the imposition of IMF conditions. There was a real prospect that the 1986 women's uprising could escalate into a national general strike. Consequently the state responded more decisively against Ekpan women than against the much smaller scale uprising of 1984. Taking into account this contrast in scale, comparisons between the two uprisings are made with reference to (1) their targets and racial dynamics, (2) alliances which women struck with men, (3) their peasant versus proletarian character, and (4) the dialects of gender and class. These comparisons explore and corroborate the three arguments presented in the introduction: that the uprisings were clashes resulting from class formation; that the gender character of the uprisings followed from the process of capitalist development; and that the degree of success enjoyed by women reflected both the degree of proletarianization and the degree of male solidarity.

First, Ugharefe women confronted a foreign oil company. In contrast, the Ekpan clash was between women and the government, as represented by the state oil corporation. In Ekpan the state effectively shielded the international oil industry from displaced peasants while Pan Ocean in 1984 did not enjoy a government buffer between its operations and peasant women. The state functions simultaneously as a class and a race buffer. The Ugharefe-Pan Ocean confrontation was a black-white racial faceoff. African women, using the specifically gendered weapon of collective nudity, insisted on justice from representatives of white US men. However, there is no doubt that black men were thought to be equally susceptible to being rendered impotent by the sight of naked women. The ethnic dimensions of the 1986 clash were more complex and subtle. Ekpan women did employ the apartheid analogy to contrast the luxury housing enjoyed by African state oil personnel, with their own homes which lacked water and electricity. While Ekpan women employed a racial analogy to highlight class difference among black people, they also concentrated on ethnic bias in hiring and contract awards.

Second, Ekpan women were not supported by a council of youth as were the Ugharefe women. While Ekpan women moved against the government only to be surprised at the depths of betrayal by their chiefs; Ugharefe women had already acted independently and against the chiefs. In the Ugharefe clan women and youth had allied themselves against weak, sell-out chiefs and this alliance won broad social support.

A separate aspect of women's alliance with men was tactical. Women in both uprisings took action on behalf of men who, in comparison with women, could be subject to much more severe state repression. Women took action in part because of the protection which their being female bought them. Women had been massacred, for instance in the Aba Women's War of 1928-1930, but there persisted amongst both women and men a notion of shame associated with men attacking women. Men's resistance to state exploitation, in colonial and in post-colonial times, has always met with brutal repression. Women lose from this repression in at least two ways. They lose their husbands, sons and the most able-bodied men on whom they rely for some defence against rival communities and at times of calamities. And they face a future, after the repression, in which the state may take advantage of an extended interval of unimpeded exploitation. Women were acting on their own behalf but also in the interests of their immediate families and in order to secure social amenities for the entire community. The women's uprisings were embedded in a long history of African communal strategies for expressing and resolving collective grievances.

Third, the demands of the 1984 uprising related to the interests of small farmers and traders, not waged workers. The Ugharefe women were demanding protection as farmers supplying local markets, in order to avoid being proletarianized. In contrast, the Ekpan women who had lost much of their land, were demanding better conditions as proletarians and small contractors, at the same time as they sought protection of the eclipsed peasant way of life.

Fourth, class and gender relations differed in the two uprisings. The more intensive class formation of Ekpan bolstered the power of elite men. In contrast, the persistence of peasant relations in Ugharefe preserved the power of ordinary men who continued to control land. The Uvwie community immediately adjacent to the oil city of Warri bore the brunt of land loss as the oil boom exploded. Land deals by the hundreds were executed. There was a high level of involvement of indigenous men who were well placed to broker these land deals. Men in positions of power within the local class configurations, became very rich through organizing the alienation of communal land. In 1986 Ekpan women revolted against these men.

The displaced peasantry was largely female. This follows from the fact that women did most of the farming, fishing and marketing. With land loss these women could neither reap profits from farming nor could they ensure the survival of their own households. As traders, food processors and artisans, Uvwie women depended on farming and the landed household for produce and labour. These women moved against the class of land alienators, all male, and against the men of the state to whom land rights had been ceded.

Men related to the women's uprisings in various ways depending on their class. In Ekpan men sought waged work. In their uprising, Ekpan women demanded jobs "for the sons and daughters of Uvwie." The oil industry is a male preserve. Waged jobs (apart from those in agricultural labour) usually require literacy and girls have had to face much greater obstacles than boys to graduate from schools [Rouse-Amadi 1993a]. The colonial and neocolonial states in Nigeria preferred male to female waged workers, at least in most jobs [Fadayomi 1991:187]. Consequently, few women had waged work open to them as an alternative to peasant farming and own-account trading. When oil belt women came under pressure they responded, defending their own interests as economic and social actors. Among these interests were more jobs. Men from the peasantry did join women in the 1984 Ugharefe uprising, supporting them against the chiefly elite aligned with foreign capital. This class division among men was also evident in Ekpan. But there, unlike in Ugharefe, elite men prevailed. They intervened successfully in the negotiations. The 1986 Ekpan women's uprising was moderated and diverted by influential men based in the indigenous power structure responsible for land alienation, and linked through 'male deals' to capital and the state.

In sum, the class struggle amongst men was won in 1984 by the Ugharefe peasant men aligned with women. But it was lost by men from the exploited classes in the case of Ekpan in 1986. This pattern suggests that class gains depend on solidarity between women and exploited men on the terms according to which women are prepared to exercise their social power. The pattern contrasts sharply with the stalinist formula which relegates women's issues to a status subordinant to the so-called 'overall class struggle.'

Conclusion

In the years since the 1986 uprising, Nigeria's political and economic crisis has become more acute. Women and all poor people came under more severe attack as the state sought to implement the IMF structural adjustment program. As the collapse of oil prices reduced government revenues, the economy deteriorated even more and the environment came under more severe threat [NEST 1991]. Privatization included some denationalization of oil. Militant Nigerian oil-workers were retrenched enmass and replaced by North American and European personnel. Foreign companies gained power as the state establishment shrank and became delegitimized from the perspectives of both capital and the grassroots. At the same time the weakened state became more repressive, while promising, but not delivering on, a return to civilian rule. The military regime in the early 1990s was clearly a refuge for indigenous chiefs who are targeted by their subjects as enemies. Uprisings have been frequent as Nigerian society becomes even more polarized along gender and class lines. The multiplication of insurgencies is especially evident in the oil belt where groups of villagers have been massacred by police because they protested corporate depredation [CDHR 1990:31-32, CDHR/NADL 1991, *Newswatch* 1990, 1993]. Nigerian authorities covered up an October 1990 police massacre of 80 un-

armed villagers that occurred after Shell Oil appealed to the police
for intervention against protestors demanding compensation for lost
land [*Platt's Oilgram News* 9 October 1992:6]. As oil belt women
establish that they are prepared to use the ultimate weapon of
collective nudity, men increasingly support women's initiatives and
capital's counterinsurgency tactics are increasingly directed towards
the demobilization of women. The state and foreign aid donors
persist in attempts to mute feminist militancy with reformist 'women
and development' projects [Trager and Osinulu 1991]. Nigerian
women are sharply divided into a bourgeois elite backed by the state
and a mass of women in the exploited classes. With the destruction
of civil society and the middle class, indigenous religious and clan
organizations have become more politically important. Underneath
the surface of religious uprisings are class conflicts with crucial
gender dimensions [Dauda 1992].

As noted in the introduction, the Ugharefe and Ekpan women's
uprisings were events within a process of political mobilization. The
process continues. The patterns of women's resistance in the colonial
period reappeared in the 1980s: women shut down markets, took
over buildings, blocked roads and attacked indigenous male leaders
for siding with the state against the people. The process by which
sections of the exploited classes work out methods for unified struggle is also a process of developing gender and class consciousness.
This consciousness is international because it is replicated in other
oil exporting societies in the responses of people, women and men,
to the same actions and social relations imposed by multinational
petroleum firms and the International Monetary Fund.

The process of political mobilization continued in the late 1980s
under the impetus of two new external forces. The first of these forces
was an innovation from the IMF. Structural adjustment programs
were to have not only economic but political conditions attached to
them. Governments were required to make a kind of democratic
transition to civilian multiparty governance. This was part of the
IMF-Bank concern to put a human face on the process of implementing structural adjustment [Plewes and Stuart 1991:107; Shettima
1993:88]. The second external force was the meteoric rise of
democracy movements which challenged Soviet and other centrally
planned states' power. In the space provided by these external
developments, Nigerian political mobilization has produced a range
of human rights and civil rights organizations some of which have

both grassroots and international links [Turner and Ihonvbere 1993; Abdullah 1993:35-37]. And it has produced incipient popular movements, notably in the oil belt. In the 1990s protests against oil company pollution have mobilized thousands of people with over 100,000 Ogoni women and men massing for a day long demonstration in January 1993 in the oil region near Port Harcourt [*Newswatch*, 25 January 1993]. The uprisings against oil companies in Nigeria were initiated by oil belt women and have now been joined by all sections of the impoverished communities.

While these external developments did widen the political space within Nigeria, they were soon confronted by counter developments. The peace and democracy dividends which were expected to flow from the collapse of Soviet state power were blocked by US militarism in the Middle East and elsewhere. US and other imperial states changed their orientations from being apparently pro-democracy involving support for fair elections and a transition to civilian rule, to being content with the military status quo in Nigeria. The change follows from the strength of internal resistance to structural adjustment policies combined with the dramatic lesson of state disintegration provided by Somalia in the early 1990s [Africa Watch 1993:3]. It became apparent in 1993 that in Nigeria only the military could maintain order, impose IMF policies especially with regard to the oil industry and foster a form of federal state coherence in the face of demands for the creation of more states and the growing sophistication of popular insurgency.

Both the 1984 and the 1986 uprisings confirm the ability of women to wrest concessions from exploitative authorities. Ugharefe and Uvwie-Ekpan women's actions should be seen as part of the class struggle that has persisted in both colonial and post-colonial Nigeria. The women constituted an autonomous force within the class struggle. The women's uprisings against the oil industry are especially important because they reveal the transformational impulse inherent in capitalist development. This impulse transforms gender relations so as to create possibilities for the forging of class solidarity on the basis of women's militancy.

The women's uprisings against the oil industry in Nigeria in the mid 1980s confirm the double complexity of capitalism's denigration and empowerment of women. On the one hand, the extension of exploitation worsened the situations of women. Earlier relative reciprocity between men and women dissipated into intensified sexism. The rise of local capitalists from the indigenous elite was paralleled by a transformation in gender relations. A kind of gender reciprocity was broken by elite men's private appropriation of land, the fundamental basis of poor people's livelihood and community. With the deepening of capitalist relations, unequal gains of men and women were echoed by unequal opportunities among ethnic groups.

On the other hand, industrialization led to land alienation which motivated women's fight back. It elevated women's political impact by offering them vulnerable oil industry targets against which to concentrate their collective social power. It prompted feminist militancy which reforged the reciprocity between women and men, but this time on the new basis of class solidarity. Out of this experience is emerging a new society with the force and reason of women, and their organization and consciousness, at its forefront.

Chapter 11

Servicing mankind: women and domestic labour in Port Harcourt, Nigeria

Hilary Rouse-Amadi

Rapid urban growth has been one effect of the oil industry on Eastern Nigeria in the post-civil war period. Port Harcourt, as the administrative centre of the major oil, construction and servicing and supply companies, has increased dramatically in size and density of population. Estimates vary between one and one and a half million people; but there are no current, reliable census figures. The teeming squalor of the sprawling slums of Diobu, testifies to the poverty and brutalizing conditions experienced by the vast majority of the city's inhabitants. What are the employment opportunities for young girls and women, who come to this town, in the hope of enhancing their life-styles and improving their standards of living? With little or at best rudimentary formal education and marketable skills, the majority enter domestic service, while some work as salesgirls, waitresses, barmaids, clerks and typists. For many, prostitution may present itself as a preferable alternative or may be taken up on a part-time basis to supplement poor wages. Any adequate investigation and analysis of the impact of neocolonialism on female labour must address itself to the conditions and experiences of young girls and women in domestic service. The following pages attempt to focus on these experiences and locate them within the total economic structure of the Nigerian comprador state, with particular reference to the period from the mid 1970s to the mid 1980s.

Child Labour

In pre-capitalist, subsistence and semi-subsistence societies, child labour was an integral part of the agricultural and domestic economy. Today, child labour continues to be a feature of rural and urban life, in many parts of the continent, both in the traditional form within the extended family unit and within the typically urban-based wage labour system. It is especially in the latter that girls are often severely disadvantaged and acutely vulnerable.

For the majority of African children, childhood is essentially a period of purposeful apprenticeship, leading gradually to adult status and responsibilities. It is not a period in which the child, reduced to the status of a nursery toy, is reified and reared on a television diet of aggressive, confusing escapist fantasies. Consequently, the African child learns to contribute economically, as a working member of the family, from a much earlier age than his/her North American and Western European middle class counterparts, or indeed the children of the comprador bourgeoisie.

In Malawian villages, it is common for a procession of women and girls fetching water from streams and wells to end with the toddlers, balancing small cups or cigarette tins, brimful, on their heads, with an earnest concentration which eloquently testifies to their early and carefully nurtured sense of social responsibility. In Nigerian cities, children of primary school age ply their assorted wares as petty traders in the interminable 'go-slows,' clogging the urban highways, or move from compound to compound in the affluent suburbs selling bread, oranges and kolanuts, or mind a roadside stall for an absent relative for long hours at a stretch.

Gender divisions are learned early, or as a former colleague from Mbaise, Imo State succinctly put it, boys are taught in early childhood to regard themselves as socially superior to their sisters and I must add, the primary agent of socialization at this stage is the mother [Njoku November 1979]. Typically, among Igbo and other ethnic groups in the East, girls fetch wood and water, help their mothers with farming, food processing, general domestic work, trading and child care. Although they followed a predictable pattern, gender divisions in child labour in rural economies were, according to Sylvia Leith-Ross, not necessarily rigid or absolutely clear-cut in Nneato (Owerri province) during the late 1930s:

> "In the home, the boy may sweep the yard, even the house 'if he be good boy and want to help his mother,' he may possibly help to pound the fufu but he would never cook, nor have I seen one washing or scraping cassava. The girl helps in all

domestic work, including the cooking, and both boys and girls fetch wood and water, though on the whole it is more usual to see the boys doing outdoor work while the girls are more use at home [Leith-Ross 1965:89]."

As for child-minding, in the absence of a sister or a grandmother, a brother or a cousin would function as nursemaid, while the infant's mother farmed or went to market. "These children take their position as nursemaid very seriously, even the small boys will be seen wiping the baby sister's nose with the utmost care and quickly twisting a little grass together so that it should not sit down on the bare ground," and the author waxes lyrical in her description of "the younger children (of a family), patiently hushing a tiny form to sleep, sitting motionless and cramped, a tiny head in the crook of their own tiny arm [Leith-Ross 1965:104]."

Capitalist relations in the colonial and neocolonial periods have in many instances, altered the nature of child labour in particular and domestic labour in general, creating in the process, new and increasingly oppressive forms for utilizing and controlling female domestic labour. Evolving class relations in Igbo society have intensified the exploitation of female domestic labour, both unwaged and waged, and have generally fostered in the children of the urban petty bourgeoisie, an arrogant contempt towards the domestic servants employed by their parents. In societies still strongly influenced by gerontocratic traditions, gender divisions, age-grades and ranking, this trend in the life-styles of the rich and privileged demonstrates the disruptive and alienating impact of 'naira power' on domestic relations and kinship ties. The extended family cannot be simply and simplistically labelled as a stabilizing and cohesive social force, or as providing a preferable alternative to excessively bureaucratic state welfare systems. True, it may sometimes fulfil some of these functions, but entangled in a social web of giant contradictions, it more often mirrors and reflects the explosive tensions and latent class and gender conflicts characterizing the larger society.

In many villages such as Umueze, Ogwa, near Owerri, capital of Imo State, traditions have evolved whereby "poorer relations give their young children to their more well-to-do kinsmen to help rear for them [Onyemaobi August 1981]." Often, this in effect has meant the exploitation of cheap labour from the villages, by an urban based elite, manipulating kinship ties within the extended family to its own advantage, while posing as benevolent patrons, ostensibly providing access for poorer relatives to 'modern' and 'sophisticated' urban lifestyles. Sometimes, in exchange for some basic formal education, these children "do all the odd jobs and also face a lot of deprivation. One can't blame the parents for they couldn't do otherwise. And in the families where there are these 'wards' (relations-cum-househelps) to clean, cook and carry, the 'children of the house' relax and never do a thing [Onyemaobi August 1981]." The promise of education is often honoured more in the breach than in the observance, especially where there are no kinship ties between employer and 'ward.' Young girls from the rural areas may work in town for 'strangers,' under the guardianship of an older relative, already established in urban employment. Very often, their labour is ruthlessly exploited. They may suffer acute deprivation and never so much as 'smell' their wage packet, which will be handed over to the 'guardian' at each 'monthend,' part for onward transmission to parents in the village and part, no doubt, into the pocket of the 'guardian' whose role, in certain respects, is frequently analogous to that of the pimp.

Skilled and semi-skilled male artisans can make good profit on the side, acting as agents for their employers' or customers' friends, by seeking out young girls fresh from the village to work as nannies and maids. Such agents normally charge the prospective employer for procuring and recruiting the girl and, in addition, demand for themselves a portion of the maid's wage, at the end of the first month. Even members of the affluent business and bureaucratic class are known to demand their pound of flesh, when helping a friend or acquaintance find a maid. One senior civil servant in Port Harcourt, a family man in his early fifties, offered a young girl of fourteen from Imo State, the choice between forfeiting the bulk of her first wage packet to his voracious purse, or granting him sexual favours. Since she refused to accept his terms, he refused to take her to her potential employer on the agreed day. It was only through determined detective work that she located this Madam, with whom she eventually worked and lived for several years [Iwuchukwu April 1975]. The girl in question had already worked as a nanny for the family of a prominent member of the local power elite, whose persistent sexual harassment ironically was a major factor impelling her to seek alternative employment. Even after she had established herself with her subsequent employer, if the man caught sight of her in town, he would 'wind down the glass of his Mercedes and beckon her to enter and join him'. Her account of this incident was accompanied by much laughter and it was clear that, although the man in question was a well-known public figure, in his mid forties, she, a mere child by comparison, regarded his antics as ludicrous, childish, immature and typical of men in his class and position of power.

In Port Harcourt, I encountered another particularly pathetic case of a young girl, aged between fourteen and fifteen, from Cross River State, who found herself abruptly uprooted from family and community after completing her primary education. Her brother worked as a driver in Port Harcourt, cast around and found his junior sister a job as nanny in the home of a prosperous Ikwerre entrepreneur. She was categorically told by her mother that the family was not in a position to fund further post-primary education or training; but that if she worked well in her new job, a portion of her wages would be set aside each 'monthend' and kept in her brother's savings account, so that she could later attend commercial school and learn typing and shorthand. Initially, she discovered that her Madam, fluent in Kalabari and competent in Ikwerre and English, knew no Efik, her own mother-tongue. The cook, gardener, driver and other household employees were either Igbo or Ikwerre speakers. Her early experiences in the household were both humiliating and terrifying. Mocked by her co-workers, she described to me how one of them had tied a rope around her neck, pulled her along in the cement yard adjoining the servants' quarters at the back of the compound, laughing and abusing her in a language that was totally incomprehensible to her. Soon, she complained to her brother that her Madam was not feeding her properly, that instead of allocating her some soup from the family pot, as agreed, Madam often gave her gari (an Eastern Nigerian fast food staple derived from cassava) with tinned sardines. Extracting pocket-money from her brother to buy toiletries and the odd packet of biscuits was a monthly nightmare which often left her tearful and frustrated. Her clothing on arrival was old; she had expected her Madam to provide her with a basic, modest wardrobe. Her Madam, a high-society, fashion-conscious bank employee, eventually bestowed on her little nanny a blouse, skirt and dress, all rejects from her own extensive wardrobe, which had to be altered to ensure they did not part company from the skinny, adolescent body of their temporary owner, like a ship adrift from its moorings! Her brother told his little sister it was Madam's responsibility to clothe her, and Madam told her to ask her brother to use some of her wage packet for the purpose. The result was that stranded between the devil and the deep blue sea, she remained underfed, overworked, inadequately clothed and poorly shod.

A virtual prisoner, she was locked into her place of work day and night. The two mansions in the compound were walled around with thick fortifications and watchmen were on patrol twenty four hours a day, backed up by a fierce alsatian and glaring searchlights. (The incidence of armed robbery with violence has risen steadily with unemployment and retrenchment). Her own vivid description of her working environment conveyed the impression of a confused child, reduced to servitude in a luxury concentration camp. She was not permitted to move freely out of the compound and was expected to sleep with the two children in her care every night. Her one regular weekly break from this routine was church on Sunday. Within six months of this regimen, she had formed the habit of sneaking out of her employer's house sporadically in the evening and sleeping around with male stewards, nightwatchmen, drivers and artisans living in the servants' quarters of neighbouring compounds. The response of employer and guardian alike, was to beat her and sermonize. When she left the service of her first Madam, she was asked to return the clothing which she had assumed the woman had given her to keep. Her second employer, on discovering her in the most compromising of positions with the gardener from the neighbouring compound, summoned the brother and advised him to take his sister back home to the village and explain to her fully and carefully, the security risks and health hazards she was running. He showed no shock or surprise at the accounts of his sister's persistent nocturnal absences and activities and after failing to persuade the employer to retain his sister's services, lost no time in finding her a third job as a nanny. At this point, she was no nearer to realizing her educational ambitions than when she first came to town and many of her friends were convinced that, while her family back home in the village enjoyed some of the fruits of her labour, the brother 'chopped' the rest. How else, they asked, was he able to acquire a brand new motor bike?

For many girls from poor backgrounds trapped in a vicious circle of domestic servitude, prostitution may be the only viable means of acquiring some form of post-primary education, as the following case amply illustrates.

Domestic service and prostitution

In December 1979, I carried out a number of informal interviews with young prostitutes, frequenting one of Port Harcourt's most prestigious and expensive hotels, in their search for clients. The tenacity and courage shown by many of these young women in the harsh struggle to contribute to the welfare of their families and acquire skills and education for alternative urban employment is ignored, overlooked and disregarded, within the prevailing prescriptive, moralistic ideology propagated by the comprador bourgeoisie and its institutions, including the NCWS (National Council of Women's Societies). At an open-air church service, organized by the NCWS at the Port Harcourt Temporary Stadium on the 28th of April 1985, Mrs. Elizabeth Membere, a Chief Magistrate in Port Harcourt, claimed that: "Nigerian women were responsible for 70% of the nation's ills." Her fire and brimstone vitriol was directed against "delinquent housewives and mothers," women trafficking in drugs and foreign currencies, prostitutes and all women who 'disgrace their sex,' by engaging in criminal activities to obtain money [Koko 29 April 1985]."

Ngozi, aged twenty, from Imo State, the daughter of poor peasant farmers who were finding it increasingly difficult to make ends meet, was the eldest of ten children, four of whom had died. Before she was able to complete primary school education, her parents arranged for her to start work as a houseservant for a family moving to Lagos. She worked for a year in Lagos, looking after the baby and cooking for the family, at the end of which, the family moved to Port Harcourt. At this point, there were two children to look after. During the next two years, Ngozi completed her primary schooling while continuing to work as a houseservant. Her monthly wage was 50 naira (at that time approximately US $50), out of which she would send between 20 naira and 30 naira home to her parents, food and lodging being provided by her employers. Ngozi felt bitterly disappointed when, at the end of this period, they were unwilling to pay for her to attend commercial school and learn typing and shorthand, while she continued working for them on that basis, established over the preceding two years. Since she had worked conscientiously and continuously for the family for over three years and had always made her long-term plans and expectations clear, she was left feeling cheated, convinced that she merited help and had earned it.

Boldly, she took the decision to leave domestic service and turn to part-time prostitution to cover her living expenses, school fees and contributions to the family. At the time of the interview, Ngozi rented a room in the Garrison area of Port Harcourt for 20 naira per month. Living on her own, she was vulnerable to theft and complained that thieves had broken in and stolen her clothes on several occasions. From her earnings as a part-time prostitute, she estimated that she had made between 300 naira and 400 naira per month, out of which a minimum of 70 naira would go into her personal savings account "in case of sickness." In addition, she was supporting a sister and brother, in Class 2 (secondary school) and Elementary 3, respectively. Having assumed responsibility for training them, she was at that stage of the process, paying for one set of secondary school fees and two sets of school textbooks and uniforms. Every month, she would send home money to cover these expenses, as well as continuing to contribute to her parents' income. Her own school fees amounted to 30 naira per term. Through careful management of her financial resources, she had already completed three years out of a four year programme when I conducted the interview. Her classes were scheduled between twelve noon and 5:30 p.m., so she would visit the hotel in question three or four times a week in the evening, sometimes taking a week off if she felt tired or run down.

To Ngozi, it was obvious that prostitution provided her with the only possible means of acquiring further education and ensuring that her brother and sister stayed in school. Since there was no-one in the family to help her financially and since her employer had, in her opinion let her down, she simply had to struggle on her own as best she could. Her average monthly income from prostitution appears to have been in the region of 350 naira. Compared to a typist with basic qualifications and several years working experience, in the employ of a state institution and earning 125 naira per month, or a laboratory assistant taking home 78 naira per month, she was, in purely financial terms, highly successful. Many lower-grade clerical workers and typists operate as part-time prostitutes to supplement meagre incomes. Prostitution, in Ngozi's experience, unlike domestic service, provided her with the opportunity 'to improve herself' and the potential for upward social mobility. Her family also benefited enormously from their daughter's 'naira power' and devotion. While functioning in vulnerable isolation within the competitive, urban cash nexus, this young woman like so many others who share the fruits of their labour with their families and finance junior brothers and sisters through training programmes and apprenticeships, provided for others the very support and help she herself had been denied.

While polygynous arrangements in pre-colonial Africa were primarily "designed to capture the labour (and reproductive) power of women [Rodney 1972:247-248]" systematically and comprehensively, there was within the system, at least for the freeborn, a code of reciprocity with regard to domestic labour, for as a father, mother, grandfather or grandmother, the elder became the recipient of the very services he or she once rendered as a child. Needless to say, within the patriarchal, gerontocratic social structure, men benefited at each stage of the process, from the services of others, to a much greater degree than women. Nonetheless, there were certain safeguards, what might be referred to as a system of checks and balances built into the patriarchal structure of the "democratic republican villages" and "constitutional village monarchies" [Afigbo 1972], characterizing pre-colonial Igbo society, which ensured a certain cohesion. The young child performing a variety of arduous and tedious household tasks, knew that in years to come, adulthood and old age would confer and guarantee certain recompenses, rewards and privileges. In the present wage labour system, class divisions automatically confer on the children of the affluent the dubious privilege of leisured childhood, while the young maid or nanny not only finds herself at the bottom of the hierarchy of domestic service, but also subject to the whims, caprices and superiority complexes of Madam's spoilt offspring, some of whom are her agemates and juniors and who all too often perceive her as a servicing robot, belonging to a species apart.

Domestic labour and rural-urban migration

Many middle class, professional women in Port Harcourt, purposefully seek out homehelp, direct from the rural areas and villages of Cross River State and Imo State. Certainly, in the case of Imo State, density of population and rural poverty are the prime economic factors behind this system of migrant domestic labour and the overwhelming preference, on the part of the parents, to invest scant financial resources in the education and post-primary training of sons, rather than daughters. One explanation commonly given by employers is that girls new to township life prove more amenable to discipline, more honest and diligent in their work and easier to train and supervise, or to put it more bluntly, they are likely to prove more easy to control and will accept a lower rate of pay than their older, more experienced, urbanized counterparts. Before a mother hands her daughter over to a new Madam, a bargain may be struck to the effect that the girl's future training and education will be paid for and provided by her employer after a certain period of service, or if her children are old enough, the maid may study part-time while working. One of the prostitutes I interviewed in December 1979, lived with her widowed mother in Mile Two, Port Harcourt and employed a ten year old girl as houseservant and nanny to her three children, aged five, three and two. In exchange for her services, the employer, a young woman from Calabar in her early twenties, fed, clothed, housed and sent her to school. Thus, from the very outset, the little maid paid for her primary education through her labour power.

Very often, as in Ngozi's case, these girlservants experience bitter disappointment when their educational goals and ambitions remain unfulfilled and they find themselves unable to improve their skills and employment opportunities. Marriage, like a seductive mirage may then appear to offer a happy escape from underpaid domestic labour and poverty. Like the young adolescent girl from Cross River State, the vast majority of minors in domestic service have no control over their earnings, which will be collected from the employer by a senior member of the family or guardian appointed by the family. Sometimes, the relative assures his sister that part of her salary is being put aside to be invested in her education, at some unspecified time in the future. Very often, she discovers, when she leaves the job in thorough frustration, that there are no such savings, that her wages have been eaten up by the burgeoning demands of her family for medical bills, school fees for junior brothers, even the brideprice an elder brother is struggling to pay. The instability that characterizes female domestic service testifies to the frustration of the employees and their conditions of service, rather than to any inherent deficiency in their personalities and where such are manifest, they are for the most part a product of inhuman and brutalizing treatment and not its cause.

Sexist stratification of domestic labour

Male cooks and stewards, especially those engaged by the oil and construction companies generally command higher wages than their female counterparts, partly because they are regarded as more stable and partly because they are seen to constitute a lower risk factor (i.e. they will not be subject to sexual harassment, either within the employer's home or outside, with the accompanying risk of pregnancy and possible litigation by the girl's family). The large companies normally pay an allowance for domestic servants to their expatriate contract officers. I have heard of numerous cases where the employer pays his domestic employee/employees perhaps half or two thirds of the allowance allocated by the company, pocketing the remainder. In addition, following patriarchal tradition in advanced capitalist societies, it is assumed that a male adult is earning a family wage, but that the same does not apply to female workers. In reality, girls in domestic service in Eastern Nigeria are expected to contribute a substantial proportion of their wages to dependent and disadvantaged members of their family, sometimes also feeding and supporting unemployed boyfriends and retrenched husbands during the present period of economic depression.

Urbanization and domestic labour

Thus rapid urbanization, in a dependent capitalist economy, based on the wild fluctuations in revenue derived from the petroleum industry, has brought major changes to family life and increased the exploitation of female domestic labour in the cities. A girl's access to formal education is often sacrificed so that a brother may pursue academic studies, an apprenticeship or technical training. The training of these sons is a heavy financial burden for the average family to shoulder; and they remain more dependent on parental support for a much longer period than within the rural subsistence economy, where, as I have emphasized, children, especially female children, are productive from an early age, contributing significantly to the general well-being of their community, rather than functioning purely as consumers of family wealth. This increase in cost and investment is not simply born by fathers and mothers and elder brothers but sisters, who are often under pressure to enter the urban wage labour system at a very early age and become economically self-sufficient, and who in many cases end up supporting less able brothers through post-primary training programmes, for which they themselves have more aptitude and potential.

Hilary Rouse Amadi

The relationship between educational disadvantage and domestic labour

In the final analysis and viewed from a long-term perspective, it is the state that must take up the challenge and responsibility for training its citizens and providing adequate opportunities for all, regardless of sex. As long as the onus is anachronistically left to the overburdened extended family system, with its male-dominated priorities and perspectives, girls will remain subject to sex discrimination and will be acutely educationally disadvantaged, no matter their merit or ability. In an address to the 1970 graduating class of Owerri-Nkwoji Girls' Secondary School, Nkwerre/Isu Local Government Area, Imo State, the guest speaker called for major changes in attitudes towards the place and role of women in Igbo society: "Education must no longer be seen by women as the exclusive preserve and prerogative of the men." And he continued, "Parents must realize that the more education their daughters acquire, the more their earning power, the surer their confidence in themselves and the greater their leadership chances and roles in society and the lesser their dependence on exploitive individuals [Emenyonu 20 July 1979]."

Admirable though these sentiments and ideals undoubtedly are, they cannot be realized through moral appeals to parents, whose perceptions of reality derive from an economic system, which by its very nature exploits all existing social relations, both 'traditional' and 'modern' in the overwhelming pursuit of short-term profit, material gain and sheer, basic survival. It is a system in which every social relation, be it that of husband and wife, father and son, mother and daughter, employer and employee, doctor and patient, lawyer and client... is subject to the same ruthless laws which govern the wheeling and dealing between the local comprador politico-business class and their metropolitan masters.

As I sat helping the bored, truculent, pampered son of a Senior Civil Servant from Rivers State revise for the Common Entrance Examination for entrance into secondary school, the young housemaid joined our side and quickly and easily supplied answers to the arithmetical problems that the child was unable to solve. Sluggishly, the boy assumed that since his father was a 'big man' in town, he could and would, if necessary, bribe and badger the Principal of a suitable secondary school for admission. Several years earlier, the housemaid

172

had performed well in the final year of primary school, but typically, her family with severely limited resources, preferred to educate some of the sons and at the same time of the incident referred to, in 1985, she was paying fees for one brother in secondary school and feeding, clothing and housing another brother, who had recently started his apprenticeship as a panel-beater in Port Harcourt.

The underdevelopment of African women and the simultaneous, wholesale exploitation of their labour power becomes a compelling symbol of neocolonial waste and degradation in Mongo Beti's moving novel, *Perpetua and the Habit of Unhappiness*. The heroine whose ambition it has been to become a doctor, finds herself withdrawn abruptly from secondary school so that her widowed mother can cash in on her brideprice. She is mercilessly married off to a low-grade clerical worker whose intellectual stupidity and sexist malevolence highlight the criminal waste of her own human and academic potential. "The intolerable knowledge that his wife was his superior [Beti 1978:89-106]," drives Edward to humiliate Perpetua in public and in private at every turn. Incensed by the jibes and mockery he receives from his male peers, Edward feels threatened and undermined, even though Perpetua's domestic servitude in marriage prevents her from putting her latent and dormant intellectual powers to creative use, both to her benefit as an individual and to the benefit of society as a whole.

Domestic labour in the home

In the home, it is assumed that girls will carry a heavier domestic load than their more privileged brothers. Sometimes, indeed quite often, the latter are exempt from domestic chores and household tasks altogether. This means that even where a girl is lucky enough to receive formal education, she has far less time for homework and leisure pursuits than her brothers. Girls may also be expected to perform domestic services for their brothers, for example cooking for them, washing their clothes and dishes, fetching and heating water for bathing. Little wonder that an Ikwerre father, alarmed at the poor academic performance of one of his daughters in secondary school, discovered that one of the causes was that she was spending a disproportionate amount of time after school, carrying out household tasks for her mother, who at the same time made no such similar demands on the son of the family. The boy, primarily because of the mother's norms and expectations, lorded it over his sister and eventually, the father decided to send the daughter in question to boarding school so that she would have more time to herself to study in the evening and at weekends. It is all too often the mothers, who perpetuate the inequity of gender roles in the patriarchal family structures of Eastern Nigeria, mistakenly but understandably, concentrating on the interests and needs of their sons, to the neglect and detriment of their daughters, essentially because it is through 'male issues' that a woman's long-term social and economic security in her husband's family and home are established. By custom, sons not daughters inherit landed property in many parts of Eastern Nigeria:

> "As recently as 1977 an Ibo Customary Law manual, drawn up by 461 men and 2 women, actually prohibited all women in certain areas of Imo and Anambra States from owning land or landed property. It prohibited all married women from divesting themselves of any landed property without their husband's consent and stopped married women in certain areas from owning land [Obadina 10 April 1983:5]."

Consequently, the Eastern Nigerian women traditionally looks to her sons for security and comfort in her old age. The daughters, after all, will 'marry out' and their priority like hers will be to establish their position in their new families.

Contradictions in the ideology of female subordination

From these conditions, a profound contradiction emerges in that, while a daughter is socially, economically and educationally disadvantaged compared to her brothers, she may be expected to contribute substantially to their training, through her domestic labour power, either unwaged in the home or waged in the household of her employer. In general, she has scant opportunity to develop her skills and potential, yet the maximum profit and use is extracted from her labour power by her family, before she marries, and indeed by her husband in the interests of his family after she marries. And ironically, it is the mother who most often transmits and implants the ideology of female subordination into the minds and hearts of her own daughters. Perhaps the very knowledge that her daughters will soon 'marry out' impels many a mother to extract the maximum domestic labour from them, for the relatively short period she has them under her control. A mother's attitude to her son or sons may border on idolization, it will almost certainly be indulgent, compared to her treatment of her daughters. As one young Igbo woman graphically stated, when a woman has only one son "she go handle'am like egg." Paradoxically then, while male children are essential for a woman's long-term security in her marital home, girls are desired in part for the intensive, short-term contribution of their labour power in domestic service. In an interview with Millie Adisa of *The Guardian*, forty three year old Madam Fatumata Adesoya of Oshodi Market, Lagos, the mother of seven boys and two girls claimed the size of her family would not have been so large if she had had the girls earlier:

> "Madam Adesoya says, although boys are a life-long protec-
> tion to their parents, the immediate gains of a mother from her
> children are mostly delivered by the girls. 'Look,' she says
> pointing to her eleven year old daughter in her stall, 'she has
> just returned home from school and she's here to help with
> the sales. After that, she'll go home to start the cooking before
> my return. How many boys will do that for their mother?'
> [Adisa 22 April 1984:5]."

How often, one wonders, are girls like this able to find time to study at home, read without interruption, prepare schoolwork undisturbed? And yet, since the typical Nigerian mother is "saddled with close to 100% responsibility for the care and maintenance [Ayandele 8 April 1984:15]" of her children, and in Eastern and Western Nigeria, required to make a substantial economic contribution to the family income, one cannot blame low wage earners for depending on the support and service of their daughters. The problem will only be solved when gender roles in the home are radically redefined and perceived to constitute in their present form an integral aspect of the human waste that characterizes neocolonial, patriarchal society in Nigeria. To tackle the problem of domestic labour effectively, it must be treated as a basic economic, political and ideological issue, for it is a problem that is central not peripheral to any agenda for progressive social change.

Class and gender

Class divisions in present-day Nigeria, affect women to an even greater degree than their menfolk, for at the end of the working day, the peasant or proletarian man becomes lord of his compound, boss in his overcrowded rented room, as does the rentier in his suburban mansion in the G.R.A. (Government Reservation Area). Daughters, therefore continue to be exploited by both poor and even affluent mothers, and middle class women exploit their working class and rural 'sisters,' with little compunction or compassion. Because of gender, women share certain experiences, but because of class, their interests diverge and come into conflict. Wages for female domestic labour are pitifully low, off-duty periods irregular and relations between an employee and her Madam, typically feudal in character. Paid domestic service is non-unionised, unstable, isolated, insecure and potentially dangerous, since it is common for maids to be sexually harassed by Madam's husband or other male members of the household. What finally emerges however, is not simply a picture of oppression, but also a picture of the strength, courage and individual creativity in adversity and stress, of young girls and women in domestic service.

In theoretical terms, they constitute classic examples of alienated labour, for the kernel of Marx's theory of alienation highlights the impotence of the worker to harvest and enjoy the fruits of his or her labour, to determine its value and use and hence play a creative role in the politics of work and production within capitalism. The child nanny has no bargaining power in terms of contract and rate of pay, decided on her behalf by senior relatives. In the first instance, she is the victim of pre-capitalist social structures demanding her unquestioning loyalty and dedicated service to the interests of the patriarchal extended family of which she is a member. Secondly, and of paramount importance, she is also a victim of a capitalist wage labour system, which in its neocolonial form voraciously utilizes and distorts all social relations, both those it has created and those which belong essentially to pre-capitalist modes of production and consumption. In the new order, the exploitation of pre-capitalist social and economic arrangements is intensified to the extent that they contribute to the accumulation of wealth and increase the consumer power of the petty bourgeois comprador class of neocolonial Nigeria.

The lower the wage paid to the child nanny, the greater the spending power of her Madam. The longer the nanny minds her charges, the greater the opportunity her employer has to further her own career interests, enhance her chances of promotion and increase her salary. Madam's kitchen is equipped with a deepfreeze, gas cooker, liquidizer, washing machine, dishwasher and air-conditioner. Her maid's room in the servants' quarters at the back of the compound has wooden shutters in a bare window frame. She cooks by kerosene lamp on a small kerosene stove and fetches water from a common tap in the backyard. At night she barricades her door against the persistent sexual harassment of Madam's husband and the other male employees resident in the compound. If she becomes pregnant, she is liable to instant dismissal and blamed for immoral conduct. If she exposes herself to an illegal backstreet abortion, she risks 'spoiling her womb', damaging her health, or even losing her life. She knows that back home in the village the livelihoods and lifechances of younger brothers and sisters, or the health and well-being of an ageing widowed mother depend substantially on the financial support she can give. And so she suffers and serves, sometimes rebels, but for the most part stoically endures, learning to play the role of mother, even when she herself is still a child. In so many ways, Marx's account of the problematic position of the alienated, proletarian worker applies aptly to her:

> "In what does this alienation of labour consist? First, that the work is external to the worker, that it is not a part of his nature, that consequently he does not fulfil himself in his work but denies himself, has a feeling of misery, not of well-being, does not develop freely a physical and mental energy, but is physically exhausted and mentally debased....His work is not voluntary but imposed, forced labour. It is not the satisfaction of a need, but only a means for satisfying other needs. Its alien character is clearly shown by the fact that as soon as there is no physical or other compulsion it is avoided like the plague. Finally, the alienated character of work for the worker appears in the fact that it is not his work but work for someone else, that in work he does not belong to himself but to another person [Marx in Bottomore and Rubel, eds. 1963:177]."

But unlike the male worker who "feels himself at home only during his leisure, whereas at work he feels homeless [Marx 1963:177]," her state of 'homelessness' by comparison, is absolute and her insecurity overwhelming. Child and domestic labour thus, sharply illustrate the developing underdevelopment of women in oil-dependent Eastern Nigeria, in the post-civil war, neocolonial period.

Chapter 12

Women and Work
in an oil exporting community

Hilary Rouse-Amadi

In sickness and in health.
(For Eunice who refused to abandon her sick husband)

She came to town and earned her pay
As maid to a sociologist from the U.S.A.;
And when her madam finally
Packed her bags and went away,
She tried her luck with an Ikwerre family.
But the noise, turmoil, confusion
And strife and nagging intrusions
Into her puny patch of private life
Made her decide to retire from the fray
And stay with her electrician in Mile Three,[1]
While together they figured out a way
To pay some of the heavy brideprice
Her father adamant would demand
For his favourite daughter's precious hand.
Better by far to stay with your man
Than be accused by your loud-mouthed mistress
Of stealing her husband from under her nose,
While God in his heaven surely knows
You feared those furtive, nightly knockings
Persistent on your padlocked door.

Some of her savings
She siphoned Silas' way,
As initial downpayment
On the hefty brideprice
He had reluctantly agreed to pay.

And from her sewing, cooking and trading
Determined, she transformed
His hovel into a home,
Where he was happy to invite his friends
Sip beer and coke on a Sunday afternoon,
After singing and dancing the morning away
In Holy Gabriel's Cathedral where
Many came to drown their despair
In the rapture and frenzy
Of ecstatic worship and feverish prayer.

But when the fits of coughing
Robbed him of work and sleep,
Stripped the flesh from his limbs
And threatened the ground under his feet,
His wife consulted with a doctor in town,
Whose modest bill and sympathetic frown
Warned her stormclouds were gathering fast
To drive away the smiling skies
That had blessed and caressed her
For a few carefree days and paradise nights.
Trouble has packed into her home,
When the marriage has only just begun.
Her neighbours, relatives and friends
Sighed, sympathized and shook their heads
At the painful plight of the newly weds.

Anxious, her father summoned
His beloved daughter to his side
To whisper in her ear practical advice.
You are young and beautiful
And you'd be an idiot and fool
To waste your precious life
On a man who is not likely to survive
This killer curse they call T.B..
At best he'll linger ailing over the years
A pitiful invalid who'll bring you only
Sickly babies, debts and tears,
Leaving you quenched and drained,
Mourning in vain the youth
You wasted and threw away.
This miserable marriage must be untied.

The brideprice payments so far made
Can quickly and easily be repaid,
After which I shall inform his people
Reluctantly, I've changed my mind
And decided to keep you by my side.
In a few months, the gossip will subside
And then discreetly I'll tell family friends
You are willing to consider marriage again.

She went to his people secretly
And pleaded for money for the medical fees.
But his father and uncle both refused,
Reasoning to each other pragmatically
They had nothing to spare, nothing to scatter
To the wild winds and relentless rains,
For a cause so hopeless, so utterly vain.
They justified their refusal with proverbial refrain,
Masking their bulldozing business mentality
With the capitalist logic of limited liability:
For he who knowingly invests foolishly
Has only himself to blame
When the serpent bankruptcy swallows
His naira[2] and poisons his name.

First her costly wrappers[3] left her box,
Then her sewing machine was the next loss
And after all her savings were eaten away
She looked for another job as a maid,
Begging the landlord she would soon repay
The arrears of rent left unpaid.
Determined to ensure Silas' stay
In Enugu in specialist care,
She reverted to the role of domestic machine
For a young German bachelor engineer
Working for a mighty multinational company.
She went to her father and put her case,
She needed his help to avoid disgrace.
If he sold a small portion of his land
The ancestors would surely understand,
The sacred duty to save the life of an in-law
And prevent their desperate daughter turning whore.
For if you turn a deaf ear to my plea,

Then I'll share my oga's[4] bed for a regular fee
To help pay for the medicine, food and long-term rest
I have sworn to continue to provide,
Until my husband returns healthy to my side.
For the love of his daughter
He sold precious farmland,
 Commanding her to warn Silas
That should he ever dishonour his wife,
The wrath of their ancestors would strike
And swiftly snatch back his ransomed life.

 A year later Silas' relations spent lavishly
On a thanksgiving service and sumptuous feast,
To praise the Almighty for a job well done
In miraculously sparing their dying son,
While Silas' father-in-law whispered in fury
But for my daughter they'd have only bones to bury!

Continuation classes

(Poetry for voices, first performed at the third annual 'Women in Nigeria' Conference, Port Harcourt, April 1984. The theme of the conference was 'Women and Education.')

Part I

Daughter

Mother where shall I find
The fees for continuation classes?

Mother

Daughter, I have asked your father
For the money, but he tells me:

Father

Senior wife, business is bad,
Very bad and getting worse;
 No government contract again.
Now we must look first to our sons,
Who will carry my name,
In this hard world when I am gone.
 Let some prosperous N.P.N.[5] man marry
Your daughter and pay those continuation fees.
Has one not shown his eagerness already?
Why should your daughter drive away
His love and naira from this house?

Daughter

Mother, teacher says, no continuation fees
No way to pass School Cert.[6]

Mother

Oh daughter, why must your teacher
Harass us for these continuation fees?
I have sold fine George and wrapper

To buy a cupboardful of books,
Uniforms, provisions and give my share
To the P.T.A., sports fund, library,
Bore hole project, dining hall development plan.
Nothing now remains for continuation fees,
In this hard time of austerity.
My purse is hollow like a beggar's bowl,
Lined dry with harmattan dust.

Daughter

Mother, teacher says, no salary
For more than four months now.
Teacher complains stomach and bank account
Empty and strength no dey again.
Energy at low tide and ebbing lower
And lower like the failing waters
Of Kainji dam. Teacher says
Make we fuel'am proper
Before his motor fit start,
Before he fit teach us serious.
Mother plead with my father again.

Mother

Daughter, your father says
His head aches too much and
His nerves shriek nasty like
Our Governor's siren noising
Up and down this garbage city.

Father

Woman, shut your mouth,
Close'am well well
Like the lid on your cooking pot,
You hear. My building site sits silent
And empty like a burial ground.
Plumbers, masons, carpenters, bricklayers
Come check their arrears, refuse to
Work until I pay. And you know
Very well where these arrears

Found their way: to pay for
Books, uniforms and boarding
For your sons. I am drained
And dry as harmattan dust,
Dry as the old beer cans
Our neighbour upstairs tosses
From his window onto the street below.
Woman, I must complete that house
For my impatient customer-party-man.
Because of your daughter, he is angry,
Unwilling to advance more until
He sees results. He complains I am
Insulting his manhood, his position,
His reputation. He complains I am
The one advising our daughter
Against the marriage he proposed.
He shouts that I don't want
To build him a house, now that
He has made it known he wishes
To live there with my daughter.
He says old wines taste best.
He asks me if I want my daughter
Mixing with young riff-raff
Without naira or sense,
Who will loot and leave her
And laugh at the swelling sewn
Carelessly, casually into her ripening womb?
He threatens to send some of his boys
To deal with me well well.
He roars for all to hear,
That I have refused to complete his house
And won't accept him as a son-in-law,
Because we are age-mates and
Because my foolish pride prevents
My sending our daughter as his bride
To live with him under the roof
I have built. He shouts in my face
That it is better that a girl becomes
Third wife of a powerful party man,
Than a school dropout or unemployed
School-leaver. He promises her trips
To London to do her shopping

Hilary Rouse Amadi

At the month-end. He promises me
That I will move closer and closer
To the people that count,
After this marriage is made.
He insults me and snarls in my ear
That he can crush a petty petty ant person
Like me, in one second flat under
The leather heel of his made-in-Italy shoe.
Ah woman, shut your mouth, shut 'am
Well well, tight tight, you hear.
Don't turn this house into another
Building-site-dispute-confrontation,
Another strike, another wage claim,
Another centre of conflict and confusion.
You say you won't receive your husband
In bed until I pay continuation fees,
There are other doors well oiled,
Smooth, freshly painted which will
Open willingly to my knock.
The hinges of your own are rusty
And grate on my tired nerves.
Tell that stubborn she-goat daughter
Of yours to bring us the brideprice fees
Her impatient 'husband' has promised
And not I to pay for her continuation classes.

Mother

Husband, wait, wait, rest and cool
Your temper in your own home.
Don't carry your fire to the beer-parlour
And return swaying, swinging, horning
At the gate of our compound
In tomorrow's early-morning hours.

Father

Woman, leave me, remove your hand
Let me relax far from
 Your sour face and
Naira swallowing mouth.
Let me go, I say.

Mother

Daughter, your father has lost all sense,
Your father, furious in frustration,
Pushes me aside roughly, like
An old broom, worn out with age and use.
I know where some of the money flows
Now our junior wife has put to bed.
I know my thighs cannot hold him here.
I know I barricaded the way
To force his hand to pay your fees.
Let him not carry disease to my bed!
Let him not disgrace this family-oh!

Daughter

Mother, my sweet mother, make you no cry,
Quiet my mother, rest my mother,
Peace my own mother.
Let me return to the boarding house.
I shall find a way.

Mother

Daughter, my pickin, how you go manage?
How you go manage self?
Why not marry that N.P.N. man,
Your father's own customer?
He go 'gree pay brideprice to your father,
Big mighty one, express delivery,
Two thousand naira cash down.
With that your father fit pay
His workers, complete his house,
Buy the remaining books for your brothers.
Daughter, your youth and beauty
Will bring from that man's purse
Naira to pay more than
A few small continuation fees.

Daughter

No mother, no, I no fit marry
A man my father's age.
I no fit suck the naira
From an aging sugar-daddy,
And make myself the third slave-wife
To that bloated, greedy grandfather goat.
Mother, I will find a way.
And mother, I will pass my School Cert..

Part II

Father

Ah Madam Paradise, my dear,
Bring me one of your loveliest,
Freshest, juiciest angels.
Bring me one new untasted morsel
To make the blood pound furiously
Again in my aching veins,
And remind me of the days
Before austerity stole so many contracts
From my outstretched hands.
Bring soft new flesh
To allow me to forget
My unpaid workers, unfinished house,
Angry customer, stubborn daughter.
Bring me something special
From your menu as you always do.
Ah Madam Paradise, your Eden Heights
Hotel is a second home to me.
Yes, Madam, you are my wife,
Your girls, my sisters, sweethearts, daughters.
Let me forget the absence of a younger wife,
The presence of the older, rough-tongued witch,
Whose tired breasts and lifeless thighs
Drive me to your tempting delicacies.
Bring me my menu for tonight
And take your money for the night.

Madam Paradise

Come daughter, it is your first time
With us tonight, come
I have brought you an easy customer
To please. Speak sweetly, softly,
Make this old customer of ours
Forget his collapsing belly and broken contracts.
Tell him he moves in you
With the strength of a young lion,
With the power of a warrior in his prime.
He will not work you hard.
His blade is blunt, his battery flat.
His motor may not even groan
And splutter into slow-motion start.
But remember to tell him
He is the answer to a young girl's
Prayers and dreams.
And here is your twenty naira
To pay those continuation fees.
You have softened my heart.
Your luck shines like the full moon.
A new girl and part-time casual
Gets only ten naira the first time
And must prove her skills. But I like
A girl who is serious with her studies.
To room number seven my dear.

Father

Come in my beauty, come remove
Them all, every stitch, every piece
Of garment must be uncovered.
Come, I will be as gentle as a father.
Step forward, leave shyness in
The corridor outside. Let me know
Your name, come, come, my sweet.

Daughter

Father, is this the only way
To make you pay my continuation fees?

Hilary Rouse Amadi

Child Labour.
(For Nkechi who lived it.)

Her legs, two match sticks,
Pin thin, poverty toughened,
Propel her slight form,
Ballooned in faded cotton,
Forward with her load.

Her arms, two slender arcs,
Curving fluid to fingertips,
Steadying the headpan
Brimful with sand,
Brought to the contractor's
Busily bustling building site,
Raise and lower, lower and raise,
Times without number,
Her small stubborn loads.

She is only ten, or is it eleven?
She wants to read and write,
Learn arithmetic, knack small English.
But her father ruinously roared
To her mother's mute kneeling form,
That he would pay no school fees
For daughters whose skills,
Would only fatten another man's
Compound after marriage.

The mother, monument of resigned regret
Told her little daughter pleading
Prostrate with impotent passion,
That her small small money from trading
Was long since spent on her sons'
Books and biros for secondary school.
Her aunt claimed the forthcoming marriage
Of her son to his bride
Meant no kobo to spare
At-all-at-all at this time.
But her grandmother smiled away
Her tears with a rainbow of hope:

Bring money for books and I'll
Find the money for your fees.

So daily, her match stick legs
Stubbornly propel her thin form
Ballooned in the flapping tent
Of her senior sister's discarded dress,
As she carries a trickle of
Sand steady and slow to
Eze's[7] palace-in-the-building.
And so the youngest of his casual
Workers with the help of her mama's mama
Made it through those last two years
Of the local primary school.

But soon her grandmother died
And soon she was hired out to
Relatives in town to cook and clean
And tend their young, like any other
Obedient domestic machine.
That said her father,
Is the best school there is
For my young daughter before marriage.

Her legs are still thin
Though they carry two lives,
And often she silently swears
To the guardian spirit of her
 Grandmother on the other side,
That if God gives her a girl,
Her daughter will learn book
Aplenty for secondary school
And will not be rented out
As a cheap domestic machine.

Endnotes:

[1] Mile Three, a high density area of Port Harcourt associated with poverty, poor housing and rapid urbanization. Mile Three mushroomed in the post civil war years of the oil boom.

[2] The naira is the standard unit of currency in Nigeria.

[3] Wrapper, an ankle length cloth, worn by men and women, though tied differently according to gender. Eastern Nigerian women traditionally accumulate costly wrappers as savings and insurance against hard times since they can be traded for cash or kind.

[4] Pidgin English meaning sir, master, boss.

[5] The National Party of Nigeria, in power from October 1979 to end December 1983.

[6] Secondary School Leaving Certificate.

[7] Igbo word meaning King.

Chapter 13

It is not O.K. to hurt a woman

Leigh S. Brownhill

**Dedicated to Lisa Grimshaw, freedom fighter, in prison
for the murder of her batterer**

I was sitting in the common room
in Nairobi
trying to ignore the buzzing box in the corner
until my ears pricked
for some reason.
I looked up.
A North American news program,
U.S. voices.
I watch.
Two men, an interview, vigil ante-ism
I've missed the introduction.
"But how did you feel that you
weren't actually killing a
CRIMINAL?
I mean this was no Charles Manson,
this was just a case of
domestic violence!"
Whoa, my mind is thrown into a haze.
What is he saying?
I must have missed something.
The man reacts,
"What I saw was a brutal murder
and I wanted to do something about it!"

Break for commercials,
UPS flashes clean propaganda.
I ask the other watchers
"What's this guy done?"
"He killed a guy in the parking lot

who'd just killed his own girlfriend."
Oh. So killing your own girlfriend
is not a criminal act?
But this man stood up.
Stood against another man.
He killed him. Shot him dead.
One man killed another man
who'd just killed his girlfriend.
"domestic violence is not a crime!"
But this man said, "Yes it is."
He didn't ask if the woman
was the killer's girlfriend, wife,
property.
He didn't need to know that.
A woman, a person had just been killed.
And this man reacted. Interfered.
And he let the world know that
killing your girlfriend
can get you shot dead.

Strangeways Prison riot in England.
News reports.
Demands shouted. Banners
displayed. Bricks thrown.
Inhumane conditions. "Give us
medical care when we're sick!"
Violence.
One prisoner shot by the rebels.
A rumour flies that
Six sex offenders have been hung
with bed sheets.
These men are mad.
These prisoners are
really pissed off.
They don't want men running around
raping or molesting
their sisters, mothers
daughters, grandmothers, wives,
friends.
And they've shown how they feel
about sex offenders.
These men are standing up.

Standing against other men.
These men are really pissed off.
They've told the world that
rape
can get you hung with a bedsheet.

I weed through the trash
that is the World Report,
the International News.
I weed through
and pick up on the seeds
that are sprouting,
growing, bursting violently through
and letting the world know,
twice in one news hour, that
IT IS NOT O.K.
TO HURT A WOMAN.

Thousands of women around the world are in prison for murder or attempted murder of their batterers. The fight against violence against women is global and growing. The signs of men joining the resistance to these crimes tells us of the strengthening of the fight. The presence of these men in the fightback reinforces us not only by their added numbers, but more importantly by their proximity to the population of other men that so persistently attempts to crush women.

Chapter 14

The 1991 Gulf War
and popular struggles

Terisa E. Turner

"What is the new world order?" asked one Baghdad woman in the week after the fighting stopped, her voice rising in rage. "Is it based only on killing and money? Bush insisted on this war, and now he has what he wanted. We are nothing." Quoted in Ridgeway 1991:239.

"Almost every post-World War II American president has had a doctrine on the Middle East, and has also seen his grand design challenged by Middle Eastern nationalists - Mossadegh in Iran, Abdel Nasser in Egypt, Qassem in Iraq. For example the Baghdad Pact, a seminal American scheme, was held at bay by Abdul Nasser, and rendered ineffectual by the 1958 nationalist uprising in Baghdad. The anti-imperialist component of Middle Eastern nationalism has frustrated U.S. designs on the region throughout the post-World War II period. In turn, it has been the prime target of American interventions, both covert and overt. ... It also seems that U.S. policymakers significantly underestimated the power of the Arab street. They seemed to assume that the Arab street was not powerful, that there was no civil society functioning in the Arab world. They seemed to believe the Arab countries were not like Iran, not like Pakistan, where popular opposition overcame unpopular leaders; thus they believed that there would be no serious challenge to the U.S. alliance mounted in Egypt or Saudi Arabia, or elsewhere in the Arab world." Eqbal Ahmad 1991:12,18.

Introduction

Analysis of the 1990-1991 crisis in the Middle East has focused on reasons for Iraq's annexation of Kuwait, and reasons for US intervention in Saudi Arabia. Some of the implications of the US war against Iraq have been considered. What has not sufficiently been the focus of analysis is the politics of ordinary people.

This chapter argues that popular mobilization, or what may be termed the 'global intifada,' throughout the Arab world and Iran created the context in which the US government intervened militarily to secure Middle East oil under its control. Part of this argument has to do with the inability of compliant states in the region to act as buffers between the citizenry and foreign oil companies.

The analysis covers four periods. First, between 1900 and 1945 the British and French ruled the region. The decolonization of the Middle East after WWI was partial and unsatisfactory. The second period covers 1945 to 1960. Nationalists in the 1940s and 1950s expelled French and British colonialism from the region. They formed uneasy alliances with Soviet and US interests. Many of the states in the region developed further these alliances. They sought to ensure their stability in the face of continued militancy from below and from the populations of neighbouring states.

In the third period, 1960 to 1980, nationalist states forged a policy of oil nationalism through OPEC. This entailed creating state oil companies. It involved buying participation shares in existing foreign oil companies. The governments of the region thereby inserted themselves between the people and the international oil majors. This pattern was broken by the Iranian revolution of 1978-1979.

In the fourth period, 1980 to the present, the mobilization of the peoples of the region against international oil and against their compliant states grew in strength, although there were setbacks. When the deterrent of the Soviet Union was removed in 1989, the US military established itself in the region to exercise direct control over oil.

The prospects for this new edition of direct imperial occupation are poor. Not only is the US military presence a target for Arab radicalism, Islamic fundamentalism, terrorism and other political manifestations. It is also incapable of ruling in place of the states it discredits by its presence. It is not possible to run an oil industry through unmitigated repression as the experience of the Shah's attempt to break the oil strike in Iran in 1978-1979 demonstrated [Turner 1980; 1990]. Consequently, the current stage in the unfolding of popular power in the Middle East is likely to be dominated by military clashes, perhaps leading to oil embargoes imposed by workers themselves. Eventually the wealth and politics of the region will be brought under the charge of democratic popular organization. This trajectory can be traced in more detail.

Decolonization: 1900-1945 - Arabia is broken up

Arabia, stretching from the Persian Gulf to Algeria on the Atlantic, was created by the spread of Islam. The Middle East and North Africa constitute a region unique in the third world in that peoples are unified by the religion, Islam and the language, Arabic. Iran is outside this pan-Arab unity but does share geography, oil and Islam. Diversity also characterizes the region. But the unity of the pan-Arab heritage is important for today because it is the rallying cry of political militants and of those who believe that all wealth in Arabia is the heritage of all Arabians.

Countering this attitude is the British colonial strategy which sought to break up the region into small states. WWI ended Ottoman rule over Arabia. While many of the peoples of the region expected national independence to follow the war, the British arranged through the Sykes-Picot treaty of 1920 to maintain colonial control.

In 1922 the current borders of Saudi Arabia, Kuwait and Iraq were drawn by Sir Percy Cox, the British High Commissioner to Iraq. He intentionally limited Iraq's access to the Persian Gulf so that Iraq could not exercise a significant degree of independence vis a vis the British. The remaining boundaries were drawn to break up oil reserves among several small, weak sheikdoms. Large populations were concentrated in states surrounding the Persian Gulf: Pakistan with its 120 million, Iran with its 60 million, Egypt with 72 million and one of the smaller states, Iraq with 18 million. Small family ruled states with vast reserves of oil were created: Kuwait with 600,000, the United Arab Emirates with 500,000 and Saudi Arabia with between four to eight million people. Ahmad [1991:20] has pointed out that Middle Eastern people ask "How did it happen that this wealth of the Middle East was de-coupled from its people? Why separated the wealth of the Middle East from the people of the Middle East? Why is it, in the same region, that Kuwait's per capita annual income is $16,000 a year, and Egypt's is $650 a year?"

Family patriarchs were set up as rulers and these were highly dependent on British support in order to remain in power. It was a deliberate policy of the British and later of the US oil majors to reinforce and preserve reactionary elements of Islamic culture [Nore and Turner 1980]. This facilitated indirect rule whereby the patriarchal and theocratic structures were turned into supports for external dominance.

The United States secured a foothold in the region in 1928 when major US oil companies acquired oil concessions in Iraq. In 1938 oil production in Saudi Arabia began under Chevron and Texaco who were later joined by Mobil and Exxon. These four major US firms operated under Aramco, the Arabian American Oil Company. They secured US government funding for the King of Saudi Arabia during the Second World War, thus diverting him from British patronage.

In 1946 oil production began in the tiny sheikdom of Kuwait under a joint venture owned by British Petroleum and Gulf Oil. The world oil industry has historically been dominated by seven large corporations, sometimes described as 'the seven sisters.' The five US majors, Gulf, Texaco, Exxon, Mobil and Chevron were represented in Saudi Arabia and Kuwait. The two European majors, BP and Shell were also heavily involved in the region.

US policy in the Middle East was expressed through a State Department report in 1945 which said that "The oil of the Middle East is a stupendous source of strategic power and one of the greatest material prizes in world history." The drive to maintain control of this great prize has been the centre of US policy in the Gulf ever since. George Kennan, head of policy planning at the State Department in the late 1940s, "was particularly prescient in identifying Middle Eastern oil as having a future leverage in defining America's relations with its Western allies" [Ahmad 1991:10]. Every US president since Franklin Delano Roosevelt has promoted the view that the defense of Saudi Arabia is vital to US interests. The US built an airbase in 1944, within reach of the Soviet Union, but this was not used because Saudi Arabia's rulers were unwilling to discredit themselves in the face of rising nationalism, by consenting to a US military presence.

1945-1960: Pan Arabism and the formation of OPEC

The post war period saw the rise of Arab nationalism. The US stepped into British shoes as the major power in the region. In 1948 the Israeli Palestinian war resulted in the formation of the state of Israel. This presence of an outdated white settler state divided Arab unity and has continued to plague the region with the conviction that the business of decolonization is unfinished.

In 1956 the Algerian people began an armed struggle against the French who were desperate to maintain their closest and most important oil supply [Fanon 1961:90]. A tenth of the population or over one million Algerians were killed in this liberation struggle. The Algerian revolution had as an ambassador, Franz Fanon, a West Indian psychiatrist from Martinique. Fanon wrote about Algerian Islamic women's crucial part in the armed struggle. But in reality he championed Islamic patriarchal culture as it challenged French colonial macho culture [Burris 1973:353]. Women in this Arab war of liberation were, after securing victory, subordinated to their men. Although celebrated, they remained secondary in Algerian society after independence in 1962 [Mernissi 1987, 1991, Sabbah 1984].

In 1951 Mossadeq in Iran nationalized the oil industry only to face an international boycott. CIA action resulted in the overthrow of this democratically elected leader in 1953. Norman Schwarzkopf, under cover in Tehran as a police trainer, organized the thugs who trashed Iran's parliament. The New York Times of August 6, 1954 editorialized that "underdeveloped countries with rich resources now have an object lesson in the heavy cost that must be paid by one of their number which goes berserk with fanatical nationalism [Stork 1975:74]. The Shah was placed in power in Iran. The US majors secured 40 percent of Iranian oil from European companies with the agreement of their governments. The presence of a US client state on its borders galvanized the Soviet Union into more aggressive support for Pan Arab nationalism, and for oil takeovers by governments in the Middle East.

Arab nationalism was most powerfully articulated by Egypt's Gamal Abdul Nasser who came to power by coup in July 1952. Nasser nationalized the Suez Canal in 1956. Israel, France and Britain tried to reverse the situation militarily, but withdrew under US pressure. Through the Eisenhower Doctrine, announced in January 1957, the US invited pro-Western regimes in the Middle East to attribute domestic challenges to "international communism" manipulated by the Soviet Union or its agent Egypt. The US invaded Lebanon in 1958 to quell militancy there. US troops were poised to invade Iraq if the regime which had taken power there by coup on July 14, 1958 moved against foreign oil interests. The Iraqi regime declared that oil interests would not be touched. However Colonel Qassem's government seized foreign oil interests in 1961 and formed a state oil company only to be overthrown by a CIA sponsored coup in 1963. Stork [1975:82] notes that "The US-British military intervention [into Lebanon and Jordan] demonstrated the lengths to which they were willing to go once their oil interests were directly threatened. On the other hand, their rather ignominious withdrawal served to emphasize again that the balance of political forces was changing in the Middle East and in the world, and that Western control over Third World resources could no longer be assured by military means." The strength of Pan Arab nationalist and anti colonialist sentiment prevented the United States from establishing a military presence in the Middle East. Soviet retaliatory capacity increased cold war tensions in the 1950s.

In April 1959 the second congress of the Federation of Arab Labour Unions called for a union among all oil exporting countries in the region. The workers demanded that Arab oil be considered the birthright of the pan Arab nation, that Saudi oil income be spent on the needs of the whole Arab people and that oil concessions be changed to bring them in line with national aspirations [Stork 1975:92]. Stork observed that foreign oil companies "could ignore only at their peril the popular attitudes and political sentiments expressed by the demands of the labour unions congress and other openly political movements. Equally threatened by the prospect of a more equitable distribution of wealth and power were the regimes of the oil-producing states themselves. The political transformation of the Middle East during the 1950s was characterized by increasingly radical popular demands regarding the future of the oil industry that threatened companies and governments alike [1975:92]."

The Arab workers' challenge to foreign oil companies and US interests was headed off by the formation in September 1960 of the Organization of Petroleum Oil Exporting Countries. The militancy of workers was muted by pre-emptive action by the region's governments. OPEC throughout the 1960s functioned much like a company union and was viewed by the oil majors as of little consequence.

1960-1980: revolution and militarism

The Algerian revolution won a popular victory in 1962. The war had so weakened and divided France, that in the 1950s it conceded to Vietnamese freedom fighters and pulled out of Vietnam. The US replaced France in South East Asia and pursued the war. This galvanized anti imperialist sentiment worldwide. In 1961 Iraq was taking unprecedented steps to control national oil resources. When Britain granted independence to Kuwait in 1961, Iraq massed troops on the border, but withdrew after Arab League negotiations.

In 1965 the British pulled its military out of the Middle East, leaving the US as the only enforcer of the status quo. The 1967 Arab Israeli war was the first demonstration of military power secured by Israel through US patronage. As a result of the war, Israel occupied three Arab countries. In 1968 Saddam Hussein came to power in Iraq. By this time politics in the Middle East were marked by the emergence of what Edward Said [1990] calls "the national security state."

The national security state refers to states such as those found in Iraq, Syria, Lebanon and Egypt. It is largely a response to Israeli militarism. It is rationalized as necessary to meet this threat and to restore to the Palestinians a homeland. The unfinished business of decolonization is the business of the national security state. This mission of protection and decolonization is used to justify its dominance of civil society, its abrogation of democracy, its military buildup and the suspension of development on many fronts. Said has pointed out that "the monopoly on coercion given the state has almost completely eliminated democracy in the Arab world, introduced immense hostility between rulers and ruled, placed a much higher value on conformity, opportunism, flattery and getting along than on risking new ideas, criticism or dissent.... There are first-rate novelists, poets, essayists, historians, yet all of them are not only unacknowledged legislators, they have been hounded into alienated opposition" [Said 1991:4-5].

OPEC was jolted from its complacency in 1969 by Gaddafi's coup against Libya's King Idris. Since August 1954 the United States had its largest foreign base at Wheeler Field near Tripoli. The US Marine Corps hymn invokes this imperial reach with the stanza 'from the halls of Montezuma to the shores of Tripoli.' Gaddafi's first action was to expel the US military. Next he nationalized British Petroleum's holdings. A new era of oil radicalism began in the Arab world.

It is significant that the organizational basis for the Libyan revolution came from imperial militarism and international oil. Gaddafi was trained at Sandhurst by the British and he engineered a perfect coup. His lieutenants were trained by Exxon, British Petroleum and other global oil organizations with their high tech and sophisticated management practices.

Throughout the 1960s oil prices, and hence revenues to oil rich states, had been eroding. This was due in part to excess production on the world market. Many new, smaller US and European oil companies had secured access to oil. The Soviet Union had been aggressively pricechopping in order to capture market shares. It had also bartered oil for tea with India, sugar with Cuba and other commodities with various countries in the third world.

Arab exporters demanded that oil companies pay more, raise prices, and relinquish both territory and shares to state oil corporations. The majors negotiated hard against this "creeping nationalization," but the radicalism of Libya and Iraq supported by Algeria resulted in important gains for OPEC.

Then in 1973 the October 8th war erupted. When the US resupplied Israel, which had pre emptively destroyed Egypt's airforce; the Arab governments, united in OAPEC (Organization of Arab Petroleum Exporting Countries), imposed an oil embargo. South Africa, the US, Britain and Portugal were targeted. The price of oil quadrupled to about $13 per barrel (all figures in US dollars).

Panic ensued in the oil market as Japan, West Germany, Italy and other oil "have nots" scrambled for supplies. Civil disturbances and strikes broke out in the US. Electricity supplies in Britain were restricted to three days a week. Callahan's government fell in the UK as the British coal miners struck to further strangle energy supplies. Haile Selassie's regime in Ethiopia was crippled by strikes against higher fuel prices and in 1974 he was deposed [Kapuscinski 1983:121-122].

Western governments responded by forming the International Energy Agency (IEA) which France boycotted. This agency governed oil stockpiles and their distribution to member countries in the event of another oil shortage. The OPEC governments quickly took control over oil sales. They nationalized concessions by buying shares in the foreign companies' operations. In some cases state oil companies took 100 per cent ownership. Prices continued to rise. The OPEC countries made lower priced oil available to some hard hit third world countries, usually on condition that the recipients sever relations with Israel.

The OPEC price revolution of 1973 and its aftermath were major shocks for the oil companies. Their control over physical crude plummeted from about two thirds of world production to about one third. OPEC appeared able to set international oil prices.

However, the majors responded rapidly with a multi pronged strategy. First, the oil companies too had wanted prices to rise, and they reaped tremendous profits from oil under their own control, for instance in the Caribbean, Angola, Egypt, and Mexico. Second, the companies fought back, by dividing OPEC through appealing to the corruptibility of rulers in these undemocratic states. Special allocations of oil would be arranged by the companies, and corrupt officials or members of the royal families would receive kickbacks in their foreign accounts [Turner 1976].

Third, western finance capital executed a strategy of integrating the financial interests of the oil rich states with the interests of both private and public capital. Global inflation ate into the buying power of OPEC oil revenues. Concerted efforts were made by western banks to recycle oil money, and soon indebtedness characterized many oil exporting states. Efforts by Western governments and corporations to encourage oil exporters to invest revenues paid off handsomely. In 1990 Kuwait had $125 billion invested in the West, while Saudi Arabia was reaping income from $225 billion in investments. Many OPEC members had major downstream investments in the industrialized countries. Kuwait had by 1990 established a strong position in petroleum product distribution in the United Kingdom. The Kuwaiti ruling family, the al-Sabahs, and their investment arm, KIO (Kuwait Investment Office) pursued an investment strategy aimed at securing political allies as well as investment income [Scott 1991:162]. Kuwait owns stock in almost all of the top 70 firms on the New York Stock Exchange. "In addition to owning the U.S. oil and gas exploration firm Santa Fe International, the Kuwait Petroleum Company by 1981 had invested some $250 million in other U.S. oil companies, including almost 3.89 percent of Atlantic Richfield and 2.39 percent of Phillips Petroleum. Meanwhile another arm of the al-Sabah government, the Kuwait Investment Office (KIO), has become the largest foreign investor in Spain, and reputedly the largest foreign investor in Japan. In Great Britain, the KIO now holds 9.9 percent (down from a high of 22 percent) of British Petroleum, Britain's largest corporation, and 10 percent of the Midland Bank. Such investments do not purchase control, but they do buy financial and political allies" [Scott 1991:161-162].

Fourth, international oil companies diversified into safe sources of oil such as the North Sea and Alaska, now profitable because of higher prices. Fifth, the majors set up technical and service contracts with "nationalized" oil companies. In this way the seven sisters frequently made more money per barrel produced than they had under earlier direct ownership arrangements. In addition energy conservation cut consumption by about a third per unit of GDP, in the industrialized economies. Production of types of energies which could be used as alternatives to oil was accelerated.

By 1975 the oil companies again had the upper hand. The 1975 OPEC meeting in Algiers passed a declaration of national sovereignty over natural resources. But it was little more than rhetoric. As demand for OPEC oil contracted, the Arab states along with other oil exporters, willingly offered lower and lower prices to the oil buyers. The market was flooded with oil and as prices fell, so did OPEC revenues.

Foreign oil companies countered nationalism with the key strategy of allowing concessions to come under the legal control of state corporations via a process of "participation." This strategy bought time and stability by embracing superficial "nationalizations." The state oil corporations in OPEC countries were run by technocrats or state capitalists. These united with foreign oil companies in a new kind of alliance to run the oilfields. In 1979 I wrote that "It appeared on the surface that national sovereignty over natural resources had been exercised. The oil corporations, in many self-congratulatory statements from 1974 to 1977, heralded a long future without upheavals in the oil business. For instance, the chairman of Shell stated in 1977 that with participation 'the oil industry now has a more comfortable role than it used to have....OPEC successfully removed the oil companies as a target from that particular firing line'[Turner 1980:289]."

By the late 1970s the majors had succeeded in placing OPEC state oil corporations between them and the citizens of the oil rich societies. OPEC state ownership was a shield, a smokescreen, behind which the majors continued to exercise control. Pundits began speaking not of the seven, but of the fourteen sisters.

The price revolution generated vast sums of money which swelled OPEC state coffers. The use of this oil revenue had profound effects in exporting societies. The implications of rapid capitalist develop-ment were particularly negative for women and children. People were bound more tightly into the net of the world market. The economies became more highly monetized. People of the region became more internationalized through labour migration, inten-sified travel including the Hadj to Mecca, and the use of global communications technology. Construction projects, militarization, infrastructural development and rampant consumerism resulted in profound social dislocation. For instance, the Shah's White Revolu-tion in Iran gave capitalist farmers land and drove thousands of rural people to the cities. The crowded cities were controlled through severe repression. The Shah's state was built up by the US who formed one of the world's most barbaric agencies of repression, the SAVAK.

Having lost the Vietnam war in 1975, the US government was unable to intervene elsewhere in the world. Popular outcry at home and abroad curtailed US militarism. It was in this context that the Nixon Doctrine, which originated in 1968 was put into effect. In 1968 the Viet Cong launched the successful Tet Offensive, and brought home to the US administration the likelihood of defeat in the Vietnam war. The Nixon Doctrine accepted the difficulty of winning a guerrilla war or politically sustaining direct military intervention in the third world. It relied on creating surrogate regional powers which would police territories on behalf of the US. Israel's utility to the US in this task was limited because of the explosive popular response of the Arab people to Israeli aggression. The US oil companies cautioned the State Department to play down the Israeli connection lest the prize of Saudi or Kuwaiti oil be lost.

Egypt was expected to provide this gendarme service for the United States. But more important, the Nixon Doctrine concentrated on the Shah's Iran as the regional surrogate for US military power. The US poured millions of dollars into arming Iran and establishing multiple military and intelligence systems in that country. The Iranian people, mobilized and dislocated by change attendant on the rapid spending of oil money; were confronted by SAVAK and other repressive agencies of the Iranian state, paid for and designed by the US.

In 1978 and 1979 the Iranian revolution took shape and ejected the Shah. The revolution pulled six million barrels of oil a day off of the world market on which about 30 million barrels were traded daily. The price of oil on the spot market doubled to $43 a barrel by November 1979 [Seymour 1980:192]. The Iranian oilworkers, some 80,000 strong, had effected an historically unprecedented strike. With the involvement of two million people living in oil towns, the workers shut down the massive Iranian industry without incident. The US engineered an attempt to get oil flowing again by staffing the fields and refineries with 10,000 naval cadets trained for this purpose. The strike breaking effort failed. The striking workers refused to send oil to Israel and South Africa. Yet through a strong and intricate network of peoples' committees called Shura in Pharsi, oil products were distributed throughout Iran, though not to the Shah's military [Turner 1980:272-302].

There are two dimensions of the Iranian revolution that may be significant for the future. First is the power of oilworkers, a highly privileged stratum within the working class, to stop and restart the oil industry. The Iranian oilworkers were irreplaceable in the dangerous and highly technical operations of the oil system. They immediately coordinated amongst themselves a national operation, using the organization and communications technology of the industry itself.

Second, the society was democratically run from the grassroots by popular committees (Komitehs or Shura) for approximately two years. These Shura formed in late 1978 in all sectors of society: the schools, the military and media, the oil industry, among the rural Kurds and in the civil service as well as in local neighbourhoods. Garbage collection, bread baking and distribution, education and publishing, munitions manufacture and international relations were only a few of the social activities carried out by these radical democratic committees. Khomeini crushed them through reactivating the Shah's SAVAK. In so doing, he reasserted the power of the bazaari, the mullahs and the national bourgeoisie in Iran. He had to galvanize the country for a war with Iraq to gain the upper hand over the Shura [Turner 1990].

There is another crucial point to be made about the Iranian revolution. It destroyed the cover which state oil corporations were providing for international oil companies. The uprising was directed against the state which was explicitly identified as the agent of US and European imperialism. No longer in the Middle East, could the oil companies seek anonymity behind state capitalist agencies.

The demise of the Shah was also the demise of the Nixon Doctrine in the Middle East. Khomeini supported the kidnapping of US embassy officials and could not be relied upon to police the region in the interests of the US. On November 20, 1979 hundreds of well armed Islamist guerrillas seized the Grand Mosque in Mecca and denounced the Saudi ruling family. The guerrillas demanded the creation of an Islamic state and the severing of all ties with the US. This situation led to the launching of a new US strategy. The fear in Washington was that Islamic fundamentalism and radical sentiment would sweep the region. In September 1980 Brzezinski, then US National Security Advisor, encouraged Iraq to invade and make war against Iran. Egypt, by signing the Camp David accord in 1979, was reduced to a pariah state in the Arab world. In exchange for Israel returning the oil rich Sinai to Egypt, Sadat earned the title of US lackey, and as such was of little use, to the US, as an alternative surrogate to Iran. First the Arab League imposed diplomatic and economic sanctions on Egypt. Then on October 6, 1981 Sadat was assassinated by members of the Holy War Organization.

1980-1990: oil bust and build up to war

In his 1980 State of the Union message, US President Carter told the joint session of Congress that Saudi Arabia was a vital interest of the US, and that any attempt by an outside force to gain control of the Persian Gulf region would be viewed as an attack on the strategic interests of the United States. Any such encroachment, Carter said, would be met with military retaliation.

Carter's short lived rhetoric about human rights and the need for a North South dialogue had neutralized some domestic opposition to US intervention abroad. Now, with Vietnam being obscured in the popular memory, and terrorism being presented as an international threat, the United States was again prepared to send troops to secure its control of Arabia's oil.

Carter announced the formation of a Rapid Deployment Force. As Joel Beinin has observed, it, like the Holy Roman Empire, was neither rapid, nor deployable nor a force. It was a bureaucratic fiction. If an emergency were to arise, a force would be cobbled together from other military formations. The US attempt to rescue the hostages in the US embassy in Iran in 1980 underlined the operational incapacity of the US in the Persian Gulf.

While encouraging Iraq to make war on Iran to curb the latter's possibilities of spreading radical Islam to the smaller Arab oil producing states; the US began to arm Saudi Arabia. Reagan's administration sold some $50 billion in arms to the Saudis to construct a Gulf wide air defence system based on AWACS.

Five AWAC aircraft were sold to Saudi Arabia in 1981 over the opposition of the US zionist lobby. This is the only time the Reagan administration, in eight years in office, was prepared to implement a policy opposed by the zionist lobby. During the 1991 war the AWACs coordinated battlefield hostilities. In the 1980s the US overbuilt Saudi air bases, allowing hanger space for US aircraft, and making landing fields adequate for US planes.

The Reagan administration also expected that US troops would do most of the fighting, should a war be launched in the Middle East. A document entitled Defence Guidance 1984-1988, was leaked to the press. It contained high level instructions on US military operations and said "Whatever the circumstances, the US should be prepared to introduce American forces directly into the region should it appear that security of access to the Persian Gulf is threatened [Beinin 1990]."

Reagan transformed the Rapid Deployment Force into the Central Command which had 350,000 troops. Its area of control includes the Horn of Africa and the entire Middle East except for Israel, Syria and Lebanon which fall under the control of the US Sixth Fleet. This systematic program of preparation indicates that US military deployment in the Middle East has been planned over the past decade.

One prong of Reagan's strategy towards the Middle East in the 1980s was direct military presence. However, the threat of Islamic militancy emanating from Iran was great enough to lead Arab rulers to refuse to host US forces.

The second prong of US strategy in the 1980s was support for Iraq in the eight year Iran-Iraq war [Darwish and Alexander 1991:55-84]. In 1982 Reagan removed Iraq from the list of countries supporting international terrorism. Diplomatic recognition followed in 1984 (after being severed since the 1967 Arab Israeli war). The US encouraged France to sell massive quantities of arms to Iraq by providing Saddam Hussein with several hundred million dollars in agricultural credits so he could divert hard cash to France for arms. The US did sell civilian aircraft and helicopters to Iraq. Washington's criticisms of Iraq's use of chemical weapons against Iran and its own Kurdish population were mild in the extreme.

Yet the US could not find an opening for establishing a military presence. Then an opportunity arose in March 1987. In response to Iraq's bombing of Kuwaiti tankers, the US reflagged those tankers and dispatched a fifty ship naval flotilla to the Gulf. With the end of the Iran-Iraq war in March 1988, the flotilla remained.

What was happening in the oil market and in Arab societies in the decade of the 1980s? After the 1979 price rise due the Iranian revolution, prices fell. OPEC could not cooperate. Member countries continuously overproduced and competed with price cutting. Debt weighed on third world oil importers and on many oil exporters alike. This encouraged barter with oil being exchanged for goods. The practice, called "countertrade" led to precipitate drops in oil prices. Because oil exporting governments really owed much of the foreign exchange they would get from official oil sales to the IMF and other creditors, these states had every incentive to instead barter oil for goods at ever lower prices. In December 1985 the bottom fell out of the market. By the beginning of 1986 oil prices were down to below $10 per barrel.

The oil bust had profound implications for the societies of the Middle East. Migrant workers were idle and funds stopped flowing to their countries of origin including Pakistan, Tunisia and Egypt. Once robust local markets lacked customers. Real estate developments went bankrupt. Everywhere buildings stood half finished. Imports were cut. Infrastructure and social services deteriorated. The downturn was particularly severe in its impact on women and children. Social unrest broke out as governments sought to impose austerity measures. For instance, the IMF terms for Egypt included increased bread prices which provoked serious riots.

In 1982 Israel invaded Lebanon. In an area under the control of Israeli soldiers, the Lebanese Christian militia massacred thousands of people at Sabra and Shatilla, which were Palestine refugee camps inside Beirut. Some 128,000 Israeli soldiers defeated some 20,000 Lebanese plus a few thousand PLO irregulars. A sea rescue shipped the broken PLO force from the shores of Beirut to camps in Algeria. In 1982 the Palestinian struggle for statehood was at a very low ebb. The US refused to support a Security Council resolution to allow food and medical supplies through the Israeli blockade into Beirut on the grounds that the resolution was not sufficiently "balanced." The Israeli invasion resulted in at least 20,000 dead and 30,000 injured in Lebanon. It split Israeli public opinion and sparked a peace movement in Israel. In the US for the first time progressive Jewish people, in significant numbers, mobilized against the zionist lobby.

In 1985 Israel bombed Tunis and in Philadelphia the FBI bombed the African American community, killing 11, destroying 61 houses and leaving 250 people homeless [Caffentzis 1992:285]. This quelled the insurgent 'Free South Africa' movement which was demanding that public corporations 'divest fast.' In 1986, the US bombed Libya thereby putting an end to that country's internationalist ventures.

The end of the 1980s saw a resurgence of popular struggle in North Africa and the Middle East. In December 1987 an uprising or "intifada" broke out on the West Bank and Gaza [Bennis and Cassidy 1990]. Palestinian children stoned Israeli soldiers. Block committees were formed. The societies were highly organized. Women took the lead. It is important to note that the organizations of the intifada, the block committees, take the same form as did the Shura, the committees of the Iranian revolution [Turner 1991:161].

Of the intifada, Hulaileh noted that "the best aspect of this experience has been its multiplicity and its democracy." The Palestinian grassroots movement prosecuted the intifada through "...boycotting Israeli products, reducing rents, stabilizing the exchange rate of the Jordanian dinar, returning to agriculture and home economy, [making] new agreements between factory owners and labor unions....without any form of imposition of will, but through popular initiatives" [Hulaileh 1991:200].

The resistance of the Intifada struck responsive cords within Israel. There a growing peace movement and what Cohen [1991:211] called "its most durable and visible wing, the women's movement," spanned the spectrum from those groups which expressed sympathy with Palestinians to those which favoured the establishment of a Palestinian state [Cohen 1991:207]. This 'shared assembly point,' which is the Israeli peace movement included "Peace Now, liberals from the "left Zionist" parties, Jewish-Arab dialogue groups, Women in Black, socialist feminists, anti-Zionist or non-Zionist or post-Zionist Marxists, human rights activists, religious doves, old-style Communists, moral witnesses against the Occupation, pacifists, soldiers who refuse to serve in the occupied territories, [and] supporters of PLO factions...." [Cohen 1991:205].

The resistance of the intifada reverberated throughout North Africa and the Middle East. Arab and Muslim peoples of the region participated in the global drive for democracy which gathered momentum over the 1980s. Ahmad observed that "Within the Muslim world, there is evidence of greater creativity than has been seen for the last 300 years. It can be seen now in Arabic literature, in Arab poetry, in Arab art. We are witnessing an Arab renaissance in creative activity. It reflects the yearning for democracy that began to be expressed in the last two-and-a-half of three years of the eighties - an expression as yet insufficient, but growing all the time. The

Palestinian intifada is part of this quest for democracy. In the entire annals of the history of resistance there are very few examples like this, in which an essentially unarmed people managed to stand up and sustain resistance for years against an armed and ruthless occupying force whose aim is the exclusion and expulsion of that occupied population" [Ahmad 1991:21].

In 1988 there was a massive uprising in Algeria, the first since the FLN victory against the French in 1962. Democratic elections were demanded and held. Similar demonstrations broke out in Tunisia and Morocco. In 1988 the PLO declared itself a government of Palestine in exile and supported the creation and security of the two states, Israel and Palestine which, insisted the PLO, could live together in peace.

In the late 1980s the Soviet system collapsed under pressure from peoples' democratic uprisings. Key in the Soviet Union were strikes by coal miners, oil and energy workers [Turner 1990]. Some 80 per cent of Soviet foreign exchange is from oil sales by this, the world's largest producer (12.5 million barrels a day in 1990). Moscow entered 1990 with two pressing needs: higher oil prices and a green light from the US to repress its dissident populations with impunity. These needs lay behind Gorbachev's acquiescence to US intervention.

The Soviets exported approximately one fifth of four billion barrels produced per year. In August 1990 when the trade embargo against Iraq blocked Iraqi oil exports, and the prospect of war led to panic buying, oil prices rose and by September 26, 1990, reached $40 per barrel. Based on an expectation of average 1990 oil prices rising from about $15 to $33 dollars, the USSR stood earn some $30 billion from oil exports [Kinsley 1 November 1990]. As of January 1992 its eastern European customers were required to pay in hard currency. The Soviet oil bonanza was enhanced by a windfall from natural gas exports, the prices of which rose in tandem with those of oil. Based on a projected total world production of 21 billion barrels in 1990 and a price increase of $15 per barrel, some $300 billion a year would be transferred from oil consumers to oil producers.

Moscow, in addition to profiting from the oil bonanza, peddled its vote at the United Nations as did other Security Council members with the exception of Cuba and Yemen (which suffered a $70 million penalty imposed by the US and Gulf states). One day after the Soviets voted for the UN Security Council resolution 677 of November 29, 1990 authorizing the use of military force against Iraq, the Gulf states pledged $6 billion to the USSR in consideration for its support.

The end of the cold war not only eliminated the Soviet Union as a deterrent to the US achieving its longstanding goal of establishing a military presence in the Gulf. It also put the US military industrial complex under intense pressure to find an alternative raison d'etre. In 1990 when Iraq waxed belligerent toward Kuwait over chronic price cutting, market-flooding oil production levels, national borders, access to the Gulf, the division of oil from the cross-border Rumaila field and the war debt (Iraq borrowed $40 billion of an $80 billion war debt from Kuwait, the United Arab Emirates and Saudi Arabia); the US encouraged Saddam Hussein to put pressure on Kuwait.

The background to this encouragement includes a desire for higher oil prices by US companies which have close links with the Bush administration. With US Congressional elections scheduled for November 6, 1990, Bush may have gambled on electoral gains resulting from a mini oil boom which would follow from higher prices. A price increase was especially sought by the Texas oil industry, US independents and all oil companies dependent on high cost oil such as that from North America and the North Sea. As early as January 1990 a member of the Bush Administration's Foreign Relations Council met a top Iraqi Cabinet Minister in New York [Perspective 1991:7]. He suggested to the Minister that Iraq engineer a substantial rise in the price of oil to help pay off its war debts. Then in February 1990, US Secretary of State James Baker ordered suppressed a State Department report criticizing Iraq's human rights record. Senator Robert Dole met Saddam Hussein in Baghdad and apologized for attacks on his regime in the US media. Bush vetoed Congressional sanctions against Iraq, in connection with human rights abuses.

In March 1990 the energy director of a US foreign policy think tank with links to Iraq asserted in a report that the oil market could support a price rise to $25 a barrel. The report suggested that this price rise could be brought about by one of the Gulf states "with the power to force all the states of the Gulf to follow suit [Perspective 1991:7]." In May 1990 Saddam Hussein began to claim a right to $25 per barrel. Iraq confronted Kuwait repeatedly in OPEC meetings for deliberately undercutting prices through over production.

215

On July 19, 1990 US Secretary of Defense Cheney told reporters during a press briefing that the US was committed to defending Kuwait if attacked. Bush's spokesperson Pete Williams later explained that Cheny had spoken "with some degree of liberty" [Village Voice 22 January 1991] On July 24, State Department spokesperson Margaret Tutwiler responded to a question about US - Kuwaiti military agreements by stating that "We do not have any defense treaties with Kuwait, and there are no special defense or security committments to Kuwait." The next day, July 25, under instructions from the State Department, the US ambassador to Iraq called upon Saddam Hussein in Baghdad. It was one week before Iraq's invasion of Kuwait. By that time, Iraqi troops were massed on Kuwait's border. US Ambassador April Glaspie told Hussein, that the US desired better relations with Iraq and that it favoured $25 per barrel oil (not the existing $18, nor the $21 proposed by Kuwait).

Glaspie was quoted in an Iraqi transcript of the talks (published in early September 1990 in the New York Times and not repudiated by the US State Department and reprinted in Bennis and Moushabeck 1991, appendix b) as saying "We have many Americans who would like to see the price go above $25 because they come from oil producing states." Then she stated that the US has "no opinion on the Arab-Arab conflicts, like your border dispute with Kuwait," and that "[Secretary of State] James Baker has directed our official spokesman to emphasize this [Cockburn 1990]."

On July 26 the Washington Post quoted White House, State Department and Department of Defence officials as having "asserted yesterday that an Iraqi attack on Kuwait would not draw a US military response, but that the US would join in condemning such a move and would work diplomatically to force Iraq's withdrawal [Tyler 1990]." After this quasi official statement of US policy, in an OPEC context, Kuwait again refused to go above $21 per barrel.

On July 31, 1990 after the CIA reported that an Iraqi invasion appeared imminent; Assistant Secretary of State John Kelly, who is responsible for the Middle East in the State Department, addressed the House Middle East subcommittee of the Foreign Affairs Committee. For the second time in three months Kelly said that the United States had no military treaty or alliance with Kuwait. The text of Kelly's testimony which follows was aired by the BBC World Service thirty hours before Iraq's invasion of Kuwait [Cockburn 1990]:

Representative Lee Hamilton: "If there - if Iraq, for example, charged across the border into Kuwait and - for whatever reason - what would be our position with regard to the use of US forces?"

Kelly: "That is a hypothetical question."

Hamilton: "...is it correct to say, however, that we do not have a treaty commitment which would obligate us to engage US forces there?"

Kelly: "That is correct."

Eqbal Ahmad [1990] has argued that "Far from being anti-imperialist, Saddam Hussein is a dictator and a tyrant. And moreover, he is a fool." For Saddam opened the door to US military intervention in the Gulf. Edward Said observed that "Saddam Hussein, a dictator of the kind the United States has typically found and supported, was almost invited into Kuwait, then almost immediately demonized and transformed into a worldwide metaphysical threat" [1991:1].

The US used this "set up" to establish a massive military presence, to pursue a war and to confirm Saudi Arabia, with some 21 per cent of world oil reserves, as the price determiner in the future. The alternative was Iraq in the position of price determiner. Iraq, with control over Kuwait, accounted for some 20 per cent of world oil reserves. This alternative was not attractive to the US since Saddam Hussein could not be relied upon to cooperate with US dictates [Beinin 1990]. Equally important was Washington's determination to ensure control of a continued flow of Kuwaiti oil dollars into the investment markets of the US and other industrialized countries.

From the US perspective, the Gulf crisis turned on two issues. First was control over oil prices. Second was justifying to the Arab oil states a permanent US military presence. US Secretary of State Baker testified to the House Foreign Affairs Committee before hostilities broke out on 16 January 1991 that regardless of the resolution of the current crisis, the Bush administration "foresees the establishment of a permanent NATO-like presence in the Persian Gulf [Beinin 1990]." When hostilities ceased, US President Bush reconfirmed the continued presence of US forces in the region.

Conclusion: popular committees versus the imperial state

Now global US hegemony has been re-established militarily, although it continues to lag economically. Recession and economic crisis rage at home. There is a remarkable contrast between demonstrated US military strength and demonstrated economic weakness. Eqbal Ahmad [1990] offers the image of "the United States roaming the world, a pistol in one hand and a begging bowl in the other, a very dangerous combination."

The US controls oil supplies to its main competitors, Germany and Japan, which have promoted economic rather than military development. The US has scrambled back into the control seat after having lost economic dominance and after ceasing to have military importance to Europe as the provider of a strategic defence shield. Direct military control over Middle East oil has put the US back into a position of dominance over Europe, Japan and the third world. It has bought time for the fragile financial patchwork which passes for an international monetary system.

Edward Said observed that after the 1991 war, "the United States, triumphalist internationally, seems in a febrile way anxious to prove that it is Number One, perhaps to offset the recession; the endemic problems posed by the cities, poverty, health, education, production; and the Euro-Japanese challenge" [Said 1991:3]. The US military industrial complex has a new mission despite the absence of a Soviet threat. Fully ten percent of buying in the New York stock market surge attendant upon the start of US bombing on January 16, 1991 was of IBM shares. Other corporations heavily dependent on Pentagon and Department of Defense military contracts also participated in the stock market surge. The new world order of the Bush administration, is the old imperial order in which the US exercises military force to secure markets and resources. Militarism is costing US society, and the societies of its allies, dearly. Social programs are being cut, energy alternatives are foregone and basic ecological needs are devalued. Racism and killer machismo eclipse social values of humanism and universalism.

US militarism, itself fostered by Bush's attempt to divert attention from domestic crisis, provoked vigorous protest inside the country.

The technology of the video camera, fax machine and computer communications have been in the hands of activist organizations long enough for experience to have accumulated. The 1980s in the US were marked by the gradual coming together of a broad based social movement including activists from the anti apartheid, welfare rights, homeless, feminist, peace, anti nuclear, health, environmental and Central American solidarity movements. The international insurgency which demanded democracy in 1988-1989 found resonance throughout the USA and notably on the university campuses and in the high schools. In April 1989 fully nineteen US universities were struck by building occupations through which students sought to halt research funded by the Pentagon and the Department of Defence [Turner and Belknap 1989]. Barely a year later this anti-militarism was confronted by compulsory draft registration for all youth and a concerted regime of media enforced patriotism. Bush's drive to war must be understood in the context of state response to growing strength of a new US social movement.

Due to this momentum, mobilization of an anti war movement was immediate [Elbaum 1991:142-145]. The New York Times of January 11, 1991 headlined a front page story "Drawing on Vietnam legacy, antiwar effort buds quickly." It was militant and even extreme. On December 9, 1990 a Vietnam veteran died after setting fire to himself in Isleton, California, to protest US action in the Gulf. On February 18, 1991 a young man carrying a peace sign set himself on fire and died on the Amherst common in Massachusetts. African Americans and other people of colour in particular, opposed the war [Payton 1991, Elbaum 1991:146-147]. The women's movement and environmentalist decried the warrior culture and 'eco-war' [Ehrenreich 1991, Vine 1991, Fagan 1991, Kemp 1991]. Even conservative and pro military US businessmen and politicians were concerned about the immense risks of going to war to 'liberate' Kuwait including the "negative reaction in the Arab world, danger to the economy, [and the] potential upheaval at home" [Elbaum 1991:149]. Continued popular resistance to Bush's new world order and its domestic costs can be expected. Mike Davis may be right when he says that "L.A. was just the beginning" [Davis 1992].

In North Africa and the Middle East, the very social conditions which spurred the US to military occupation are likely to be aggravated by its existence. The oil price crash of the mid 1980s not only traumatized the societies of the Middle East. It also underlined the impotence of client regimes to manage the region's oil wealth. As popular expectations in the 1970s were disappointed, "the sheikhs became objects of contempt" [Ahmad 1991:18]. Oil management requires cooperation across national boundaries. The grassroots pan Arabism of the 1940s and 1950s is being rekindled by an imperial military presence.

So dangerous was this pan Arab reality that in early 1991, Egypt's president banned television footage of war carnage in Iraqi communities. On August 29, 1990 Syrian forces had bloody clashes with demonstrators opposed to Syrian support for US intervention. On November 6 some 47 Saudi women drove their own cars in protest against the government's ban on women drivers. Islamic religious leaders urged strong reprisals against the women and their families, on the grounds that if women's status changed the al Saud ruling patriarchy would be fundamentally undermined. Jordan's King Hussein was pushed by a near riotous population, sixty per cent of which is Palestinian, to denounce the US war against brother and sister Arabs in Iraq. Saudi Arabia, Egypt, Syria and "all those craven sheikhs of the Persian Gulf who joined the American alliance in the war face a tremendous loss of credibility as they are seen to have the blood of hundreds of thousands of Arabs on their hands, having fought at the side of a foreign power" [Ahmad 1991:19]. Eleven or nearly one half of the Arab states did not support the US invasion and war. On September 3 Arab League secretary general Chedli Klibi resigned over his organization's handling of the Gulf crisis. On September 11, Clovis Maksoud, Arab League envoy to the UN, resigned citing opposition to the foreign military buildup in the Gulf. Among those Arab League member countries in opposition were states in which democratic expression has recently gained ground. This is a measure of the anti-US sentiment in North Africa and the Middle East. The double standard of opposing Iraqi occupation of Kuwait while supporting Israeli occupation of Palestinian territory provoked anger at US cynicism among the majority of Arab people.

In the Middle East the image of Israel, wrote Ahmad, "is that of a conquering power." While some claim that Middle Eastern fears of Israel are unfounded, "the truth is that those fears are reborn in the shadow of Israeli bombs. And they see those bombs as created by American power. In other words, these anxieties, the mistrust, the legacy of America's unbalanced, biased, one-sided relationships in the Middle East, will likely lead, after the American victory in the

Gulf, to massive region-wide resistance to America and American interests" [Ahmad 1991:21].

Fear of such resistance moved the editors of the Oil and Gas Journal, which represents smaller US companies dependent on national production, to recommend caution. In its January 21, 1991 editorial [cited in Tanzer 1991:267], the journal observed that 'For the international petroleum industry, war in the Middle East means the world will never be the same:'

> "But there are huge questions beyond those involving the conflict itself. The petroleum industry must now wonder what happens once the shooting stops.... For industry, the dangers are obvious. What may be less obvious is the rapidly diminishing degree to which companies in the future will be able to rely on stability enforced from abroad. The petroleum world - and that includes consumers - has played its Western military ace. If this fight lives up to its bloody expectations who will lead the next defense of the world's economic sustenance? Not the U.S. A loud minority didn't want to fight to defend petroleum interests this time. Next time it won't be a minority. And this war, coming as it does at the beginning of a recession and well into a period of fiscal distress, will be costly. If the next crisis comes any time soon, the U.S. won't possess the military and financial resources necessary to respond. And if the world's single biggest oil consuming country doesn't respond, no one will."

The Gulf war meant intensified hardship for Palestinians. They were forced to carry restrictive identity cards, lived under curfew and were massively retrenched from Israeli jobs, which were then filled by immigrant Soviet Jews. Unemployed Palestinians from the Gulf returned to place more pressure on households now without remittances or markets. Despite these hardships, the most important achievement of the war period was "the fact of Palestinian human and institutional economic build-up, linked to the dynamics of Palestinian political resistance in the occupied territories. It is the linked texture of institutions with various visions and directions, that are coordinated and working at paving their way in the economic field...." [Hulaileh 1992:204].

The rising Intifada, organized around block committees throughout the Middle East and North Africa, has challenged regime after regime. Because of the significant part played by ordinary women in the intifada, the mobilization is unprecedentedly democratic. More than any other before it, the movement is rooted at the very bottom of society. Consequently it is virtually impossible to uproot.

A vital point is that the Palestinian intifada arose on the ashes of the 1982 defeat of the Palestinian Liberation Organization forces in Lebanon. As a community based uprising, the intifada offers alternatives and new directions to the old style nationalist broad front. Also vital is the rise of this new politics in the political space created by the discrediting and collapse of Soviet style communism. The Arab communist parties have been a divisive and conservative force. At the very moment that Solidarity was gaining momentum in Poland, the 1979 Iranian revolution rejected stalinism and Soviet communism in the guise of the Iranian Tudeh party. The clearing away of the impediments of elitist communist bureaucracy opens the way to new revolutionary forms. Central to the future of new social experiments is the popular committee. It has already proven itself capable of the exercise of power for fundamental transformation.

Ahmad drew attention to the fact that with the 1991 war, the West, "in taking on the Middle East took on a people who have a history of having quite corrupt leadership, but who, when pushed to the wall, will fight back. They fought back against France in Algeria, and defeated it. They fought back against Israel in Lebanon, and beat it. And they fought back against the Soviet Union in Afghanistan, and defeated it" [Ahmad 1991:21].

On February 27, 1991 the US military was finished with the obscene bloodshed of more than 200,000 bombing missions and the 'ground war' massacre of tens of thousands of defeated Iraqi troops. But as Ahmad observed, "reverberations from this kind of violence can be expected to spread inexorably through the aggrieved villages and cities of the Middle East. And it is this growing anger that the American people, as innocent as the Iraqi people, will reap in a bitter harvest. Everything about this environment suggests that this first Arab-American war will not be the last. Another, more protracted war could follow, making the Korean and Indo-Chinese wars look tame by comparison" [Ahmad 1991:20].

The US, not able to secure control over oil and petrodollars through surrogates and clients, has established itself through direct military occupation. This can only further discredit existing undemocratic regimes and give momentum to pan Arab radicalism and to 'one, two, three or more Vietnams.' The direction of change is toward popular power, and that is in the interests of all of us.

Bibliography

Abdullah, Hussaina. "The democratic process and the challenge of gender in Nigeria." *Review of African Political Economy* 56 (March 1993):27-37.

Abu-Lughod, Lila. *Veiled sentiments.* Berkeley and Los Angeles: University of California Press, 1986.

Abuoga, J., and A. Mutere. *The history of the press in Kenya.* Nairobi: The African Council on Communication Education, 1988.

Adams, Patricia. *Odious debts: loose lending, corruption and the third world's environmental legacy.* London and Toronto: Earthscan, 1991.

Adisa, Willie. "How parents choose size of family." *The Guardian* (London, April 22, 1984):5.

Afigbo, A.E. *The warrant chiefs: Indirect rule in southeastern Nigeria 1891 - 1929.* London: Longman, 1972.

Africa Watch, *Somalia - beyond the warlords: the need for a verdict on human rights abuses.* New York: Africa Watch, March 7, 1993.

Afshar, Haleh and Carolyn Dennis, eds. *Women and adjustment policies in the Third World.* New York: St Martin's, 1992.

Agarwal, B. Women and technological change in agriculture: the Asian and African experience. In E. Ahmed, (ed.), *Technology and rural women: the conceptual and empirical issues.* London: Allen and Unwin, 1985.

Agarwal, Bina, "The Gender and Environment Debate: Lesson from India," *Feminist Studies*, 18:1, (Spring 1992):119-158.

Agheyisi, Rachel Uwa, "The Labour Market Implications of the Access of Women to Higher Education in Nigeria" in Bappa, S., et.al. (eds.), *Women in Nigeria Today*, (London: Zed Books, 1985).

Ahmad, Eqbal. "Portent of a new century." In Bennis, Phyllis and Michel Moushabeck (eds.). *Beyond the storm: a Gulf crisis reader.* New York: Olive Branch Press, Interlink Publishing Group, 1991:7-24.

Ahmad, Eqbal. *Transcript of tape recorded lecture.* Delivered November 1990 in Boston. Recorded by Alternative Radio, Boulder, Colorado.

Ajulu, Rok. "Kenya: the road to democracy." *Review of African Political Economy* 53 (March 1992): 79-87.

Allen, Donna, and Ramona Rush (eds.). *Communications at the crossroads: the gender gap connection.* New Jersey: Ablex Publishing Corporation, 1989.

Allen, Lillian, 1985. "Revolutionary Tea Party," on the album *Revolutionary Tea Party,* Verse to Vinyl, 427 Bloor St. West, Toronto, Canada (tel: 416-922-5602, album number WRC1-4590).

Alot, M. *People and communication in Kenya.* Nairobi: Kenya Literature Bureau, 1982.

Amadiume, Ifi, *Male daughters, female husbands,* London: Zed, 1987.

Amos, V., and P. Parmar. "Challenging imperial feminism." *Feminist Review 17 (1984): 385-410.*

Anderson, D.M. "Depression, dust bowl, demography and drought: the colonial state and soil conservation in East Africa during the 1930s." *African Affairs* 83 (1984):321-343.

Antrobus, Peggy. "Reaching beyond university walls," *Development* (Journal of the Society for International Development, Rome) 4 (1984): 45-49.

Antrobus, Peggy. "Learning together/working together: a South-North dialogue," *Fifth International Forum, Association for Women in Development,* Washington, D.C., *mimeo* (21 November 1991): DAWN c/o WAND, University of the West Indies, School of Continuing Studies, Pinelands, St. Michael, Barbados.

Antrobus, Peggy. "Women and Development: An Alternative Analysis," *Development* 1 (1989): 26-28.

Apthorpe, Raymond. "Some problems of evaluation." Carl Gosta Widstrand (ed.), *Cooperatives and rural development in East Africa,* New York: Africana Publishing Corporation, 1970.

Ardener, S. "Sexual insult and female militancy," in S. Ardener, (ed.). *Perceiving women.* London: J.M. Dent, 1975.

Atwood, William. *The Reds and the Blacks: a personal adventure.* New York: Harper and Row, 1967.

Ayandele, Margaret. "Agonies of women who love to breed like rabbits." *Sunday Concord* (April 8, 1984): 15.

Badinter, E. *L'amour en plus.* Paris: Flammarion, 1980.

Bakan, Abigail B. *Ideology and class conflict in Jamaica: the politics of rebellion.* Montreal and Kingston: McGill-Queen's University Press, 1990.

Bappa, S., et. al. (eds.), *Women in Nigeria Today,* (London: Zed Books, 1985).

Barrett, Leonard. *The Rastafarians: the dreadlocks of Jamaica.* Kingston: Sangster's Book Stores, 1977.

Barrett, Leonard. *The Rastafarians: sounds of cultural dissonance.* Boston: Beacon Press, 1977.

Bassier, Dennis. "Kali-Mai worship in Guyana: a quest for new identity." In: *Second Conference on East Indians in the Caribbean: A symposium on cultural, economic and political issues.* St. Augustine: University of the West Indies, 1981.

Bates, Robert H. *Beyond the miracle of the market: the political economy of agrarian development in Kenya.* Cambridge 1989.

Bauer, D. "The dynamics of communal and hereditary land tenure among the Tigray of Ethiopia." In B. J. McCay and J. M. Acheson, (eds.), *The question of the commons*. Tuscon: University of Arizona Press, 1987: 217-230.

Beckles, Hilary McD. *Natural rebels: a social history of enslaved black women in Barbados*. New Brunswick, N.J.: Rutgers University Press, 1989.

Bell, Wendell. "Remembrances of a Jamaican past." *Caribbean Review* (Winter, 1977).

Beneria, Lourdes and Shelley Feldman, (eds.), *Unequal burden: economic crises, persistent poverty, and women's work*. Boulder: Westview Press, 1992.

Beneria, Lourdes, and Gita Sen. "Accumulation, reproduction and women's role in economic development: Boserup revisited." *Signs*, vol.7, no.2 (Winter 1981): 279-298.

Bennis, Phyllis and Michel Moushabeck (eds.). *Beyond the storm: a Gulf crisis reader*. New York: Olive Branch Press, Interlink Publishing Group, 1991.

Bennis, Phyllis and Neal Cassidy. *From stones to statehood: the Palestinian uprising*. New York: Olive Branch Press/Interlink, 1990.

Berkes, Fikret, David Feeny, Bonnie J. McCay, James M. Acheson. "The benefits of the commons." *Nature* 340:91-93.

Berkes, F. "Common-property resource management and Cree Indian fisheries in subarctic Canada." In B. J. McCay and J. M. Acheson, (eds.), *The question of the commons*. Tuscon: University of Arizona Press, 1987: 66-91.

Berkhofer, Robert F. *The White Man's Indian*. New York, 1979.

Berman, Bruce and John Lonsdale. *Unhappy Valley: conflict in Kenya and Africa*. London: James Currey, 1992.

Berman, Bruce. *Control and crisis in colonial Kenya: the dialectics of domination*. London: James Currey, 1990.

Bernardi, B. *The Mugwe: a blessing prophet, a study of a religious and public dignitary of the Meru of Kenya.* (1959) Nairobi: Gideon S. Were Press, 1989.

Beshoff, Pamela. "Conversation with C.L.R. James." *Jamaica Journal* 19:1 (February - April 1986): 23-28.

Bilby, K, and E. Leib. "Kumina, the Howellite church and the emergence of Rastafarian traditional music in Jamaica." *Jamaica Journal* 19:3 (August - October 1986): 22-28.

Bishton, Derek. *Blackheart man: a journey into Rasta.* London: Chatto and Windus, 1986.

Blake, Judith. *Family structure in Jamaica.* New York: The Free Press of Glencoe, 1961.

Blake, Barbara. "No more Rasta for me." *The Sunday Gleaner Magazine* (September 1983): 2-4.

Bloom, Allan. *The Republic of Plato.* New York: Basic Books, 1968.

Bond-Stewart, Kathy. *Young women in the liberation struggle: stories and poems from Zimbabwe.* Harare, Zimbabwe: Zimbabwe Publishing House, 1984.

Book, Brother (Hollis Peters). *The Optician.* Trinidad: Vanguard Publishing, 1977.

Boot, Adrian. *Jamaica, Babylon on a thin wire.* Oxford: Alden Press, 1976.

Boserup, Esther, *The role of women in economic development,* New York: St. Martin's Press, 1970.

Bottomore, T.B., and M. Rubel (eds.). *Karl Marx: selected writings in sociology and social philosophy.* Harmondsworth: Penguin, 1963.

Bourne, J. "Towards an anti-racist feminism." *Race and Class* 25 (1983): 1-22.

Braidotte, Rose, Ewa Charkiewicz-Pluta, Sabine Hausler and Saskia Wieringa. *Negotiating for change: debates on women, the environment and sustainable development*. London: Zed, 1993.

Brand, Dionne. "Black women and work: the impact of racially constructed gender roles on the sexual division of labour," *Fireweed* 25 (Fall 1987): 28-37.

Brodber, Erna. *Myal*. London: New Beacon Books, 1988.

Brown, Paula, Harold Brookfield and Robin Grau. "Land tenure and transfer in Chimbu, Papua New Guinea: 1958-1984 - a study in continuity and change, accommodation and opportunism." *Human Ecology* 18:1 (1990):21-39.

Brownhill, Leigh. "Poor people gonna rise up: revolutionary popular music," in Terisa E. Turner, et al, (eds.). *Revolutionary popular culture*. New York and Amherst, International Oil Working Group, 1989, 33-48.

Burns, John F. "South African rebels attack fuel plants." *New York Times* (June 2, 1980): 1.

Burris, Barbara. "The Fourth World Manifesto." (originally published in *Notes from the Third Year*, 1971) *Radical Feminism*. New York: Quadrangle, 1973, 322-357.

Bush, Barbara. *Slave women in Caribbean society 1650-1838*. London: James Currey, 1989.

Caffentzis, George. "Rambo on the Barbary Shore." In Midnight Notes Collective. (ed.), *Midnight Oil: work, energy war, 1973-1992*. Brooklyn: Autonomedia, 1992, 283-302.

Callaway, Barbara J., "Contrasting Socialization of Igbo and Hausa Women and Political Efficacy." *Women and Politics* 8:2 (1988):45-68.

Campbell, Horace. *Rasta and resistance: from Marcus Garvey to Walter Rodney*. Trenton, N.J.: Africa World Press, 1987 and Dar es Salaam: Tanzanian Publishing House, 1985.

Campbell, Guy. *The charging buffalo: a history of the Kenya Regiment, 1937-1963.* London 1986.

Campbell, B., and R. A. Godoy. "Commonfield agriculture: The Andes and medieval England compared." National Research Council, *Proceedings of the Conference on Common Property Resource Management.* National Academy Press, Washington, C.D., 1986:323-358.

Campbell, Horace. "Rastafari: culture of resistance." *Race and Class* 22 (1980):1-22.

Carby, H. "White women listen! Black feminism and the boundaries of sisterhood." In: *The empire strikes back*, Centre for Contemporary Cultural Studies (ed.). London: Hutchinson, 1982.

Carpentier, Alejo. *The harp and the shadow.* London: Andre Deutsch, 1992.

Carse, James P. *Finite and infinite games: a vision of life as a play and possibility,* New York: The Free Press, 1986.

Castro, Fidel, and Linda Jennes. *Woman and the Cuban revolution.* New York: Pathfinder Press, 1990.

CDHR (Committee for the Defence of Human Rights), "1990 annual report on human rights situation in Nigeria, Lagos (PO Box 7247): CDHR 1990.

CDHR/NADL (Committee for the Defence of Human Rights and National Association of Democratic Lawyers), Why General Olusegun Obasanjo cannot become the United Nations Secretary General!, Lagos: May 31, 1991.

Chapman, Tracy. "Matters of the heart." *Sparerib* 234 (May 1992):6-9.

Chepkwony, Agnes. *The role of non-governmental organisations in development: a study of the National Christian Council of Kenya 1963-78.* Uppsala 1987.

Clark, John Hernik. Review of "Race first - the ideological and organizational struggles of Marcus Garvey and the UNIA," by Tony Martin. *Jamaica Journal* 11:1,2 (1977): 64-65.

Clark, Edith. *My mother who fathered me.* London: George Allen & Urwin, 1969.

Clark, Carolyn M. "Land and food, women and power, in nineteenth-century Kikuyu." *Africa* 50:4 (1980): 357-70.

Cleary, Anthony. "The myth of Mau Mau in its international context." *African Affairs* 89 (1990):227-245.

Clough, Marshal. *Fighting two sides: Kenyan chiefs and politicians 1918-1940.* (Niwot, 1990).

Cobham, Rhonda and Merle Collins, (eds.) *Watchers & Seekers: creative writing by black women.* New York: Peter Bedrick Books, 1988.

Cockburn, Alexander, *The Nation.* New York, October 8, 1990.

Cohen, Stanley. "From the sealed room: Israel's peace movement during the Gulf war." In Bennis, Phyllis and Michel Moushabeck (eds.). *Beyond the storm: a Gulf crisis reader.* New York: Olive Branch Press, Interlink Publishing Group, 1991:205-214.

Combahee River Collective. "Statement." In *Home girls*, B.Smith (ed.). New York: Kitchen Table Women of Colour Press, 1983.

Commissiong, J.W. *Ganja (Marijuana).* Mona, Jamaica: Department of Extra-Mural Studies, University of the West Indies, 1978.

Cooper, Carolyn. "Chanting down Babylon: Bob Marley's songs as literary text." *Jamaica Journal* 19:4 (November 1986 - January 1987): 2-8.

Cooper, Carolyn. "'that cunny jamma oman': the female sensibility in the poetry of Louise Bennett." *Jamaica Journal* 18:4 (November 1985 - January 1986): 2-9.

Cooper, Frederick. *On the African waterfront.* New Haven and London: Yale, 1987.

Coquery-Vidrovitch, Catherine, "The African Mode of Production," *Critique of Anthropology*, 1975, 4-5, 38-71.

Cox, S.J.B. "No tragedy of the commons." *Environmental Ethics* 7, 1985:49-61.

Cox, Nicole and Silvia Federici. *Counter-planning from the kitchen: wages for housework - a perspective on capital and the left*. Bristol, UK: Falling Wall Press, 1973.

Crampton, D. R., Kenya, Acting Provincial Commissioner, Central Province, to Chief Native Commissioner, 27 May 1920: KNA, PC/CP 7/1/2.

Critical Perspectives. "Women, race, and class in a cultural context." Special Issue 2 (1984).

Croll, Elizabeth. *Women and rural development in China*. Geneva: International Labour Office, 1985.

Dadiran, Eva. "Kenya: police club women protesters unconscious." *Sparerib* 234 (May 1992):43-44.

Daily Times (Lagos, Nigeria) August 28, 1986.

Dalla Costa, Mariarosa and Selma James. *The power of women & the subversion of the community*. Bristol, UK: Falling Wall Press, 1972.

Darwish, Adel and Gregory Alexander. *Unholy Babylon: the secret history of Saddam's war*. London: Victor Gollancz, 1991.

Dauda, Carol L. *'Yan Tatsine and the male deal: Islam, gender and class struggle in Northern Nigeria*, unpublished MA thesis, Guelph, Ontario: University of Guelph, Department of Political Studies, 1992.

Daume, Daphne. *1990 and 1989 Britannica book of the year*. Chicago: Encyclopedia Britannica, 1990, 1989.

Davidson, Basil. "Columbus: the bones and blood of racism." *Race & Class* 33:3 (January-March 1992):17-26.

Davies, Miranda (ed.),. *Women and violence: a global crisis*. London: Zed, 1993.

Davin, Delia. *Women-work*. London: Oxford University Press, 1976.

Davis, Mike. *LA was just the beginning: urban revolt in the United States: a thousand points of light*. (Open Magazine Pamphlet Series #20) Westfield, New Jersey: Open Media, August 1992.

Davison, Jean. *Voices from Mutira: lives of rural Gikuyu women*. Boulder CO. and London: Lynne Rienner, 1989.

Davison, R.B. *Life and labour in Trench Town, Kingston, Jamaica in September, 1967*. Kingston: Department of Statistics, 1967.

Dawit, Seble. *Female genital mutilation: violence and women's human rights*. London: Zed, 1993.

Dearden, Anne. *Arab women*. London: Minority Rights Group Report No. 27, 1983.

Dennis, Carolyn, "Capitalist Development and Women's Work: A Nigerian case study," *Review of African Political Economy*, 27/28, 1984.

Desbarats, P. and J. Southerst. *Information/crisis/development; news from the third world*. London, Ontario: University of Western Ontario, 1986.

Dike, K. Onwuka. *Trade and politics in the Niger Delta 1830-1885: an introduction to the economic and political history of Nigeria*. Oxford: Clarendon Press, 1956.

Dodd, David. "Police and thieves on the streets of Brixton." *New Society* (March 16 1978): 598-600.

Dualeh Abdalla, R. H. *Sisters in affliction: circumcision and infibulation of women in Africa*. London: Zed Press, 1982.

Eberstadt, Nick. *Poverty in China*. Bloomington, Indiana: International Development Institute, 1979.

Edelman, Murray. *The symbolic use of politics*. Urbana: University of Illinois Press, 1964.

Editor. "Interview with Cedric Brooks." *Jamaica Journal* 11:1,2 (1977): 14-17.

Editor. "The editor interviews Robert Hill." *Jamaica Journal* 11:1,2 (1977): 52-55.

Ehrenreich, Barbara. "The warrior culture." In Bennis, Phyllis and Michel Moushabeck (eds.). *Beyond the storm: a Gulf crisis reader*. New York: Olive Branch Press, Interlink Publishing Group, 1991:129-131.

el Saadawi, Nawal. *The hidden face of Eve*. London: Zed Press, 1980.

Elbaum, Max. "The storm at home: the US anti-war movement." In Bennis, Phyllis and Michel Moushabeck (eds.). *Beyond the storm: a Gulf crisis reader*. New York: Olive Branch Press, Interlink Publishing Group, 1991:142-159.

Elkins, W.F. "Unrest among the Negroes." *Science and Society* 36:1 (1977): 70-73.

Elkins, W.F. "Marcus Garvey and the Negro World in the BWI." *Jamaica Journal* 11:1,2 (1977): 65-69.

Elson, Diane. "From survival strategies to transformation strategies: women's needs and structural adjustment," in Lourdes Beneria and Shelley Feldman, (eds.). *Unequal burden: economic crises, persistent poverty, and women's work*. Boulder: Westview Press, 1992, 26-48.

Elson, Diane. "How is structural adjustment affecting women?" *Development* 1 (1989): 67-74.

Elson, Diane, (ed.) *Male bias in the development process*. Manchester University Press and London: St. Martin's Press, 1991.

Elson, Diane and R. Pearson. "The latest phase of the internationalisation of capital and its implications for women in the third world," *Discussion paper number 150*. Institute of Development Studies, University of Sussex, Falmer, Brighton, UK, June 1980.

Emenyonu, Ernest. "The place of female education in Nigerian society." *Nigerian Statesman* (July 20, 1979): 6.

Fadayomi, Theophilus O., "Women in the Nigerian labor force," *International Journal of Sociology of the Family* 21:2 (Autumn 1991):175-188.

Fagan, Shannon. "The wasteland: environmental devastation in the wake of the Gulf war." *In These Times*, March 27 - April 2, 1991.

Fanon, Franz. *Sociologie d'une revolution*. Paris: Librairie Francois Maspero, 1969.

Fanon, Franz, *Wretched of the earth*. (original 1961), New York: Grove, 1968.

Farry, Marcel. "In Conversation with Nawal el Saadawi." *Sparerib* London, October 1990.

Fearn, Hugh. *An African economy*. Oxford: Oxford University Press, 1961.

Federici, Silvia. *Wages against housework*. Bristol, UK: Falling Wall Press, 1973.

Federici, Silvia. "The great witch hunt," *Maine Scholar* (University of Maine, Bangor) 1:1 (1988): 31-52.

Federici, Silvia. "The debt crisis, Africa and the new enclosures," *Midnight Notes* 10 (1990): 10-17.

Feeny, David, Fikret Berkes, Bonnie J. McCay, James M. Acheson, "The tragedy of the commons 22 years later." *Human Ecology* 18:1 (1990):1-15.

Feit, H.A. "James Bay Cree Indian management and moral considerations of fur bearers." In *Native People and Renewable Resource Management*. Alberta Society of Professional Biologists, Edmonton, 1986:49-65.

Fenoaltea, S. "Transaction costs, Whig history, and the common fields." *Politics and Society* 16:171-240.

Fisher, Jeanne M. *The anatomy of Kikuyu domesticity and husbandry*. Department of Technical Co-operation, London 1955.

Fiske, Jo-Anne, *personal communication*, March 12, 1992.

Ford-Smith, Honor. "Sistren: exploring women's problems through drama." *Jamaica Journal* 19:1 (February - April 1986): 2-12.

Foreign Languages Press. *The marriage law of the People's Republic of China*. Peking: Foreign Languages Press, 1952.

Frederikse, Julie. *None but ourselves: masses versus media in the making of Zimbabwe*. London: Ravan Press, 1982.

French, Joan. *Wid dis ring*. Kingston, Jamaica: Sistren Research, 1987.

French, Joan and Honor Ford-Smith. "Women's work and organisation in Jamaica, 1990-1944," *unpublished research study for the Institute of Social Studies*. The Hague, Netherlands, 1987.

Friedmann, John. *The good society*, Cambridge, Massachusetts: MIT Press, 1979.

Frost & Sullivan. *Political Risk Services: Kenya*. (January 1986, April 1987) New York: Frost & Sullivan.

Furedi, Frank. *The Mau Mau war in perspective*. Nairobi: London: James Currey, 1989.

Gailey, Harry A., 1970. *The road to Aba: a study of British administrative policy in Eastern Nigeria*, New York: New York University Press.

Gann, L., and T. Henriksen. *The struggle for Zimbabwe: battle in the bush*. New York: Praeger Publishers, 1981.

Garrison, Len. *Black youth, Rastafarianism, and the identity crisis in Britain*. London: ACER Project Publication, 1979.

Garvey, Amy Jacques. *Garvey and Garveyism*. New York: Octagon Press, 1976.

George, Susan. *The debt boomerang: how third world debt harms us all.* Boulder: Westview Press, 1992.

Ghai, D. (ed). *The IMF and the South: the social impact of crisis and adjustment.* London: Zed, 1991.

Gladwin, Christina H. (ed), *Structural adjustment and African women farmers,* Gainsville, Florida: University of Florida Press, 1991.

Glaspie - Hussein Transcript. In Bennis, Phyllis and Michel Moushabeck (eds.). *Beyond the storm: a Gulf crisis reader.* New York: Olive Branch Press, Interlink Publishing Group, 1991:391-396.

Globe and Mail (Toronto). "Women strip in bid to stop bulldozers: backed by police, South African officials level squatters' shanties." *Globe and Mail* (13 July 1990): A10.

Globe and Mail (Toronto). "Reggae records the beliefs of the rudies and the Rastas." *Globe and Mail* (June 1975): 3.

Government of Zimbabwe, Zimbabwe Women's Bureau. *We carry a heavy load - rural women in Zimbabwe speak out.* Harare, Zimbabwe: Government of Zimbabwe, 1981.

Graf, William, *The Nigerian State,* London: Macmillan, 1988.

Green, Maia. "Mau Mau oathing rituals and political ideology in Kenya: a re-analysis." *Africa* 60 (1990):69-87.

Green, Cecilia. "Marxist-feminism and third world liberation." *Fireweed* 20 (1985): 55-68.

Grimshaw, Anna, and Keith Hart. *C.L.R. James and the struggle for happiness.* New York: C.L.R. James Institute, 1991.

Grimshaw, Anna. *Popular democracy and the creative imagination: the writings of C.L.R. James 1950-1963.* New York: C.L.R. James Institute, 1991.

Grimshaw, Anna (ed.). *The C.L.R. James reader,* Oxford: Basil Blackwell, 1992.

Grimshaw, Anna. *The C.L.R. James archive: a reader's guide*. New York: C.L.R. James Institute and Smyrna Press, 1991.

Gutkind, Peter. "The energy of dispair," *Civilizations* (1968) 3.

Hanger, Jane and Jon Moris. "Women and the household economy." Robert Chambers and Jon Moris (eds.), *Mwea: an irrigated rice settlement in Kenya*. (Ifo-institut fur Wirtschaftsforschung, Afrika Studien 83), Munchen, Weltforum Verlag, 1973: 210-244.

Hanna, Judith Lynne, "Dance, protest and women's 'wars:' cases from Nigeria and the United States," in Guida West and Rhoda Louis Blumberg, (eds), *Women and social protest*, New York and Oxford: Oxford University Press, 1990, pp. 333-345.

Hardin, G. "Why plant a redwood tree?" in G.T. Milled (ed.), *Living in the environment* (2nd Ed.), Wadsworth, Belmont, 1979:206-207.

Hardin, G., and J. Baden (eds.), *Managing the commons*. San Francisco: Freeman, 1977.

Hardin, G. "Political requirements for preserving our common heritage." In H. P. Brokaw (ed), *Wildlife and America*. Council on Environmental Quality, Washington, D.C., 1978:310-317.

Hardin, G. "The tragedy of the commons." *Science* 162 (1968):1243-1248.

Harris, Olivia. *Latin American women*. London: Minority Rights Group, 1983.

Harris, Valerie. "Rastafari: issues and aspirations of the Toronto community." *Fuse* (Toronto, November - December 1982): 174-189.

Hartmann, Betsy and James K. Boyce. *A quiet violence: view from a Bangladesh village*. London: Zed, 1983.

Hayter, Alethea. *A sultry month: scenes of London literary life in 1846*. London: Robin Clark, 1992 (original 1965)

Heather, Randall. "Intelligence and counter-insurgency in Kenya, 1952-56." *Intelligence and National Security* 5:3 (1990):57-83.

Henriques, Fernando. *Family and colour in Jamaica*. London: Eyre and Spottiswoode, 1953.

Hermele, Kenneth, and Bertil Oden. *Sanction dilemma: some implications of economic sanctions against South Africa*. Uppsala: Scandinavian Institute of African Studies, 1988.

Hernton, Calvin C. *The sexual mountain and black woman writers*. New York: Anchor Doubleday, 1987.

Hewitt, Roger. *White talk black talk*. Cambridge: Cambridge University Press, 1986.

Hijab, Nadia. *Womanpower, the Arab debate on women at work*. Cambridge: Cambridge University Press, 1988.

Hill, Robert. "Leonard P. Howell and millenarian visions of early Rastafari." *Jamaica Journal* 16:1 (Feb 1983):24-39.

Hodges, Lucy. "Black community worried by medical view of 'Rastas.'" *London Times*, February 23, 1981.

Hodgkin, Thomas. "The African middle class." I Wallerstein (ed.), *Social change: the colonial situation*. New York: John Wiley, 1966.

Holt-Seeland, Inger. *Women of Cuba*. Westport: Lawrence and Hill, 1982.

Hopkins, Elizabeth. "The Nyabingi cult of southwestern Uganda." In Robert I. Rotberg and Ali A. Mazrui, *Protest and power in Black Africa*. New York: Oxford University Press, 1970, 258-336.

Hosken, F. "Female sexual mutilations: the facts and proposals for action," *Women's International Network News*. 1980.

Hutchful, Eboe, "Texaco's Funiwa-5 Oil Well Blow-out, Rivers State, Nigeria," *Journal of African Marxists*, 7 (March 1985):51-62.

Hyam, Ronald. *Empire and sexuality: the British experience*. Manchester and New York: University of Manchester Press, 1990.

IEU (Economist Intelligence Unit). *Country Report: Kenya, 2nd quarter 1993*. London: The Economist Intelligence Unit, May 11, 1993.

Ihonvbere, Julius, O., *personal communication*, August 1991.

Ihonvbere, Julius O., "Economic crisis, structural adjustment and social crisis in Nigeria," *World Development* 21:1 (1993):141-153.

Ilaloo, Sister. "Rastawoman as equal." *Yard Roots* 1(1981): 5-7.

Illich, Ivan, Gender, New York: Pantheon, 1982.

Itote, Warihin. *Mau Mau General*. Nairobi: East African Publishing House, 1967.

Iwuchukwu, *Interview* with Hilary Rouse-Amadi, Nigeria, April 1975.

James, C.L.R. (1956). *Facing reality*. Detroit: Bewicked editions, 1973.

James, C.L.R. (1963) *Beyond a boundary*. New York: Pantheon, 1983.

James, C.L.R. (1960). *Modern politics*. Detroit: Bewicked editions, 1970.

James, C.L.R. *Spheres of existence*. London: Allison & Busby, 1980.

James, C.L.R. *The future in the present*. London: Allison & Busby, 1977.

James, C.L.R. (1958). "New society: new people," in *At the rendezvous of victory*. London: Allison & Busby, 1984, 73-84.

James, C.L.R. (1975). "Presence of Blacks in the Caribbean and its impact on culture, in *At the rendezvous of victory*. London: Allison & Busby, 1984, 218-235.

James, C.L.R. (1937). *World revolution*. Nendeln: Kraus, 1970.

James, C.L.R. (1938) *A history of the Pan African revolt*. London: Race Today, 1986.

James, C.L.R. (1948) *Notes on dialectics: Hegel, Marx, Lenin.* London: Allison & Busby, 1980.

James, C.L.R. *What is happening every day: 1985 conversations.* edited by Jan Hillegas, Jackson, MS: New Mississippi Inc. (available from CLR James Institute, 505 West End Ave. #15C, New York, NY USA 10024) 1986.

James, C.L.R. *At the rendezvous of victory.* London: Allison and Busby, 1984.

James, C.L.R. (August 1981) "Three black women writers: Toni Morrison, Alice Walker, Ntozake Shange," in *At the rendezvous of victory.* London: Allison & Busby, 1984, 264-270.

James, C.L.R. (1950) *State capitalism and world revolution.* Chicago: Charles H. Kerr Co., 1986.

James, C.L.R. (1938) *The Black Jacobins: Toussaint L'Ouverture and the San Domingo revolution.* London: Allison & Busby, 1980.

James, C.L.R. (1958, 1960) *Nkrumah and the Ghana revolution.* London: Allison & Busby, 1977.

James, C.L.R. (1964) "Rastafari at home and abroad," in *At the rendezvous of victory.* London: Allison & Busby, 1984, 163-165.

James, C.L.R. *Gender and relationships with women: tape recorded interview* by Terisa E. Turner with CLR James, March 1989, Brixton, London.

Johnson, D., and D. Anderson, (eds.), *The ecology of survival: case studies from Northeast African History.* London: Crook, 1988.

Kalima, Rose. *Where women are leaders: the SEWA movement in India.* London: Zed, 1992.

Kamester, Margaret and Jo Vellacott, (eds.), *Militarism versus Feminism: writings on women and war by Catherine Marshall, C.K. Ogden and Mary Sargant Florence.*, (original: 1915, London: Allen & Unwin), London: Virago, 1987.

Kanogo, (a) Tabitha. *Squatters and the roots of Mau Mau 1905-1963.* London: James Currey, 1987.

Kanogo, (b) Tabitha. "Kikuyu women and the politics of protest: Mau Mau," in Sharon Macdonald, Pat Holden and Shirley Ardener, (eds.). *Images of women in peace and war.* London: Macmillan, 1987, 78-99.

Kapuscinski, Ryszard. *The emperor: downfall of an autocrat.* New York: Vintage International, Random House, (1978) 1983.

Kaufman, Michael. *Jamaica under Manley, dilemmas of socialism and democracy.* London: Zed books, 1985.

Kelkar, Govind and Dev Nathan. *Gender and tribe: women, land and the forests.* London: Zed, 1992.

Kemp, Penny. "For generations to come: the environmental catastrophe." In Bennis, Phyllis and Michel Moushabeck (eds.). *Beyond the storm: a Gulf crisis reader.* New York: Olive Branch Press, Interlink Publishing Group, 1991:325-334.

Kenya, *Laikipia District Annual Report,* 1953

Kenya, *Labour Department Annual Report,* 1955.

Kenyatta, Jomo. *Suffering without bitterness: the founding of the Kenya nation.* Nairobi: East African Publishing House, 1968.

Kershaw, Greet. "The changing roles of men and women in Kikuyu family by economic strata." *Rural Africana* 29 (1975-76):173-193.

Kershaw, Greet. "The land is the people: a study of social organization in historical perspective" (Chicago University Ph.D thesis, 1972).

Kertzer, David I. *Rituals, politics and power.* New Haven: Yale University Press, 1988.

Kimmel, Michael S., (ed.). *Men confront pornography.* New York, London: Penguin Meridian, 1991.

King, Alexander and Bertrand Schneider. *The first global revolution: a report by the Council of the Club of Rome*. New York: Pantheon, 1991.

King, Audvil. *One love*. London: Bogle-L'Ouverture Publications, 1971.

Kinsley, Michael. "Winners in the oil crisis." *The Washington Post*, 1 November 1990.

Kinyatti, Maina wa, (ed.). *Thunder from the mountains: Mau Mau patriotic songs*. London: Zed, 1980.

Kinyatti, Maina wa, (ed.). *Kimathi's letters*. Nairobi: Heinemann Kenya and London: ZED Press, 1986.

Koko, Patterson. "Women blamed for societal ills." *Nigerian Tide* (Port Harcourt, April 29, 1985).

Kolko, Joyce. *Restructuring the world economy*. New York: Pantheon, 1988.

Lan, David. *Guns and rain: guerrillas and spirit mediums in Zimbabwe*. Harare, Zimbabwe: Zimbabwe Publishing House, 1985.

Latin American and Caribbean Women's Collective. *Slaves of slaves - the challenge of Latin American women*. London: Zed Press, 1980.

Lawless, Richard. *North Africa*. New York: St. Martin's Press, 1984.

Leacock, Eleanor Burke, *Myths of Male Dominance: collected articles on women cross-culturally*, New York: Monthly Review Press, 1981.

Lee, Barbara. M. *Rastafari: the new creation*. Kingston: Jamaica Media Production, 1981.

Leith-Ross, Sylvia. *African women. A study of the Ibo of Nigeria*. London: Routledge and Kegan Paul, 1965.

Lem, Winnie, and Janet Salaff. *Women at work in pre- and post-1949 China*. Toronto: University of Toronto, 1981.

Levin, Tobe. "Women as scapegoats of culture and cult: an activist's view of female circumcision in Ngugi's The River Between." In Carole Boyce Davies and Anne Adams Graves (eds.), *Ngambika: studies of women in African literature*. Trenton, New Jersey: Africa World Press, 1986, 205-223.

Lewis, B. The impact of development policies on women. In M.J. Hay, S. Stichter, (eds.), *African women south of the Sahara*. London: Longman, 1984.

Lewis, Linden, F. "Living in the heart of Babylon: Rastafari in the U.S.A." *The Bulletin of Eastern Caribbean Affairs*, University of West Indies, 1989.

Lewis, Rupert. "Review: Henry Sylvester Williams: imperialist Pan-Africanist by J.R. Hooker." *Jamaica Journal* 11:1,2 (1977): 56-57.

Leys, Colin. *Underdevelopment in Kenya*. London: Heinemann, 1975.

Likimani, Muthoni. *Interview: the real Mau Mau* by Terisa E. Turner, August 1991, Nairobi.

Likimani, Muthoni. "Unsung heros," in Turner, Terisa E., Leigh S. Brownhill, with Teena J. Neal (eds.), *Mau Mau Women, their mothers, their daughters: a century of popular struggles in Kenya*, forthcoming 1993, 1-8.

Likimani, Muthoni. *Passbook number F.47927: women and Mau Mau in Kenya*. Basingstoke: MacMillan, 1985.

Lloyd, W. F. *Lectures on population, value, poor-laws, and rent. Delivered in the University of Oxford during the Years 1832, 1833, 1834, 1835, and 1836*. Reprints of Economic Classics. New York: Kelley, 1968.

Macgoye, Marjorie Oludhe. *Coming to birth*. Nairobi: Heinemann, 1987.

Macgoye, Marjorie Oludhe. *The present moment*. Nairobi: Heinemann, 1986.

Mackenzie, Fiona. "Local initiatives and national policy: gender and agricultural change in Murang's District, Kenya." *Canadian Journal of African Studies.* XX:3 (1986):377-398.

Mackenzie, Fiona. "Gender and land rights in Murang'a District, Kenya." *Journal of Peasant Studies* 17:4 (1990):609-643.

Mackie, Linsay. "My boyfriend threw my pills in the fire." *The Guardian* (Nigeria, June 1982): 8.

Makeda, Lee. "What is a Rastawoman?" *Caribbean Times* (June 1982): 15.

Malcolm X, (with assistance and epilogue by Alex Haley), *The Autobiography of Malcolm X.* (London: Penguin) New York: Grove Press, 1964.

Mamozai, M. *Herrenmenschen: Frauen im deutschen Kolonialismus.* Reinbeck: rororo Frauen aktuell, 1982.

Mangsingh, Ajai. "Rasta-Indian connection." *Daily Gleaner* (August 1982 Kingston, Jamaica): 22.

Mansingh, Lakshmi, and Ajai Mansingh. "Indian heritage in Jamaica." *Jamaica Journal 10* (1976): 10-19.

Mansingh, Laxmi. "Cultural heritage among the East Indians in Jamaica." In: *Second Conference on East Indians in the Caribbean: a symposium on cultural, economic and political issues,* Trinidad: University of the West Indies, 1981.

Maroney, H.J., and M. Luxton. *Feminism and political economy: women's work, women's struggles.* Agincourt, Ontario: Metheun Publications, 1987.

Martin, David. *The struggle for Zimbabwe: the Chimurenga war.* London: Faber and Faber, 1981.

Marx, Karl. (1852) *The 18th Brumaire of Louis Bonaparte.* New York: International Publishers, 1963.

Marx, Karl and Frederick Engels. *The Marx and Engels Reader*, Tucker, (ed.), New York: 1978.

Mazrui, Ali. *The Africans*. Narration, film series, "Tools of exploitation." 4:1986.

Mba, Nina Emma. *Nigerian women mobilized: women's political activity in southern Nigeria, 1900-1965*. Institute of International Studies, 215 Moses Hall, University of California, Berkeley, CA 94720, 1982.

Mba, Nina," Kaba and Khaki: Women and the Militarized State in Nigeria", in Parpart, Jane L. and Kathleen A. Staudt, (eds.), *Women and the State in Africa*, (Boulder: Lynne Rienner, 1989).

McCabe, J. Terrence. "Turkana pastoralism: a case against the tragedy of the commons," *Human Ecology* 18:1 (1990):81-90.

McCay, B.J. and J.M. Acheson (eds.), *The question of the commons. The culture and ecology of communal resources*. Tucson: University of Arizona Press, 1987.

McClean, Maxine. "Rastafarians: the revivers of leather craft in Barbados." *The Bulletin of Eastern Caribbean Affairs*, University of West Indies, 1989.

McDonnough, Maxine. "Sister Samad: living the Garvey life." *Jamaica Journal* 20:3 (August - October 1987): 77-84.

McPherson, E.S.P., and L.T. Semaj. "Rasta chronology." *Caribbean Quarterly* 26:4 (Dec. 1980): 97-98.

Meillassoux, Claude. *Maids, meals and money: capitalism and the domestic community*. Cambridge: Cambridge University Press, 1986.

Meillassoux, Claude. *The Anthropological Economies of the Gouro of the Ivory Coast*, Paris: Mouton, 1964.

Mernissi, Fatima. *The veil and the male elite: a feminist interpretation of women's rights in Islam*, New York: Addison-Wesley, 1991.

Mernissi, Fatima. *Beyond the veil*. Bloomington and Indianapolis: Indiana University Press, 1987.

Middle East Report, (formerly MERIP), Washington D.C.: Middle East Research and Information Project. Bimonthy.

Midnight Notes Collective. (ed.), *Midnight Oil: work, energy war, 1973-1992.* Brooklyn: Autonomedia, 1992.

Midnight Notes Collective. "Introduction to the new enclosures," in *Midnight Notes* 10, Special issue on New Enclosures, Jamaica Plain, MA (1990): 1-9.

Mies, Maria. *Patriarchy and accumulation on a world scale: women in the international division of labour.* London: Zed Press, 1986.

Mies, Maria and Vanadana Shiva. *Ecofeminism.* London: Zed, 1993.

Mies, Maria, Veronika Bennholdt-Thomsen and Claudia von Werlhof. *Women: the last colony.* London: Zed, 1988.

Mies, Maria. "Capitalism and subsistence: rural women in India, in *Development* (Journal of the Society for International Development, Rome) 4 (1984): 18-25.

Mies, Maria, "The Dynamics of the Sexual Division of Labor and Integration of Rural Market Women into the World Market" in Lourdes Beneria, (Ed.), *Women and Development,* The Sexual Division of Labor in Rural Societies, New York: Praeger Publishers, 1985.

Migot-Adholla, S.E. "Ideology and national development: the case of Kenya." *Ufahamu* II:1 (Spring 1971):1-25.

Migot-Adholla, S.E. "Traditional society and cooperation." Carl G. Widstrand (ed.), *Cooperatives and agricultural development in East Africa.* Uppsala: Scandinavian Institute of African Studies, 1970.

Miller, Karen A., "The effects of industrialization on men's attitudes toward the extended family and women's rights: a cross-national study," *Journal of Marriage and the Family* 46:1 (February 1984):153-160.

Minty, Abdul S. "Apartheid and oil." *Freedomways* 25:3 (1985): 135-144.

Mitchell, Sir Philip. *African afterthoughts*. London, 1954.

Mohammed, Patricia. "The "Creolization" of Indian women in Trinidad," in Selwyn Ryan, (ed.). *Trinidad and Tobago: the independence experience*. St. Augustine, Trinidad: Institute of Social and Economic Research, 1988, 381-398.

Mohanty, Chandra Talpade, Ann Russo, Lourdes Torres, (eds.). *Third world women and the politics of feminism*. Bloomington: Indiana University Press, 1991.

Mongo, Beti. *Perpeptua and the habit of unhappiness*. Translated by J.Reed and C. Wake. London: Heinneman, 1978.

Monroe, Trevor. "The Bustamante letters 1935." *Jamaica Journal* 8:1 (March 1974): 4-15.

Morris, Mervyn. "Interview with Linton Kwesi Johnson." *Jamaica Journal* 28 0:1 (February - April 1987): 17-28.

Mugo, Micere. "The role of women in the struggle for freedom," in Achola Pala, Thelma Awori and Abigail Krystal, (eds.). *The participation of women in Kenya society*. Nairobi: Kenya Literature Bureau, 1978, 210-219.

Murray, Jocelyn. "The Kikuyu female circumcision controversy with special reference to the Church Missionary Society's sphere of influence." (University of California, Los Angeles PhD thesis, 1974).

Murray, Jocelyn. "The Kikuyu spirit churches." *Journal of Religion in Africa* 5 (1974):198-234.

NACLA Report on the Americas. *Going foreign - causes of Jamaican migration*, 1981, 2-8.

Nama, Charles. "Daughters of Moombi: Ngugi's heroines and traditional Gikuyu aesthetics." In Carole Boyce Davies and Anne Adams Graves (eds.), *Ngambika: studies of women in African literature*. Trenton, New Jersey: Africa World Press, 1986, 139-150.

Napier, Robert. "The first arrest of Bedward," *Jamaica Historical Society Bulletin* II:1 (March 1957).

Nash, June, and Helen Safa. *Women and change in Latin America*. South Hadley, Mass.: Bergin and Garvey, 1986.

National Research Council. *Proceedings of the conference on common property resource management*. National Academy Press, Washington D.C., 1986.

Ndegwa, G.K. and D.C. Waihenya. "Trading by girls and women in Nairobi: the beginnings of insubordination." *Muigwithania* i:8 (December 1928-January 1929):7,9.

NEST (Nigerian Environmental Study/Action Team), *Nigeria's threatened environment: a national profile*, Ibadan: NEST, 1991.

Nettleford, Rex. *Mirror, mirror: identity, race, and protest in Jamaica*. Kingston: William Collins and Sangster's, 1970.

New York City Police Department. "Rasta crime: a confidential report." *Caribbean Review* 14:1 (1985).

Newswatch Magazine (Lagos), "Sticky, Oily Problem," July 2, 1990; "Killing the Geese," October 15, 1990; "War of Words," October 29, 1990; "Exploitation: The Agony of the Ogoni," January 25, 1993.

Nicholas, T. *Rastafari: a way of life*. Garden City, New York: Anchor Press Doubleday, 1979.

Nichols, Grace. *i is a long memoried woman*. London: Caribbean Cultural International, 1983.

Nigerian Tide, (Port Harcourt) April 18, 1986.

Njama, Karari and Donald Barnett. *Mau Mau from within*. London: Macgibbon and Kee, 1966.

Njau, Rebecca and Gideon Mulaki. *Kenya women heroes and their mystical power*. Nairobi:East Africa Literature Bureau, 1984.

Njoku, *Interview* with Hilary Rouse-Amadi, Nigeria, November 1979.

Nnoli, Okwudiba, *Ethnic Politics in Nigeria*, Enugu: Fourth Dimension Publishing Co. Ltd., 1978.

Nwabara, Samuel Nkankwo. 1965. *Ibo Land: a study in British penetration and the problem of administration, 1860-1930*, Ph.D. diss., Northwestern University. Ann Arbour, Mich.: University Microfilms.

O'Gormon, Pamela. "On reggae and Rastafarianism - and a Garvey Prophecy." *Jamaica Journal* 20:3 (August - October 1987): 85-88.

Obadina, Elizabeth. "No condition is permanent." *The Guardian* (Nigeria, April 10, 1983): 5.

Ogot, B.A. "Politics, culture and music in Central Kenya: a study of Mau Mau hymns 1951-1956." *Kenya Historical Review* 5:2 (1977):275-286.

Ogot, Bethwell. "British administration in the Central Nyanza District of Kenya." *Journal of African History*, IV:2 (1963).

Onyemaobi, *Interview* with Hilary Rouse-Amadi, Nigeria, August 1981.

Oppong, Christine, ed. *Sex-roles, population and development in West Africa: policy-related studies on work and demographic issues.* London: James Currey and Heinemann Educational Books, 1987.

Osei, G.K. *Caribbean women.* London: The African Publication Society, 1979.

Oshare, M. O., "The Ekpan women's uprising of August 1986." *Unpublished paper.* Jos, Nigeria: University of Jos, Sociology Department, 1986.

Parmar, P. "Gender, race, and class: Asian women in resistance." In: *The empire strikes back*, Centre for Contemporary Cultural Studies (ed.). London: Hutchinson, 1982.

Parrinder, G. *African mythology.* London: Paul Hamlyn, 1975.

Patterson, Orlando. *The Sociology of Slavery*. London: Magibbon and Kee. (Also published in Rutherford, NJ: Farleigh Dickenson University Press.) 1967.

Patterson, Orlando. *Freedom in the making of Western culture*. New York: Basic Books, 1991.

Patterson, Orlando. *The children of Sisyphus*. London, 1963.

Payton, Brenda. "The Black antiwar movement: looking for a post-Gulf war role." *The Nation* (New York) July 1, 1991.

Perchonock, Norma, "Double Oppression: Women and Land Matters in Kaduna State" in *Women In Nigeria Today*, S. Bappa, et. al. (eds), London: Zed Books, 1985.

Perham, Margery. 1937. *Native administration in Nigeria*. London: Oxford University Press.

Perry, Shawn. "The Rasta man." *New Internationalist* (January, 1985): 14-15.

Perspective. Lester Pearson Institute, Halifax, Nova Scotia, 1:1 (February 1991).

Petter, V.R. "The tragedy of the Sahel commons." *Science* 185 (1974):813.

Pittin, Renee, "Houses of Women: a Focus on Alternative Life-Styles in Katsina City", in Christine Oppong (ed.), *Male and Female in West Africa*, London: George Allen & Unwin, 1983.

Platt's Oilgram News, 19 March 1992, 9 October 1992.

Plewes, Betty and Rieky Stuart, "Women and development revisited: the case for a gender and development approach," In Swift, Jaimie and Brian Tomlinson. (eds). *Conflicts of interest: Canada and the third world*. Toronto: Between the Lines, 1991, 107-132.

Pollard, Velma. "Word sounds: the language of Rastafari in Barbados and St. Lucia." *Jamaica Journal* 17:1 (February 1984): 57-62.

Post, Ken. *Arise ye starvelings: the Jamaican labour rebellion of 1938 and its aftermath.* The Hague: Martinus Nijhoff, 1978.

Pratt, Mary Louise. *Imperial eyes: travel writing and transculturation.* New York: Routledge, 1992.

Presley, Cora Ann. "The Mau Mau rebellion, Kikuyu women and social change," *Canadian Journal of African Studies* 22: 3 (1988): 502-527. Also in Turner, Terisa E., Leigh S. Brownhill, with Teena J. Neal (eds.), *Mau Mau Women, their mothers, their daughters: a century of popular struggles in Kenya,* forthcoming 1993.

Raeburn, Michael. *We are everywhere: narratives from Rhodesian guerrillas.* New York: Random House, 1979.

Randall, Margaret. *Women in Cuba.* New York: Smyrna Press, 1981.

Ransby, Barbara. "Columbus and the making of historical myth." *Race & Class 33:3* (January-March 1992):79-88.

Reckford, Verena. "Rastafarian music: an introductory study." *Jamaica Journal* 11:1, 2 (1977): 3-13.

Reckford, Verena. "Reggae, Rastafarianism and cultural identity." *Jamaica Journal* 46 (1982): 70-79.

Reddock, Rhoda. "The quality of life: a commentary," in Selwyn Ryan, (ed.). *Trinidad and Tobago: the independence experience.* St. Augustine, Trinidad: Institute of Social and Economic Research, 1988, 495-503.

Reddock, Rhoda. *A history of women and labour in Trinidad and Tobago,* London: Zed Press, 1993.

Reddock, Rhoda. *Women, labour and struggle in 20th century Trinidad and Tobago 1898-1960.* The Hague: Institute of Social Studies, 1984.

Reddock, Rhoda. "Women and slavery in the Caribbean: a Feminist Perspective," *Latin American Perspectives,* 44:12, No. 1, Winter 1985, 63-80.

Reynolds, Roy C. "Tacky and the great slave rebellion of 1760." *Jamaica Journal* 6:2 (June 1972): 5-8.

Ridgeway, James. "The unquiet peace." In James Ridgeway (ed.), *The march to war*. New York: Four walls eight windows, 1991, 227-239.

Ridgeway, James. (ed.), *The march to war*. New York: Four walls eight windows, 1991.

Robertson, Claire, ""Women's Education and Class Formation in Africa, 1950-1980", in Robertson, Claire and Iris Berger (eds.), *Women and Class in Africa*, New York: Holmes & Meier, 1986.

Rodney, Walter. *The groundings with my brothers*. London: Bogle-L'Ouverture Publications, 1969.

Rodney, Walter. *How Europe underdeveloped Africa*. London: Bogle-L'Ouverture, 1972.

Rogers, Barbara. *The domestication of women*. New York: St. Martin's Press, 1980.

Rosberg, C. G. and Nottingham, J. *The Myth of Mau Mau: Nationalism in Kenya*, Nairobi: East African Publishing House, 1966.

Rowe, Maureen. "The woman in Rastafari." *Caribbean Quarterly* 26:4 (December, 1985): 13-21.

Rubin, Gayle. "The traffic in women: notes on the 'political economy' of sex," in Rayna R. Reiter, (ed.). *Toward an anthropology of women*. New York: Monthly Review Press, 1975.

Ruddle, K. and R.E. Johannes, (eds.), *The traditional knowledge and management of coastal systems in Asia and the Pacific*. Jakarta: Unesco, 1985.

Russell, Bertrand. *Mysticism and logic and other essays*. London: Unwin Books, 1963.

Rutanga, Murindwa. *Nyabingi Movement: people's anti-colonial struggles in Kigezi 1910-1930*, Kampala, Uganda: Centre for Basic Research, Working Paper, 1991.

Ryman, Cheryl. "The Jamaican heritage in dance." *Jamaica Journal* 44:4 (1979).

Sabbah, Fatna A. *Woman in the Muslim unconscious*. New York: Pergamon Press, 1984.

Said, Edward W. "Thoughts on the war: ignorant armies clash by night." In Bennis, Phyllis and Michel Moushabeck (eds.). *Beyond the storm: a Gulf crisis reader*. New York: Olive Branch Press, Interlink Publishing Group, 1991:1-6.

Salaff, Janet W., and Mary Sheridan (eds.). *Lives - Chinese working women*. Bloomington, Indiana: Indiana University Press, 1984.

Sale, Kirkpatrick. *The conquest of paradise: Christopher Columbus and the Columbian legacy*. New York and London: Hodder and Stoughton, 1990.

Salkey, Andrew. "Political spider," in Ulli Beier, (ed.), *Political Spider: Stories from Black Orpheus*, London: Heinemann Educational Books, 1969.

Santilli, Kathy. "Kikuyu women in the Mau Mau revolt: a closer look." *Ufahamu* VIII:I (1977):143-174.

Saunders, A.C. de C.M. *A social history of Black slaves and freedmen in Portugal 1441-1555*. Cambridge: Cambridge University Press, 1982.

Scott, P. "Debunking saphire: toward a non-racist and non-sexist social science." In: G. Hull, (ed.), *But some of us are brave*, Old Westbury: Feminist Press, 1982.

Seagal, Aaron. *Politics and population in the Caribbean*. Rio Piedras, Puerto Rico: University of Puerto Rico, 1969.

Semaj, Leachim T. "Rastafari: from religion to social theory." *Caribbean Quarterly* 26:4 (December, 1980): 22-31.

Semaj, Leachim T. "Inside Rasta: the future of a religious movement." *Caribbean Review* 14:1 (1985).

Sen, Gita and Caren Grown. *Development Crises and Alternative Visions: Third World Women's Perspectives.* New York: Monthly Review Press, 1987.

Seymour, Ian. *OPEC: Instrument of change.* London: Macmillan, 1980.

Shettima, Kole Ahmed, "Structural adjustment and the student movement in Nigeria." *Review of African Political Economy* 56 (March 1993):83-90.

Shiroya, O.J.E.. *Kenya and World War II: African soldiers in the European war,* Nairobi: Kenya Literature Bureau, 1985.

Shiva, Vandana, P. Anderson, H. Schuckling, A. Gray, L. Lohmann, and D. Cooper. *Biodiversity, social and ecological perspectives,* London: Zed. 1991.

Shiva, Vandana. *Staying alive: women, ecology and development.* London: Zed, 1989.

Shiva, Vandana. "Development: the "new colonialism," in *Development* (Journal of the Society for International Development, Rome) 1 (1989): 84-87.

Shiva, Vandana. *The violence of the green revolution: third world agriculture, ecology and politics,* London: Zed, 1991.

Silvera, Makeda. "An open letter to Rastafarian sistrens," *Fireweed,* a feminist quarterly, 16, (Spring 1983): 115-120. This issue was republished as *The issue is 'ism: women of colour speak out, Fireweed's Issue 16.* Toronto: Sister Vision, 1989, in which Makeda's open letter appears on pages 140-148.

Simpson, George E. "Political cultism in West Kingston, Jamaica." *Social and economic studies,* University of the West Indies 5:2 (1955).

Simpson, George E. "The Rastafari movement in Jamaica: a study of race and class conflict." *Social Forces* 34 (1955): 167-170.

Singh, Makhan. *History of Kenya's trade union movement to 1952.* Nairobi: East African Publishing House, 1969.

Sistren with Honor Ford-Smith, *Lionheart Gal: life stories of Jamaican women*. Toronto: Sister Vision, 1987.

Smith, M.G., Roy Augier, and Rex Nettleford. *The Rastafari movement in Kingston, Jamaica*. Mona, Jamaica: Institute of Social and Economic Research, University of the West Indies, 1960.

Sparr, Pamela (ed.). *Mortgaging women's lives: feminist critiques of structural adjustment*. London: Zed, 1993.

St.-Hilaire, Colette, "Canadian air, women and development: rebaptizing the Filipina," *The Ecologist* 23:2 (March/April 1993): 57-60.

Stamp, Patricia. "Kikuyu women's self help groups: towards an understanding of the relation between sex-gender system and mode of production in Africa." In C. Robertson and I. Berger, (eds.), *Women and class in Africa*. New York: Holmes & Meier, 1986.

Stamp, Patricia. *Technology, gender, and power in Africa*. Ottawa: International Development Research Centre, 1989.

Stevenson, Michael. "Columbus and the war on indigenous peoples." *Race & Class 33:3* (January-March 1992):27-48.

Stichter, Sharon. "Workers, trade unions and the Mau Mau rebellion." *Canadian Journal of African Studies* 9 (1975):259-275.

Stichter, Sharon. *Migrant labour in Kenya 1895-1975*, Harlow Essex: Longman, 1982.

Stone, Elizabeth. *Women and the Cuban revolution. Speeches and documents by Fidel Castro, Vilma Espin, and others*. New York: Pathfinder Press, 1981.

Stork, Joe. *Middle East oil and the energy crisis*. New York: Monthly Review Press, 1975.

Sunday Gleaner. "The 1960 U.W.I. report - Rastafarians." (Kingston, Jamaica), August 20, 1960.

Sunday Telegraph. (Warri, Nigeria) August 31, 1986.

Swift, Jaimie and Brian Tomlinson. (eds). *Conflicts of interest: Canada and the third world*. Toronto: Between the Lines, 1991.

Tafari, Ikael. "Rastafari in tradition: cultural confrontation and political change in Ethiopia and the Caribbean 1966-86," *The Bulletin of Eastern Caribbean Affairs*, University of West Indies, 1989.

Talbot, L.M. "Rangeland destruction in East Africa." *Population and Development Review* 12 (1986):441-452.

Tanzer, Michael. "Oil and the Gulf crisis." In Bennis, Phyllis and Michel Moushabeck (eds.). *Beyond the storm: a Gulf crisis reader*. New York: Olive Branch Press, Interlink Publishing Group, 1991:263-267.

The Vanguard (Lagos, Nigeria), April 4, 1986.

Trager, Lillian and Clara Osinulu. "New women's organizations in Nigeria: one response to structural adjustment," in Christina H. Gladwin, (ed.). *Structural adjustment and African women farmers*. Gainesville: University of Florida Press, 1991, 339-358.

Truong, Thanh-Dam. *Sex, money and morality: prostitution and tourism in South-East Asia*. London: Zed, 1990.

Tunde, Carmen. "Dreadlocks Lesbian." In Shabnan Grewal, Jackie Kay, Lilaine Landor, Gail Lewis and Pratibha Parmar, (eds.). *Charting the journey: writings by black and third world women*. London: Sheba Feminist Publishers, 1987: 205-206.

Turner, Terisa E., Leigh S. Brownhill, with Teena J. Neal (eds.), *Mau Mau Women, their mothers, their daughters: a century of popular struggles in Kenya*, forthcoming 1993.

Turner, Terisa E. *"Mau Mau and the new Rastafari: tape recorded interview with officials of the Tent of the Living God,"* Nairobi, Kenya, August 1991.

Turner, Mary. *Slaves and missionaries: the disintegration of Jamaican slave society 1787-1834*. London, 1982.

Turner, Terisa and Pade Badru, "Oil and instability: class contradictions and the 1983 coup in Nigeria," *Journal of African Marxists,* 7 (March 1985):4-34.

Turner, Terisa E. and Timothy A. Belknap (eds.), *Takeover! Students USA mobilize for the 90's: documents from the movement.* New York and Amherst, MA: International Oil Working Group, 1989.

Turner, Terisa E. "Workers, oil and economic development in Iran," In Sorab Sadri (ed.). *Oil and economic development.* Kuala Lumpur: Forum, 1991, 141-161.

Turner, Terisa E. "Multinational corporations and the instability of the Nigerian state," *Review of African Political Economy* (London) 5 (January-April 1976):63-79.

Turner, Terisa, "Commercial capitalism and the 1975 coup in Nigeria," in Keith Panter-Brick, (ed.), *Soldiers and Oil,* London: Frank Cass, 1978.

Turner, Terisa E., "Petroleum, Recession and the Internationalization of Class Struggle in Nigeria," *Labour, Capital and Society* 18:1 (April 1985):6-42.

Turner, Terisa E., "Women, Rastafari and the New Society: Caribbean and East African roots of a popular movement against structural adjustment." *Labour, Capital and Society* 24:1 April 1991):66-89.

Turner, Terisa E. *The politics of world resource development in the 1990s.* International Oil Working Group, New York, 1990.

Turner, Terisa E. "Nigerian oil workers and the oil bust," *Africa Today.* (Denver) 33:4 (1987):33-50.

Turner, Terisa E. "Nigeria: imperialism, oil technology and the comprador state," In Petter Nore and Terisa Turner (eds.). *Oil and class struggle.* London: Zed Press, 1980:199-223.

Turner, Terisa E., M.J. Collins, T.A. Belknap, L.S. Brownhill, L. Belanger, J. Hanson (eds.). *Revolutionary Popular Culture.* New York and Amherst, Massachusetts: International Oil Working Group, 1989.

Turner, Terisa E., Leigh S. Brownhill and Teena J. Neal, "The fight for fertility: Mau Mau as gendered class struggle," in Terisa E. Turner, Leigh S. Brownhill with Teena J. Neal (eds.), *Mau Mau Women, their mothers, their daughters: a century of popular struggles in Kenya*, forthcoming, 1993.

Turner, Terisa E. and Daniel O. Ihonvbere, "Environmental crises and gender relations in Nigeria: women and ecology struggles in the oil belt," paper presented on the "Gender and Urban Insurrection" panel, 22nd Conference of the Canadian Association of African Studies, University of Toronto, May 14, 1993.

Turshen, Meredeth. (ed.), *Women and health in Africa*. Trenton, New Jersey: Africa World Press, 1991.

Tyler, Patrick, *Washington Post*, July 26, 1990.

Uglow, Jenny. "Small lives." *The Independent on Sunday* (London: 5 July 1992):30.

United Movement for Democracy in Kenya. *A. Moi's reign of terror: a decade of Nyayo crimes against the people of Kenya*. London: UMOJA, 1989.

Uvwie Community. "Why Our Women Folk Demonstrated on Monday 25th August, 1986: A Case of Displacement, Neglect and Non Rehabilitation by NNPC." Warri, Nigeria, *mimeo*, August 1986.

Van Allen, Judith, "'Sitting on a Man:' colonialism and the lost political institutions of Igbo women," *Canadian Journal of African Studies*. 6:2 (1972):165-181.

Village Voice. (New York) 22 January 1991.

Vine, Peter. "The ecological disaster in the Gulf." *Middle East International*, April 5, 1991,

Waciuma, Charity. *Daughter of mumbi.* Nairobi: East African Publishing House, 1969.

Wade, R. "Common property reserve arrangement in South Indian villages. National Research Council. *Proceedings of the conference on common property resource management.* National Academy Press, Washington D.C., 1986, 231-257.

Wade, R. *Village Republics: economic conditions for collective action in South India.* Cambridge: Cambridge University Press, 1987.

Wairimu, N. *tape recorded interview,* (Terisa E. Turner), Nairobi, 6 August 1991.

Wanjau, Gakaara wa, 1988. *Mau Mau author in detention,* Nairobi: Heinemann.

Weiss, Ruth. *The women of Zimbabwe.* Harare, Zimbabwe: Nehanda Publishers, 1986.

Welcome, Patricia. "Prejudice, discrimination and the Rastafarian experience." *The Bulletin of Eastern Caribbean Affairs,* University of West Indies, 1989.

White, Timothy. *Catch a fire: the life of Bob Marley.* New York: Henry Holt, 1983.

White, Luise. "Separating the men from the boys: constructions of gender, sexuality, and terrorism in Central Kenya, 1939-1959, *The International Journal of African Historical Studies* 23: 1 (1990): 1-25.

White, Luise. *The comforts of home: prostitution in colonial Nairobi.* Chicago and London: Chicago University Press, 1990.

Williams, Eric. *Capitalism and Slavery.* Chapel Hill: University of North Carolina Press, 1944.

Williams, Eric. *A history of the people of Trinidad and Tobago,* London: Andre Deutsch, 1963.

Wiltshire, Rosina. *Environment and development: grass roots women's perspective.* WAND, St. Michael, Barbados: DAWN, 1992.

Wipper, Audrey. "Riot and rebellion among African women: three examples of women's political clout," in Jean O'Barr, (ed.). *Perspectives on power*. Durham, N.C.: Duke University Press, 1982.

Wipper, Audrey. "The Maendeleo ya Wanawake Organization - the co-optation of leadership," *African Studies Review* 18: 3 (1975): 329-355.

Wisner, Ben. "Mwea irrigation scheme, Kenya: a success story for whom?" Anthropological Research Council, Boston, MA. USA. *Newsletter*, 1982.

World Bank, *Report to the World Bank Joint Audit Committee*, directed by Willi Wapenhans, confidential and unpublished, Washington D.C.: World Bank, 1992.

Yawney, Carole D. "Violence against women." *Canadian Woman Studies* 6:1, (1984):13-16.

Yawney, Carole D. "Remnants of all nations." In: F. Henry, (ed.). *Ethnicity in the Americas*. The Hague: Mouton, 1976.

Yawney, Carole D. "Moving with the dawtas of Rastafari: from myth to reality." *El Caribe y America Latina* (1987): 193-199.

Yawney, Carole D. "Strictly Ital: Rastafari livity and holistic health." unpublished paper, Atkinson College, York University, 1985.

Yawney, Carole D. "Who killed Bob Marley?" *Canadian Forum* (December, 1984):29-31.

Yawney, Carole D. "Dread wasteland." In: *Ritual, symbolism and ceremonialism in the Americas*, edited by R. Crumrine. University of Northern Colorado Occasional Publications in Anthropology, Ethnology Series #33, Museum of Anthropology, 1979.

Yawney, Carole D. "Rastafarian sistren by the rivers of Babylon." *Canadian Woman Studies* 5:2 (1983):73-75.

Yawney, Carole D. "To grow a daughter: cultural liberation and the dynamics of oppression in Jamaica," in A. Miles and G. Finn, (eds.). *Feminism: from pressure to politics*. Montreal: Black Rose Books, 1989.

Young, Gay and Bette Dickerson, (eds.). *Color, class and country: experiences of gender*. London: Zed, 1993.

Index

F

N

O

P

Palestinian, 201, 203, 212, 213, 220, 222
pan African, 4, 28
Pan African Conference, 59
Pan African Congresses, 4
pan Africanism, 3, 4, 5, 15, 19
Pan Arab, 201, 202, 220, 223
paternity, 1, 31
patriarchal, 3, 65, 169, 176, 200
patriarchy, 49
peace movement, 212, 213
peasant, 15, 27, 39, 123, 124, 133, 139, 146, 154, 156, 157, 175
  comunities, 136
  farmers, 136, 153, 167
  women, 6, 43, 46, 133, 153, 154
peoples' committees, 208
Persian Gulf, 199, 210, 211, 217
petals of blood, 112, 122
petroleum, 134, 135, 137, 139, 171, 206
plantation, 11, 12, 18, 26, 27
police, 30, 32, 36, 45, 62, 69, 70, 85, 141, 146, 157
  brutality, 15, 64, 100
political economy, 17, 21, 43, 123, 131, 134, 136
political repression, 45
pollution, 123, 134, 140, 141, 145, 159
polygynous, 169
popular
  mobilization, 198
  movements, 4, 39, 159

  power, 42, 199, 223
  struggles, 3, 4, 5
populism, 4
populist expressions, 4
pornography, 54
Port Harcourt, 134, 192
precapitalist, 11, 52
privatization, 125, 157
profits, 3, 26, 31, 37, 55, 128, 156, 205
proletarianization, 124, 129
proletariat, 37, 46
prostitution, 33, 106, 107, 108, 143, 161, 166, 167, 168
protests, 40, 124, 134, 140

Q

queen, 22, 30, 67, 68

R

racism, 3, 14, 23, 26, 29, 48, 53, 65, 69, 72, 73, 126, 218
rape, 5, 25, 26, 51, 53, 195
rapso, 5, 14
Rastafari, 1, 5, 12, 17, 29, 32, 46, 50, 62, 65
rebellion, 25, 29, 43, 57
recession, 30, 53, 218
reggae, 12, 13, 14, 15, 32, 44, 45, 52, 76, 79, 81
reproduction, 3, 18, 19, 37, 38
resistance, 2, 16, 22, 26, 29, 38, 64, 104, 105, 124, 129, 155, 195, 213, 219
  networks, 40
resource defence, 49
resources, 41, 201, 202, 203,

U

Uganda, 22, 23, 24, 32, 33
underdevelopment, 3, 73, 173, 177
unemployment, 29, 32, 35, 166
UNIA, 28, 32, 59, 61, 63
universal, 54, 71, 75, 78, 87
  adult suffrage, 61
  new society, 13
universalism, 53, 218
unpaid work, 2, 53, 54, 188
urban, 32, 40, 135, 145, 161, 168
  employment, 164, 167
urban highways, 162
urbanization, 171, 192
urbanized, 170
USSR, 37

V

vegetarianism, 14
Vietnam, 203, 207, 210, 219

W

wage goods, 3, 19, 129
Wailers, 14, 70
WAND, 48
Warri, 123, 136, 141, 152
Weber, 11
West Africa, 18, 154
white
  man, 105, 106, 120
White Highlands, 36
white man, 24, 25, 68

White Power Message Service, 70
white settlers, 33, 35, 36, 44
white women, 3, 15, 16, 49
widowed, 170, 173, 177
widows, 137
witchcraft, 23
witches, 18
woman warrior, 27
Women's Institute, 31
women's movement, 47, 48, 72, 131
World Bank, 15, 37, 39, 104, 127
world market, 1, 4, 10, 19, 27, 204, 207, 208
world systems, 125
WW3, 87

Y

Yoruba, 148

Z

Zimbabwe, 14, 38, 64, 81
Zion, 32
zionist, 210, 212